Computer Communications and Networks

T0134997

For other titles published in this series, go to
www.springer.com/series/4198

The **Computer Communications and Networks** series is a range of textbooks, monographs and handbooks. It sets out to provide students, researchers and non-specialists alike with a sure grounding in current knowledge, together with comprehensible access to the latest developments in computer communications and networking.

Emphasis is placed on clear and explanatory styles that support a tutorial approach, so that even the most complex of topics is presented in a lucid and intelligible manner.

Javier Aracil · Franco Callegati

Editors

Enabling Optical Internet with Advanced Network Technologies

 Springer

Editors

Prof. Dr. Javier Aracil
Universidad Autonoma de Madrid
Escuela Politecnica Superior
Depto. Ingeniería Informática
C / Francisco Tomas y
Valiente, 11
28049 Madrid
Spain
javir.aracil@uam.es

Prof. Franco Callegati
Alma Mater Studiorum –
   Università di Bologna
Dipto. Elettronica, Informatica e
   Sistemistica (DEIS)
Via Venezia, 52
47023 Cesena
Italy
franco.callegati@unibo.it

Series Editor
Professor A.J. Sammes, BSc, MPhil, PhD, FBCS, CEng
CISM Group, Cranfield University,
RMCS, Shrivenham, Swindon SN6 8LA, UK

ISSN 1617-7975
ISBN 978-1-84882-277-1   e-ISBN 978-1-84882-278-8
DOI 10.1007/978-1-84882-278-8
Springer Dordrecht Heidelberg London New York

British Library Cataloguing in Publication Data
A catalogue record for this book is available from the British Library

Library of Congress Control Number: 2009926515

Cover design: SPi Publisher Services

Printed on acid-free paper

Springer is part of Springer Science+Business Media (www.springer.com)

Foreword

This book provides a broad overview of IP over WDM technologies, as seen by a group of experts participating in the e-Photon/ONe+ and BONE Networks of Excellence funded within the VIth and VIIth Research Framework Programmes (FP6 and FP7) of the European Union. Both Networks of Excellence are aimed at the integration of research teams active on optical networks at a pan-European level, with the creation of virtual centers of excellence in optical networks, technologies, and services. The working groups on optical core networks gathered about a 100 researchers from more than 20 universities and research institutions in Europe. The multifaceted viewpoints available in this community on the current state and future evolution of large WDM networking infrastructures are reported in this book. The book is organized in chapters, with chapter editors, listed on pp–, having the responsibility to collect and harmonize contributions by different research groups. The whole work was made possible by the coordination efforts of Javier Aracil and Franco Callegati, leaders, at the time when the book writing was begun, of the working groups on optical core networks and on optical burst switching in e-Photon/ONe+. We are thankful to them for their efforts. We hope that this manuscript will serve as a valuable reference for students and practitioners in the field of optical networking. Beyond this, we are proud to deliver it as a tangible outcome of the integration efforts within the European research community, which were enabled and boosted by the introduction in FP6 of the network of excellence instrument. We are thankful to our project officers at the European Union for the continuous support to our projects.

Fabio Neri and Peter Van Daele

October 2008   Project leaders of e-Photon/ONe + and BONE

Preface

Research in optical networking has always been lively and effective in Europe and some research projects achieved very pioneering results in the field. Such projects were funded by the national government and, most of all, by the European Commission. Starting from the VIth Framework Programme (FP6) the EC defined so-called *new instruments* besides the traditional research projects, with the aim to foster the integration of the research expertise and industrial R&D in Europe. The Network of Excellence is the instrument devoted to fundamental research.

Many of the research groups active in the field of optical networking succeeded in finding an agreement over a rather wide workplan and submitted a proposal for a large NoE devoted to the topic. This proposal was funded in 2004 under the e-Photon-ONe name. It was a large project, involving about 40 institutions and 500 researchers belonging to most of the EU countries, from Portugal to Turkey. It was originally funded for 2 years (2004–2005), a rather short period for the ambitious task to put together and integrate the work of so many people. Nonetheless e-Photon-ONe+ proved successful and, thanks to the good scientific results, the e-Photon-ONe+ consortium gained visibility and reputation worldwide. An example is the cosponsorship (with COST and NSF) of the "US/EU Workshop on Key Issues and Grand Challenges in Optical Networking," held in June 2005 at the European Commission (EC) premises in Brussels, with the goal to determine future research directions in optical networking and explore methods to facilitate stronger research collaboration between US and EU researchers.

The funding was renewed for 2 more years (2006–2007) under the e-Photon-ONe+ name with very similar goals and for 3 more years (2008–2010) under the BONE name, this time with a refocusing of technical objectives to follow the advances of technology.

The dimension and the wide technical scope of these projects raised significant problems of management. A model based on virtual groups of interest (called *virtual departments (VDs)* in e-Photon-ONe and *virtual centre of excellence* in BONE) was defined as the container and promoter of activities aiming at achieving durable integration, such as promoting *joint research activities (JAs)*, identifying new *research topics*, creating *common expertise and research methodology*, etc.

Within the VD devoted to optical core networks, titled *virtual department on optical core networks and technologies*, stemmed the idea to merge the many research expertises in a book presenting an up-to-date overview of the various optical technologies that will be the core of the future internet. The authors of this work are active participating into the aforementioned initiatives and were and are involved in the majority of European research projects in optical networking. They also have strong collaboration with the optical networking industry and operators. The result of such a wide, hands-on experience is the current manuscript.

Intended audience

The book is intended for practitioners in the field and graduate students in electrical engineering and computer science. It is written in a concise and clear language, avoiding unnecessary complexity and technical terms. Thus, the book is also a very valuable reference for newcomers to the field. Actually, the first chapter of the book provides an overview of internet protocol (IP) over wavelength division multiplexing (WDM) technologies and protocols, before going in-depth into optical packet switching (OPS) and optical burst switching (OBS) technologies.

Scope

The book covers architectures, technologies and protocols for optical networks and also physical layer issues, to a lesser extent. It has a strong focus in switching technologies, as they are key to understanding the all-optical transmission paradigms brought by optical packet switching (OPS) and optical burst switching (OBS).

On the other hand, the book also covers performance evaluation issues and analytical models that serve to assess network performance. A number of simulation results are also presented along the chapters. Finally, prototypes are also reported that advance the state-of-art in optical networking equipment.

Structure

This book is organized into five chapters plus an introduction.

Chapter 2 provides an introduction to IP over WDM. First, the chapter justifies IP over WDM in terms of the demand for high speed. Actually, very interesting analysis is performed in [170]. While the myth of "internet traffic doubling every 100 days" is probably too optimistic, it turns out that the traffic in the US and Australian backbone is doubling every year. Then, traffic models for internet traffic are described, as they will constitute the input for IP over WDM networks. The chapter goes on with the description of current synchronous optical networking (SONET)/synchronous digital hierarchy (SDH) networks, which have active electronic equipment. SONET/SDH represent the most mature transport technology. However, it is a rigid standard that provides a limited set of data rates (e.g., 155 Mbps, 622 Mbps, 2.5 Gbps, 10 Gbps). From such SONET/SDH networks, automatic switched optical network (ASON) and generalized multi-protocol label switching (GMPLS) networks have arisen as the most likely migration path to all-optical networks. Indeed, international telecommunication union-telecommunication (ITU-T) has defined the concept of automatic switched optical network (ASON) as an optical transport network that has dynamic connection capabilities. Both ASON and GMPLS networks are described in-depth in the chapter. Finally, we deal with the routing and wavelength assignment (RWA) problem, which has been identified as a fundamental issue in all-optical networking.

Chapter 3 is devoted to optical packet switching (OPS). In OPS networks, the basic transmission unit is the optical packet, which is transmitted end-to-end without leaving the optical domain. The major challenge is to decode the packet header and facilitate routing in very low timescales. In fact, on-the-fly switching is required for the optical packet that traverses the switch without incurring opto-electronic conversion. It is worth remarking that OPS is based on *in-band signaling*, where control information is carried by a *header* transmitted on the same wavelength as the *payload.*

The chapter provides a general description of the issues concerning OPS. Then, it goes on to header coding techniques, which can be classified into time-domain, frequency-domain, and code-domain coding. Finally, contention resolution techniques are described. Fiber delay line (FDL) buffers are introduced for the first time in the book. FDL buffers provide all-optical packet storage by means of a loop of fiber, in which the storage time is limited to the propagation time in the loop. Switch architectures are presented next, with emphasis on the wavelength conversion capabilities, either share-per-link or share-per-node. Finally, the chapter analyzes buffered switch architectures and arrayed waveguide grating-AWG based space switching architectures.

Chapter 4 covers the OBS topics, describing the architecture of OBS networks. It then discusses the burst assembly algorithms at the edge node, which have a significant impact on the network performance and presents signaling and channel reservation protocols in the core network. Then different contention resolution schemes are inspected, followed a review of the issues of quality of service (QoS) provisioning in OBS. Based on the provided material the reader should be able to understand the principles of operation of an OBS network and the main performance issue that affects its behavior, together with examples of state of the art research results in the field. It is also worth noting that the chapter discusses the interplay between transmission control protocol (TCP) and OBS in-depth.

In contrast to OPS, OBS is based on *out-of-band signaling*, whereby the control packet is sent on a separate, dedicated wavelength. Such a control packet is sent at an offset time before the actual data burst. By the moment the data burst reaches an intermediate switch it is expected that resources for switching the burst have been previously set up by the control burst.

Chapter 5 describes a possible field of application of optical networks that is considered quite significant by the scientific community. It shows how an OBS network can support a ubiquitous grid platform which is able to address the requirements of large number of dynamic users. The network architectures and OBS routers requirements in a grid-enabled OBS network are discussed, followed by consideration of the control plane and of the transport protocols to support advanced grid functionality. Given its importance in OBS, traffic aggregation and burst assembly methods to support grid services requirements are discussed, followed by the descriptions of different OBS network scenarios and their specific implementations and ability to support advanced grid functionalities and distributed applications. Based on the provided material the reader should be able to understand how OBS can be used to actually provide a distributed computing service with tight bandwidth and delay requirements.

Chapter 6 is devoted to implementation issues of optical switching fabrics and and their applicability in the real world. It presents some key performance indicators of optical switches components and then describes different applications of optical switches focusing on the two main network elements that are used in optical networks, namely optical cross connects (OXC) and optical add/drop multiplexers (OADM). Special attention is also given to protection switching, an attribute that is the most important factor for the provided quality of service. Based on the provided material, the reader should be able to understand simple as well as complex optical network topologies based on OXC and OADM nodes.

Acknowledgments

The material presented in this book provides a thorough overview of optical technologies and protocols for the future internet, which is presented from experts in the field from the e-Photon/ONe+ and BONE Networks of Excellence of the European Union. The authors wish to thank the European Union VII Framework Programme for the support in writing this book.

Contents

List of Contributors

Book Editors

Javier Aracil Department of Computer Science, Universidad Autónoma de Madrid, Spain, javier.aracil@uam.es

Franco Callegati Department of Electronics, Computer Science and Systems, Università di Bologna Italy, franco.callegati@unibo.it

Chapter Editors

Chapter 1

Franco Callegati Department of Electronics, Computer Science and Systems, Alma Mater Studiorum – Università di Bologna, Italy, franco.callegati@unibo.it

Chapter 2

Davide Careglio Department of Computer Architecture, Universitat Politècnica de Catalunya, Barcelona, Spain, careglio@ac.upc.edu

Chapter 3

Carla Raffaelli Department of Electronics, Computer Science and Systems, Università di Bologna, Italy, craffaelli@deis.unibo.it

Chapter 4

José Alberto Hernández Department of Computer Science, Universidad Autónoma de Madrid, Spain, jose.hernandez@uam.es

Víctor López Department of Computer Science, Universidad Autónoma de Madrid, Spain, victor.lopez@uam.es

Chapter 5

Reza Nejabati Department of Computing and Electronic Systems, University of Essex, Colchester, United Kingdom, rnejab@essex.ac.uk

Chapter 6

Kyriakos Vlachos Computer Engineering and Informatics Department, University of Patras, Greece, kvlachos@ceid.upatras.gr

Book Contributors

Slavisa Aleksic Institute of Communication Networks, Vienna University of Technology, Austria, Slavisa.Aleksic@tuwien.ac.at

Javier Aracil Department of Computer Science, Universidad Autónoma de Madrid, Spain, javier.aracil@uam.es

Franco Callegati Department of Electronics, Computer Science and Systems, Alma Mater Studiorum - Università di Bologna, Italy, franco.callegati@unibo.it

Davide Careglio Department of Computer Architecture, Universitat Politècnica de Catalunya, Barcelona, Spain, careglio@ac.upc.edu

Piero Castoldi Scuola Superiore SantAnna, Pisa, Italy, castoldi@sssup.it

Walter Cerroni Department of Electronics, Computer Science and Systems, Universit di Bologna, Italy, walter.cerroni@unibo.it

Marc De Leenheer Department of Information Technology, Ghent University, Belgium, marc.deleenheer@intec.UGent.be

Juan Fernandez Palacios Division of Network Planning and Techno-Economic Evaluation, Telefónica I+D, Madrid, Spain, jpfpg@tid.es.

José Luis García Dorado Department of Computer Science, Universidad Autónoma de Madrid, Spain, jl.garcia@uam.es.

José Alberto Hernández Department of Computer Science, Universidad Autónoma de Madrid, Spain, jose.hernandez@uam.es.

Andrzej Jajszczyk Department of Telecommunications, AGH University of Science and Technology, Krakow, Poland, jajszczyk@kt.agh.edu.pl

David Larrabeiti Telematic Engineering Department, Universidad Carlos III, Madrid, Spain, dlarra@it.uc3m.es

Víctor López Department of Computer Science, Universidad Autónoma de Madrid, Spain, victor.lopez@uam.es

Guido Maier Department of Electronics and Information, Politecnico di Milano, Milan, Italy, maier@elet.polimi.it

Giorgio Maria Tosi Beleffi ISCOM, Italy, giorgio.tosibeleffi@comunicazioni.it

Xavier Masip Department of Computer Architecture, Universitat Politecnica de Catalunya, Vilanova i la Geltrú, Spain, xmasip@ac.upc.edu

Reza Nejabati Department of Computing and Electronic Systems, University of Essex, Colchester, United Kingdom, rnejab@essex.ac.uk

Harald Overby Department of Telematics, Norwegian University of Science and Technology, Norway, haraldov@itemntnu.no

Achille Pattavina Department of Electronics and Information, Politecnico di Milano, Milan, Italy, pattavina@elet.polimi.it

Carla Raffaelli Department of Electronics, Computer Science and Systems, Universit di Bologna, Italy, craffaelli@deis.unibo.it

Lambros Raptis Attica Telecom, Greece, lraptis@etae.com

Ahmad Rostami Telecommunication Networks Group (TKN), Technical University of Berlin, Germany, rostami@tkn.tu-berlin.de

Sergio Sanchez Department of Computer Architecture, Universitat Politecnica de Catalunya, Vilanova i la Geltrú, Spain, sergio@ac.upc.edu

Michele Savi Department of Electronics, Computer Science and Systems, Universit di Bologna, Italy, msavi@deis.unibo.it

Dimitra Simeonidou Department of Computing and Electronic Systems, University of Essex, Colchester, United Kingdom, dsimeo@essex.ac.uk

Salvatore Spadaro Department of Signal Theory and Communications, Universitat Politecnica de Catalunya, Barcelona, Spain, spadaro@tsc.upc.edu

António Teixeira Departamento de Electrónica, Telecomunicações e Informática, Universidade de Aveiro, Portugal, Teixeira@ua.pt

Luca Valcarenghi Scuola Superiore Sant Anna, Pisa, Italy, valcarenghi@sssup.it

Kyriakos Vlachos Computer Engineering and Informatics Department, University of Patras, Greece, kvlachos@ceid.upatras.gr

Jian Wu Beijing University of Posts and Telecommunications (BUPT), Beijing, China, jianwu@bupt.edu.cn

Kostas Yiannopoulos Computer Engineering and Informatics Department, University of Patras, Greece, giannopu@ceid.upatras.gr

Georgios Zervas Department of Computing and Electronic Systems, University of Essex, Colchester, United Kingdom, gzerva@essex.ac.uk.

Acronyms

AAP	adaptive assembly period
ADM	add drop multiplexer
AFLP	asynchronous fixed length packet
AQM	active queue management
ASON	automatic switched optical network
ATM	asynchronous transfer mode
AVLP	asynchronous variable length packet
AWG	arrayed waveguide grating
BCH	burst control header
BCP	burst control packet
BFUC	best fit unscheduled channel
BGP	border gateway protocol
BPF	band pass filter
CCAMP	common control and measurement plane
CCI	connection control interface
CDC	code domain coding
COAX	coaxial cable
CoS	class of service
CP	control plane
DCS	data channel scheduling
DRCL	distributed RCL
DS	direct sequence
DS-CDC	direct sequence code domain coding
DSF	dispersion shifted filters
DSL	digital subscriber line
DTSNQoS	data transport service with network quality of service
DW	dual-wavelength
DWDM	dense wavelength division multiplexing

E-NNI	external network–network interface
EH	electroholography
ESCON	enterprise system connection

FA	forwarding adjacency
FBG	fiber bragg gratings
FBM	fractional brownian motion
FDC	frequency domain coding
FDL	fiber delay line
FEC	forwarding equivalence class
FF	first-fit
FFUC	first fit unscheduled channel
FGN	fractional gaussian noise
FICON	fiber connection
FIFO	first in, first out
FP	Fabry Perot
FPLC	fixed-paths least-congestion
FTP	file transfer protocol
FTTH	fiber-to-the-home
FWC	full wavelength conversion
FWM	four wave mixing

G-OUNI	grid user optical network interface
GbE	gigabit ethernet
GFP	generic framing procedure
GGF	global grid forum
GHPN-RG	grid high performance networking research group
GMPLS	generalized multi-protocol label switching
GoS	grade of service

HDLC	high-level data link control
HDTV	high definition television

IETF	internet engineering task force
IF	input fiber
IP	internet protocol
IPD	intentional packet dropping
IPTV	internet protocol television
IS-IS	intermediate system to intermediate system
ITU-T	international telecommunication union-telecommunication
IWU	inter working unit
JET	just-enough-time
JIT	just-in-time

L2SC	layer 2 switch capable
LAN	local area network
LAPS	link access procedure for SDH
LAUC	latest available unscheduled channel
LAUC-VF	latest available unscheduled channel with void filling
LCAS	link capacity adjustment scheme
LCSHR	least congested shortest hop routing
LL	least-loaded
LLR	least-loaded routing
LP	linear programming
LSC	lambda switch capable
LSP	labeled switched path
LU	least-used
LWC	limited wavelength conversion
MAC	medium access control
MBMAP	min-burst length-max assembly period
MEMS	micro electro-mechanical systems
MILP	mixed-integer linear program
MP	min-product
MPLS	multi-protocol label switching
MR	mixed rate
MS	max-sum
MSPP	multi-service provisioning platform
MU	most-used
MW	multi-wavelength
MZI	mach–zehnder interferometer
NG	next generation
NIMS	network information and monitoring service
NMI	network management interface
NMS	network management system
NOLM	nonlinear optical loop mirror
NP	network processor
NP	nondeterministic-polynomial
NRZ	non-return zero
O-PAM	optical packet assembly mechanism
OADM	optical add drop multiplexers
OBS	optical burst switching
OBSC	optical bit skew compensator
OC	optical channel
OCDM	optical code division multiplexing
OCh	optical channel
OCS	optical circuit switching

OF	output fiber
OFH	optical frequency hopping
OIF	optical internetworking forum
OMS	optical multiplex section
OOK	ON–OFF keying
OPI	optical pulse interval
OPS	optical packet switching
OSM	optical signal monitors
OSPF	open shortest path first
OTDM	optical time division multiple
OTH	optical transport hierarchy
OTN	optical transport network
OXC	optical cross-connect
PI	physical interface
PLC	planar lightwave circuit
PLP	packet loss probability
PLR	packet loss rate
PNNI	private network-to-network interface
PoS	Packet over SONET
PPP	point to point protocol
PSC	packet switch capable
QoS	quality of service
RA	routing area
RCL	relative capacity loss
RF	radio frequency
RFC	request for comments
ROADM	reconfigurable optical add drop multiplexers
Rsv	wavelength reservation
RSVP	resource reservation protocol
RTT	round trip time
RWA	routing and wavelength assignment
SA	scheduling algorithm
SAN	Storage Area Network
SCM	sub carrier multiplexing
SDH	synchronous digital hierarchy
SFLP	synchronous fixed length packet
SHLCR	shortest hop least congested routing
SLE	static lightpath establishment
SO-ASTN	service oriented automatic switched transport network
SOA	semiconductor optical amplifiers
SONET	synchronous optical networking

SP	shortest path
SPL	shared-per-link
SPN	shared-per-node
SPW	shared-per-wavelength
SRLG	shared-risk link group
SSMF	standard single mode fiber
SVLP	synchronous variable length packet

TCP	transmission control protocol
TDM	time division multiple
TDS	topology discovery service
TE	traffic engineering
THr	protecting threshold
TMN	telecommunications management network
TNA	transport network assigned
TWC	tuneable wavelength converters

UNI	user network signaling interface

VC	virtual container
VCAT	virtual concatenation
VCG	virtual concatenation group
VF	void filling
VO	virtualized organization

WA	wavelength allocation
WAN	wide area network
WDM	wavelength division multiplexing
WLCR-FF	weighted least-congestion routing, first-fit
WR	wavelength routed
WSON	wavelength switched optical network

XGM	cross gain modulation
XPM	cross phase modulation

Chapter 1
Introduction

Franco Callegati, Javier Aracil, and Víctor López

At the present time, optical transmission systems are capable of sending data over hundreds of wavelengths on a single fiber thanks to dense wavelength division multiplexing (DWDM) technologies, reaching bit rates on the order of gigabits per second per wavelength and terabits per second per fiber. In the last decade the availability of such a huge bandwidth caused transport networks to be considered as having infinite capacity. The recent massive deployment of Asymmetric Digital Subscriber Line (ADSL) and broadband wireless access solutions, as well as the outburst of new multimedia network services (such as Skype, YouTube, Joost, etc.) caused a significant increase of end user traffic and bandwidth demands. Therefore, the apparently "infinite" capacity of optical networks appears much more "finite" today, despite the latest developments in photonic transmission.

At the same time electronic routers evolved to provide more and more capacity, and today we have machines than can provide tens of input/output ports at speeds in the range of 1–10 Gbps. Nonetheless, these systems still present some limitations due to limited packet processing speed during routing function execution and to huge power consumption [39, 41].

These limitations are the typical motivations behind past research aimed at the development of all-optical switches and routers, assuming that it could be possible to build an optical node with the same capacity as an electronic one but with a considerably smaller number of devices and limited power consumption due to the absence of O/E/O conversion interfaces [37, 72, 80, 93, 126, 142]. This switching should lead to so-called "transparent optical networks," where the photonic technology is used not only for transmission purposes, but also for implementing more complex functions, to keep data signals within the optical domain as much as possible.

Thus, a possible evolution of network architectures is towards a "core and edge" architecture where the edge is implemented by means of electronic Internet Protocol

F. Callegati (✉)
Department of Electronics, Computer Science and Systems, Alma Mater Studiorum – Università di Bologna, Italy
e-mail: franco.callegati@unibo.it

J. Aracil and F. Callegati (eds.), *Enabling Optical Internet with Advanced Network Technologies*, Computer Communications and Networks,
DOI 10.1007/978-1-84882-278-8_1, © Springer-Verlag London Limited 2009

(IP)-based networks, while the core takes advantage of the transport service provided by the optical switching layer, capable of high-capacity transmission and switching. In such a way both sections of the network could leverage on strong factors: the flexibility and widespread availability of IP for access and the very wide band effectiveness of optics for the core.

This book addresses a road map of networking topics related to transparent optical networks, with the aim to provide the reader with a good overview of the advances of the scientific research in Europe on this topic. The focus is mainly on logical networking problems but many links to physical implementation issues are present. In fact, optical networks pose a number of new problems to the network engineers that are mainly related to the peculiar characteristics of the optical technology and related devices.

As usual, one of the major networking issues of new networking technologies is that of switching paradigms, which should provide the best cost versus performance trade-off by exploitation of the available hardware technology. Similarly to what happened in the 1990s, at the time of the discussion on the switching paradigm for the Broadband Integrated Services Digital Network (B-ISDN) that lead to the definition of the Asynchronous Transfer Mode ATM, circuit-oriented, packet-oriented, and hybrid switching paradigms have all been considered in networking switching research.

A circuit-oriented approach aims at switching the whole traffic carried on a given fiber, or on a given wavelength within a fiber at any one time. In this case the routing information can be linked to the wavelength in the wavelength routed (WR) networks [39, 72]. They offer the chance of creating high-speed circuits (lightpaths) in a very flexible way. Lightpaths may be dynamically set up and torn down, allowing reconfigurations of the logical topology. In this scenario the design issues to deal with are the definition of the best logical topology (Logical Topology Design (LTD)) and the computation of the optimum set of physical links to be assigned to each lightpath (routing and wavelength assignment (RWA)) [126, 142]. These problems have being widely studied in the literature. The objective is that the design satisfy the traffic requests while complying with the technology constraints, such as the number of optical transceivers installed on each node, which limits the connectivity degree of the logical topology, and the availability of wavelength converters, which has a strong impact on the complexity of the RWA problem. The main problem still open concerns the optical bandwidth utilization, since legacy traffic flows, handled by IP routers, require much lower capacity than that available on each lightpath. Therefore, some sort of traffic grooming layer is required in the Optical Cross-Connect (OXC), which is currently implemented with electronic technology (e.g., synchronous optical networking (SONET)/synchronous digital hierarchy (SDH)), making this networking approach less attractive and less effective.

More flexibility comes together with a refinement of the switching granularity at the subwavelength level, typically exploiting the time domain. Again different approaches are possible, depending on the size of the time multiplexing unit and on the way such a unit is handled by the network (deterministically or statistically). The time domain can be exploited in some sort of static fashion, by framing and static slotted multiplexing, combining DWDM and optical time division multiple (OTDM), as proposed in [37, 93]. This solution aims at reusing the same wavelength to carry traffic generated by a single IP router and directed to several destination IP routers. In other words, different logical links are multiplexed in a single lightpath, according to a given OTDM pattern. The resulting lightpath is routed towards all the destinations that are able to extract the relevant information. Such a solution gives the advantage of keeping the optical (de)multiplexing operation quite simple [38, 80], but it obviously presents the typical flexibility limitations experienced by techniques based on deterministic resource assignment.

As opposed to the previous solutions it is possible to envisage the implementation of the same statistical time division multiplexing that characterizes the Internet, thus providing the highest degree of flexibility and network reconfigurability. These are the so-called optical packet switching (OPS) and optical burst switching (OBS) technologies [48, 83, 201, 254]. OPS applies the packet switching paradigm to optical networking [159, 201], but it has to face some major critical issues originated by the current optical technology:

- The feasibility of the switching nodes, which must be able to provide a very short switching time that can be considered negligible compared to the burst/packet duration, thus keeping the related overhead as small as possible; these nodes must also satisfy the modularity and scalability requirements that are not so easy to fulfill with monolithic optical technology.
- The implementation of the control plane, since, even assuming a Multi-protocol label switching (MPLS) scenario, the routing information decoding and processing time may still represent a bottleneck when extremely high bit rates are used, resulting in very high burst/packet arrival rates at each node.
- The resource sharing, including issues such as contention resolution schemes and quality of service differentiation techniques that do not rely upon optical random access memories, which are not available.

OBS is a switching technology that offers a dynamic mechanism to set up high capacity end-to-end optical data connections in DWDM networks. The basic idea entails a dynamically set up wavelength path for identifying a large data flow when it traverses the network: a separate control packet therefore precedes each burst by a basic offset time, carrying relevant forwarding information.

In both OBS and OPS congestion phenomena cannot be avoided and must be managed, mainly by means of the definition of proper scheduling strategies, since something similar to the electronic random access memory (RAM) is not available in optics. In OBS the choice is to plan in advance the usage of the resources, thanks to the separate signaling, in order to minimize congestion and information loss. In OPS when packets contend for the same output, ports must be multiplied either in the wavelength domain (wavelength conversion), in the time domain (delay lines), or in the space domain (deflection and alternate routing). These sorts of problems are peculiar of optical networks. Generally speaking, effective solution requires ad hoc scheduling algorithms and optical node designs [37, 48, 83, 212, 235, 269], as is discussed in the remainder of this book.

Moreover a network needs a control plane that safeguards its working conditions (providing routing, management, etc. capabilities). For future optical networks two possibilities are available [262]:

- Overlay model, where different networks are controlled by separate planes
- Peer model, where different network layers are controlled by a single control plane, for instance generalized multi-protocol label switching (GMPLS)

The former case is the easiest to adopt in a migration path from an existing to a new technology, in particular when different operators are involved. Typically the optical network operator provides pure high-speed connectivity services to one or more IP service provider. In this case the optical and IP control planes work autonomously: the former operates on the (physical) optical network and is concerned with lightpath setup and teardown functions, while the latter operates on the (logical) IP network and deals with IP packets routing. It is assumed that optical networks will be mainly WR networks at this stage and the related control plane is still in standardization phase. Solutions like MP-lambda-S and GMPLS [123] are supported by internet engineering task force (IETF), while G.872 [124] and automatic switched optical network (ASON) [124] is supported by international telecommunication union-telecommunication (ITU-T). All of them allow setting up and tearing down optical circuits. On the contrary, the IP control plane is typically based on the traditional routing protocols of the Internet, such as open shortest path first (OSPF) and border gateway protocol (BGP).

The latter case is particularly interesting in a mid-to-long-term period, given that optical networks will be capable of OBS and/or OPS operation. In this case the integration of the control plane based on a single technology is attractive, since it allows a network control with the different layers cooperating to optimize network performance in terms of data transfer efficiency and robustness against possible failures. In this scenario the scientific community seems to converge to a connection-oriented solution based on switching of labeled traffic flows in the most generic framework (GMPLS). Such an approach is suitable for different networking solutions, ensures a good degree of scalability and flexibility, and is preferable, since it is well-suited for applying traffic engineering and quality of service management techniques.

Chapter 2
Introduction to IP over WDM

Davide Careglio, Javier Aracil, Juan Fernandez Palacios, Andrzej Jajszczyk,
David Larrabeiti, Víctor López, Xavier Masip, Sergio Sanchez,
and Salvatore Spadaro

The simple idea of having IP traffic directly transported over optical WDM technology ("IP over WDM") has been envisioned as the future for the telecommunication infrastructure.

The key point in this infrastructure becomes the switching layer between ubiquitous IP-centric networks and WDM physical layer. An intense debate has been ongoing about which model to adopt, aiming at identifying the degree of optical transparency and the proper flexibility of optical interconnection. Expected migration of switching functions from electronic to optics will be gradual and will take place in several phases. The first phase is presented in this chapter. It is characterized by the use of the wavelength as a switching granularity; the terms *optical circuit switching (OCS)*, *wavelength switching*, and *wavelength routed network* recently wavelength switched optical network (WSON) are commonly used and interchangeable.

One of the major drives of network migration is the ever-growing bandwidth demands. Section 2.1 provides statistics about network growth and traffic usage that support the need for high speed in the backbone network. On the other hand, Section 2.2 presents suitable traffic models for the numerical evaluation of the IP over WDM paradigms.

The SONET/SDH network architectures are currently the most mature and widely deployed transport technologies for IP over WDM. Originally designed for voice traffic, SONET/SDH is today experiencing a migration toward an enhanced solution (next generation (NG)) able to more efficiently transport data traffic. Some examples of its application are described in Section 2.3.

Although NG-SONET/SDH equipment adds some functionality to legacy SONET/SDH, they remain largely inflexible due to the manual provisioning of resources. The introduction of intelligence by means of a distributed control plane

D. Careglio (✉)
Department of Computer Architecture, Universitat Politècnica de Catalunya, Barcelona, Spain
e-mail: careglio@ac.upc.edu

J. Aracil and F. Callegati (eds.), *Enabling Optical Internet with Advanced Network Technologies*, Computer Communications and Networks,
DOI 10.1007/978-1-84882-278-8_2, © Springer-Verlag London Limited 2009

is recognized as the necessary further enhancement to meet the requirements of fast and flexible bandwidth provisioning, automatic topology discovery, and fast restoration. The standarization process for such a control plane is currently being enacted independently by two different bodies. The automatically switched optical network (ASON) paradigm is developed by ITU-T and described in Section 2.4. The generalized multiprotocol label switching (GMPLS) suite is designed by IETF and described in Section 2.5.

In principle, ASON and GMPLS should be not competitors but complementary works. On one hand, ASON, following the aims of ITU-T, should indicate the requirements and produce the architecture for the control plane avoiding the development of new protocols when existing ones could do. On the other hand, GMPLS, following the aims of IETF, should produce protocols in response of general requirements including those coming from ITU-T. Although the relationship seems clear, the reality is not so smooth. In fact, some incompatibilities could be found in ASON and GMPLS standards and a full interoperability is currently not possible. Section 2.6 describes the challenges for the ASON/GMPLS interworking and the current standardization efforts in ITU-T, IETF, and optical internetworking forum (OIF).

To conclude the chapter, Section 2.7 overviews the state-of-the-art of the RWA problem. In fact, whatever control plane is used, the system must set up, manage and tear down all-optical paths (so-called lightpaths) throughout the network. How to establish lightpaths to cope with given performance objectives, such as blocking probability, physical impairments, quality of service (QoS), or operators' policies, is a major research interest. In fact, beside the decision on which route between source and destination nodes is the *best* performing one, the problem in optical networks also involves the selection of the wavelength. For this reason the well-known routing problem encountered in IP networks becomes an RWA assignment problem in optical networks.

2.1 The Demand for High Speed

The steadily increasing traffic demand is driving the evolution of current IP networks to IP over WDM networks. For example, according to [258] the internet protocol television (IPTV) market will be one third of the digital market by the end of the decade and a single high definition television (HDTV) channel demands a 20-Mbps bandwidth.

Concerning the best effort traffic, a very interesting analysis is provided in [170]. While the myth of "internet traffic doubling every 100 days" is probably too optimistic, it turns out that the traffic in the U.S. and Australian backbone is doubling every year. On the other hand, the "SourceForge" statistics for *e-Mule* downloads shows that the software was downloaded around 250,000 times a day from 1 October 2007 to 24 September 2008.

In this section we provide statistics about the network growth and traffic usage that support the need for high speed in the backbone network. Actually, there are public repositories that post internet usage statistics.[1] As of December 2007, internet penetration in Europe is equal to a grand total of 43.7% of the population (348,125,847 users), with a usage growth in the period 2000–2007 of 231.2%. The penetration rate in North America increased to 71.1%.

At this writing, the number of internet users is estimated at one billion people, with a fast deployment of fiber-to-the-home (FTTH) networks both in the U.S. and in Japan [86, 230], which is progressively replacing the traditional digital subscriber line (DSL) and coaxial cable (COAX) networks.

Concerning traffic volumes, the *Internet 2* initiative provides historic aggregation data[2] that shows an exponential growth both in terms of bytes and connections. Most interestingly, a large share of Internet traffic is composed of the so-called *elephants*, namely, bulk connections from P2P services, for example. Such elephants are amenable to optical switching, as the volume of data is significant.

2.2 Traffic Models

Broadly speaking, there are two families of traffic models that have been proposed for the performance evaluation of broadband networks:

- *Fluid models:* These models provide the number of bits per time interval of a given internet traffic stream. No details about the packet arrival process are provided.
- *Packet-level models:* These models provide in-depth description of the packet arrival process, including interarrival times and packet sizes.

The IP over WDM network is expected to carry traffic from a large number of users. Thus, it is expected that the multiplex level is very high. In that case, packet-level models are too detailed for performance evaluation and it is advisable to adopt fluid models. Actually, a discrete-event simulation at the packet level results in too many events to be processed. In contrast, fluid models provide a simplified traffic description, in terms of traffic volumes, that is amenable for simulation of high-speed networks.

Usually, the traffic process provides traffic distribution in the interval $[0, t)$, i.e., the traffic sample paths are increasing functions. Let $\{X(t), t > 0\}$ denote the traffic arrival process (bits) in the interval $[0, t)$. Then, the traffic increments (in intervals of length h seconds) are given by $Y(n) = X(nh) - X((n-1)h), n = 1, 2, \ldots$. Typically, the traffic increments, and not the cumulative process $X(t)$, are used in the discrete-event simulations. Time is slotted in intervals of length h, with a value

---

[1] http://www.internetworldstats.com/

[2] http://www.net.internet2.edu/i2network/daily-report/historic-aggregate-traffic.html

of h reasonably small, and the system statistics are collected at the time epochs $nh, n = 1, 2, \ldots$. For example, let us consider a single-server infinite queue system, and let $A(n)$ be the queue occupancy at time epochs $nh, n = 1, 2, \ldots$. On the other hand, let C be the server capacity, in bits per time interval of length h. Then, the simulation program simply follows the *Lindley's* equation, i.e.,

$$A(n) = \max\{A(n-1) + Y(n) - C, 0\}. \tag{2.1}$$

It is worth noting that this is only an approximation of the queue length, which is accurate for small values of h. If, for instance, the queue is empty at $n = 0$ and $C = 10$ and $A(1) = 8$, then $A(2) = 0$. However, that does not mean that the queue has been empty for the duration of the first time interval. In fact, if the traffic comes in a single burst at the beginning of the interval, the queue occupancy is not null.

Even though the simulation models resulting from the fluid approach are not totally accurate they have the advantage of being very simple and they are also insensitive to the link capacity. Actually, no matter what the link capacity is, Eq. (2.1) applies in exactly the sameway. Thus, the execution time for the discrete-event simulation remains the same regardless of the link capacity and the traffic load.

Fluid models can be characterized by the marginal distribution and the dependence structure of the traffic. We will provide a brief discussion on the statistical features of such a fluid model and applicability to model IP over WDM switches. We will primarily consider the fractional brownian motion (FBM) [170]. However, it is worth noticing that the fractional-auto regressive integrated moving average (F-ARIMA) time series are also fluid models that show long-range dependence [81].

2.2.1 Marginal Distribution

Concerning the marginal distribution, we distinguish between Gaussian processes and non-Gaussian processes. Even though the aggregation of many sources turns out to converge to a Gaussian distribution (as predicted by the central limit theorem) it may happen that the limit distribution has infinite variance. This is the case for very high speed links at a low utilization. If, for instance, the link is multiplexing heavy-tailed bursts, then the traffic marginal distribution may not be Poisson. Let the random variable X represent the number of bits per burst and let C be the link capacity. Then, the burst duration is given by X/C. If X is heavy-tailed, i.e., $P(X > x) \sim x^{-\alpha}$ for large x then X/C is also heavy-tailed. In case C is very large then many of the bursts start and finish within the time interval h. As a result, the marginal distribution inherits the infinite variance from the heavy-tailed burst.

If, however, the burst size distribution and link capacity are such that the burst duration typically comprises several time intervals, then the resulting aggregated process is Gaussian. Usually, the traffic is modeled by the FBM, which is a Gaussian process that exhibits long-range dependence. Actually, the increments of the FBM are denoted by *fractional gaussian noise (FGN)*. It is likely that many input traffic

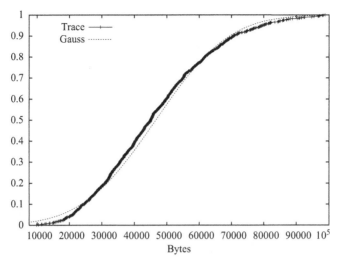

Fig. 2.1 Marginal distribution of traffic in a LAN

streams to the IP over WDM models are well-characterized by a FGN. A normalized FBM $\{Z_t, t \in (-\infty, \infty)\}$ with Hurst parameter H has the following properties, according to [168]:

1. Z_t has stationary increments.
2. $Z_0 = 0$ and $\mathbb{E}Z_t = 0$ for all t.
3. $\mathbb{E}Z_t^2 = |t|^{2H}$ for all t.
4. Z_t has continuous paths.
5. Z_t is Gaussian, i.e., all its finite-dimensional distributions are Gaussian.

Figure 2.1 shows the marginal distribution of traffic in a LAN. It turns out that there is a remarkable match between theoretical and simulation results.

2.2.2 Correlation Structure

In contrast to Poisson processes, which show independent increments, internet traffic shows long-range dependence. Considering the process Z_t defined in the previous section, it turns out that the autocorrelation $\rho(h)$ at lag $h > 0$ between Z_t and Z_{t+h} fulfills $\rho(h) \sim h^{-2(H-1)}$. On the other hand, note that $\mathbb{E}Z_t^2 = |t|^{2H}$, by the FBM definition given in the previous section. Namely, both the variance and autocorrelation show *slow decay*.

Interestingly, the fact that the variance shows a slow decay implies that the traffic burstiness does not decrease as fast as expected with an independent increments process. This phenomenon has been called *burstiness at all timescales* and has an impact in the queueing performance [65].

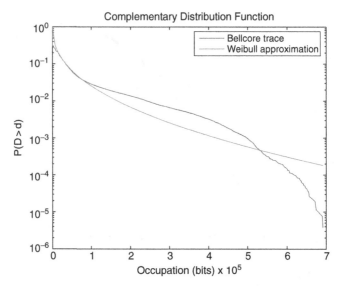

Fig. 2.2 Analytical and simulated CDF of the occupation in a fluid queue using Bellcore's trace

Actually, it turns out that the queue occupancy distribution shows Weibullian decay, namely if Q represents the queue occupancy then $P(Q > x) \sim e^{-kx^2/2}$. This is in contrast with queues fed by a process with independent increments, which show exponential decay in the queue occupancy distribution. Figure 2.2 illustrates the complementary distribution function (CDF) of the occupation in a fluid queue, when the input is the Bellcore's trace [132]. As we can see in Fig. 2.2, the analytical and the simulation fits in the body of the function.

2.3 The Currently Existing SDH/SONET Metropolitan and Core Networks

In this section we provide an analysis of current metro and core infrastructures.

2.3.1 Basic Principles

The SONET/SDH network architecture was originally designed for voice traffic utilizing a rigid hierarchy that provides a limited set of data rates (e.g., 155 Mbps, 622 Mbps, 2.5 Gbps, 10 Gbps). It actually represents the most mature transport technology and is widely utilized in both metro and core segments of modern communication networks. This implies a great number of operating infrastructures' and carriers' extensive expertise in managing and developing SONET/SDH networks and equipment.

It is therefore very attractive to use SONET/SDH network infrastructure for transporting data traffic, which continuously grew during last years. Several solutions have been indeed proposed and widely utilized with this aim. In particular asynchronous transfer mode (ATM) over SONET (ITU-T G.707 [102] defines the mapping of ATM cells in SDH frames) and Packet over SONET (PoS) (ITU-T X.85 [108] and IETF request for comments (RFC) 1661 [233], 1662 [232], 2615 [149]) represent the most utilized protocol stacks allowing data traffic transport on SONET/SDH networks. However these solutions have important drawbacks. Indeed they do not break the rigidity of the SONET/SDH hierarchy, thus implying a great waste of bandwidth in data traffic mapping. As an example, for gigabit ethernet (GbE) transport a virtual container (VC)-4-16c (composed of 16 contiguously concatenated virtual container VC-4 of bandwidth 150 Mbps) is used with a very low bandwidth efficiency of 42%.

Therefore, in the last years a set of NG-SDH functionalities, consisting of virtual concatenation (VCAT), generic framing procedure (GFP), and link capacity adjustment scheme (LCAS) has been introduced for allowing flexible and efficient transport of data traffic through the SONET/SDH infrastructure. The aforementioned functionalities also support the interoperability with the operating legacy SONET/SDH devices thus guaranteeing the possibility of a gradual migration from legacy SONET/SDH networks.

- **Virtual concatenation (VCAT).** (ITU-T G.707 [102] and G.783 [104]) VCAT provides a way to partition SONET/SDH bandwidth into several subrates to efficiently accommodate voice and data services. VCAT breaks the rigidity of SONET/SDH hierarchy enabling fine bandwidth assignment. In particular, it allows building virtual concenteration group (VCGs), which are composed of a uniform set of VCs. The several VCs holding to a particular group can follow different paths within the SONET/SDH network. Intermediate equipment does not need to support virtual concatenation for correctly managing passing through traffic. As an example virtual concatenation allows building a virtual concatenation group (VCG) composed of seven VC-4 (i.e., VC-4-7v of bandwidth 1050 Mbps), which is a good candidate for efficiently carrying GbE.
- **Generic framing procedure (GFP).** (ITU-T G.7041 [100] and G.806 [105]) GFP is an encapsulation procedure for the transport of packet data over SDH. GFP defines a flexible adaptation mechanism specifically designed to transport several types of upper-layer data clients in SONET/SDH frames. Other possible mechanisms are X.26 (ethernet over SDH using link access procedure for SDH (LAPS)) and ethernet/multi-protocol label switching (MPLS)/point to point protocol (PPP). GFP overcomes the typical drawbacks of ATM and high-level data link control (HDLC). Indeed by supporting variable length payloads GFP does not rely on client traffic segmentation typical of ATM. Moreover, by utilizing an efficient frame delineation mechanism, GFP does not need the byte-stuffing procedure utilized by HDLC framing. GFP has been developed in two versions: framed mapped and transparent mapped GFP. *Frame mapped GFP* is defined for variable-length data traffics (IP/PPP, ethernet), while transparent mapped GFP is defined for octet-aligned (8B/10B) block coded (fiber connection (FICON),

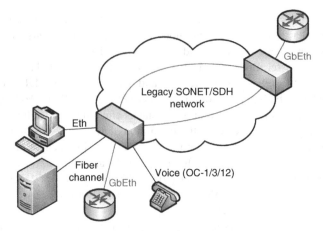

Fig. 2.3 Ethernet over legacy SONET/SDH network

enterprise system connection (ESCON), fiber channel, and GbE) traffic streams, and its main objective is the reduction of the transmission latency, which is a critical parameter in Storage Area Network (SAN)s.

- **Link capacity adjustment scheme (LCAS).** (ITU-T G.7042 [101], G.806 [105] and G.783 [104]) LCAS introduces Bandwidth on Demand services in SONET/SDH networks. It provides the possibility for one to dynamically increase/decrease the VCGs bandwidth; moreover it provides the capability of temporarily removing members that have experienced a failure. Therefore the utilization of LCAS guarantees efficiency and flexibility in bandwidth assignment for both bandwidth adjustment utilized with variable data traffic and traffic rerouting necessary under network failures or maintenance.

Network devices able to support NG-SONET/SDH (VCAT, GFP, and LCAS) are called multi-service provisioning platform (MSPP). These devices, which have to be placed at the edge of the existing SONET/SDH networks, are actually commercially available and besides the aforementioned functionalities still support ATM over SONET, PoS, and voice services.

Figure 2.3 shows a generic example where MSPPs, supporting next generation functionalities, use the legacy SONET/SDH network for efficiently transporting different types of data traffic. As an example, illustrated with red lines in the figure, a gigabit ethernet flow (1 Gbps) is routed using transparent mapped GFP in a VC-4-7v VCG (1.04832 Gbps) with a bandwidth efficiency of 95%. The several members of the VCG can be routed along different paths within the network by means of LCAS; then they will converge at the destination MSPP.

2.3.2 Installation in Provider's Networks

Today, most of traditional SONET/SDH vendors are providing NG-SONET/SDH equipment, which is extensively used especially by incumbent operators. Therefore,

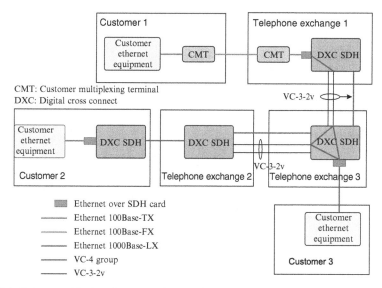

Fig. 2.4 Point to multipoint ethernet service over SDH

NG-SONET/SDH is one of the most extended technologies in metrocore and core networks and is mainly aimed at providing a bridging point between the legacy time division multiple (TDM) architectures and new IP transport networks.

There exist several implementation scenarios for NG-SDH in operators' networks:

- **Ethernet services over the transport network.** NG-SDH is used to support an end-to-end service for customers which can be point-to-point and point-to-multipoint. As shown in the Fig. 2.4, access from the customer network can be electric or optical.
- **Extension of metro access ethernet networks.** NG-SDH network extends the reach of metro access ethernet networks. In this scenario, ethernet-based services can be offered to customers that are far from the ethernet edge nodes. For example, as shown in Fig. 2.5, a customer ethernet flow can be provided over an SDH aggregation network by mapping it in a VC-12-5v group.

2.4 Automatically Switched Optical Network (ASON)

Optical backbone networks, based on SONET/SDH and WDM technologies, are designed mainly for voice applications, and do not match current needs triggered by the rapid growth of data traffic. Available resources often cannot be properly allocated due to inherent inflexibility of manually provisioned large-scale optical networks. This problem may be solved by using intelligent optical networks, which allow the automatic reconfiguration of the network resources in real time.

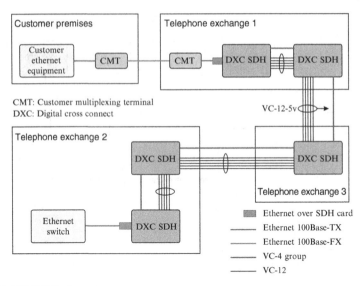

Fig. 2.5 NG-SDH in the metro access

Most limitations of current optical networks are due to the fact that they are operated manually or via complex and slow network management systems. Major drawbacks of such optical networks include: manual error-prone provisioning, long provisioning times, inefficient resource utilization, difficult interoperability between the packet client networks and the circuit-switched optical networks, complex network management, difficult interoperability between networks belonging to different operators, lack of protection in mesh-type optical networks [114].

Network operators expect the following major features from an automatically switched optical network: fast provisioning, easier network operation, higher network reliability, scalability, simpler planning and design. Provisioning of optical channels in minutes or even seconds would open new opportunities related to better resource utilization, creation of new services, such as bandwidth on demand, and a range of traffic engineering mechanisms. Optical network resources can be automatically linked to data traffic patterns in client networks. Creation of a separate control plane will significantly impact the network operation and management. Connections can be set up in a multivendor and multicarrier environment without relying on interoperability between different management systems. Such systems will be also relieved from route selection and the need to manually update the network topology. This, in turn, will increase scalability which is essential to support switched connections on a global scale. New protection and restoration schemes for mesh-type optical transport networks will improve the reliability performance measures offered to customers. Large-scale transport networks are difficult to plan and design. Lack of reliable traffic data, uncertainty of future service needs predictions, and a large variety of available protocols and interfaces make the network design process a real challenge. The standardized control plane will enable the reuse of existing protocols and will reduce the need to develop operational support systems for configuration management.

ITU-T has defined the concept of automatic switched optical network (ASON). ASON is an optical transport network that has dynamic connection capability. This capability is accomplished by a control plane that performs the call and connection control functions [107]. A related, but more generic, term is *automatic switched transport network* (ASTN) [106]. ASTN is technology-independent, i.e., it concerns more than just optical networks. The ASON architecture describes a *reference architecture* since it presents functional components and abstract interfaces.

ASON supports three kinds of connections, differing in connection establishment type: *permanent, switched, and soft permanent* [106]. The permanent connection is set up either by a network management system (NMS) or by manual intervention and is an equivalent to a traditional leased line. Therefore, such a connection does not require any intervention of the control plane and does not involve automatic routing or signaling. The switched connection is established on demand by the communicating endpoints by using routing and signaling capabilities of the control plane. The switched connection requires a user network signaling interface (UNI) and its setup may be the responsibility of the end user (the client network) [106]. The soft permanent connection is established by specifying two permanent connections at the edge of the network and setting up a switched connection between the permanent connections within the network.

A logical view of the ASON architecture is shown in Fig. 2.6. The transport plane, referred also to as the *data plane*, represents the functional resources of the network which convey user information between locations. The control plane performs the *call control* and connection control functions. The functions of the ASON control plane are automated, based on networking intelligence, that include automatic discovery, routing, and signaling. The management plane performs management functions for the transport plane, the control plane, and the system as a whole, as well as coordinates operation of all the planes [107]. These management functions are related to network elements, networks and services and, usually, they are less automated than those of the control plane.

Figure 2.6 also shows a variety of interfaces (reference points). UNI is a signaling interface between service (call) requester and service provider control plane entities. Internal network-network interface (IN-NI) is a signaling interface between control plane entities belonging to one or more domains having a trusted relationship, and external network-network interface (EN-NI) is a signaling interface between control plane entities belonging to different administrative domains. Other interfaces include: the physical interface (PI) in the transport plane, the connection control interface (CCI) between components of the control and transport planes, as well as two kinds of network management interface (NMI) between the management plane and two other planes. CCI instructs the network element, e.g., an optical cross-connect, to set up connections between selected ports. This interface is vendor-specific. Network management interfaces are used between network management systems (e.g., telecommunications management network (TMN) based) and the control (NMI-A) and transport (NMI-T) planes.

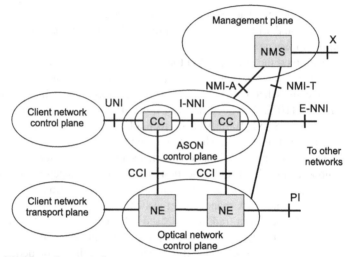

CC: Connection controller
CCI: Connection controller interface
E-NNI: External network-network interface
I-NNI: Internal network-network interface
NE: Network element
NMI-A: Network management interface–ASON control plane
NMI-T: Network management interface–Transport plane
NMS: Network management system
PI: Physical interface
UNI: User-network interface
X: Interface between management systems

Fig. 2.6 Logical view of ASON architecture

The control plane in ASON is responsible for the call and connection control. Indeed, an important feature of ASON is the separation of call and connection control functions. The *call control* is responsible for the end-to-end session negotiation, call admission control, and call state maintenance. The *connection control* is related to setup and release of connections as well as maintenance of their states.

The principal functions of the control plane to support the call and connection control include: automatic neighbor, resource and service discovery, address assignment and resolution, routing, and signaling [113].

Automatic discovery eliminates the need for explicit configuration activity. The neighbor discovery is responsible for determining the state of local links connecting to all neighbors. The *resource discovery* has a wider scope than the neighbor discovery. It allows every node to discover network topology and resources. This kind of discovery determines what resources are available, what are the capabilities of various network elements, and how the resources are protected. It improves inventory management as well as detects configuration mismatches. The *service discovery* is responsible for verifying and exchanging service capabilities of the network, for example, services supported over a trail or link. Such capabilities may include the class of service (CoS), the grade of service (GoS) supported by different administrative domains, the ability to support flexible adaptation at either end of the connection, and the ability to support diverse routing.

Routing is used to select paths for establishment of connections through the network. ASON supports hierarchical, source-based and step-by-step routing resulting in a different distribution of components between nodes and their mutual relationships.

Signaling involves transporting control messages between all entities communicating through a network's control plane. Signaling protocols are used to create, maintain, restore, and release connections. ASON defines functionality of the control plane independent of a particular choice of control protocols. Therefore, a variety of such protocols can be used in real networks, including those from the MPLS family, like resource reservation protocol (RSVP)-traffic engineering (TE), or coming from the ATM world, like private network-to-network interface (PNNI).

The ASON-based approach to the control plane for optical networks is relatively mature. The key standards are already available, although considerable work still has to be done to fill all gaps. The strength of the ASON concept is the fact that it is a reference architecture and can employ well-developed concepts like ones coming from the IP world, such as automatic discovery or routing, and allows reuse of some of its protocols, in the circuit-switched environment of optical networks. Implementation of ASON enables fast provisioning, easier network operation, increases network reliability and scalability, as well as simplifies planning and design. This, in turn, may be translated into direct benefits to operators and their clients. It should be noted, however, that along with ASON, there exist alternative approaches to the implementation of the control plane for optical networks, such as those based on GMPLS.

2.5 Generalized Multiprotocol Label Switching (GMPLS)

Generalized multi-protocol label switching (GMPLS) is an enhancement of the MPLS traffic engineering architecture, performed by the internet engineering task force (IETF). In order to properly understand GMPLS, the reader should study MPLS in depth first, as this is not within the scope of this book. In a nutshell, MPLS [217] is a technology that enhances routers to support packet forwarding based on labels rather than on destination addresses. These labels are inserted at the ingress node of an MPLS core network and removed at the egress node. The most interesting property of MPLS is that the path followed by the MPLS frames throughout the network—called labeled switched path (LSP)—need not follow what the route table dictates. In fact, any path can be set up throughout the network; this makes LSPs suitable for a number of traffic engineering applications not supported by IP.

The success of MPLS as a way to incorporate connection-oriented features to core packet networks has fueled the interest on using this technology not only as the logical bridge between MPLS-enabled packet switched and circuit networks, but more importantly, as the control paradigm to build next generation dynamic optical networks as an alternative to ITU-T ASON. Towards this goal, the common control and measurement plane (CCAMP) IETF working group[3] has been working on the extension of MPLS control protocols to properly support TDM and optical networks. This concept, formerly called MPLS, is the purpose of the GMPLS architecture and protocols [150].

2.5.1 GMPLS Concept

GMPLS extends the LSP concept to circuits in TDM and optical networks and proposes the extension of existing MPLS control protocols to control connection-oriented switches. This means that TDM and optical switches must become aware of GMPLS control protocols to translate an operation on a label forwarding entry into a change of space/lambda/time switching state. Thus a single protocol can provide end-to-end circuit provisioning across routers, SDH multiplexers, and optical switches, as well a unified framework for protection, restoration, monitoring, management, etc. including all layers and switching devices involved in a connection. The shift of paradigm is quite important. Today, circuit setup and management in optical networks is mainly performed manually by operators from a centralized operation and management center [9]. Switch configuration is static and remotely executed switch by switch from the NMS through the element network system (EMS). GMPLS changes this centralized approach to a new architecture featuring a distributed and dynamic control plane: all nodes exchange control information over a dedicated channel—using e.g. OSPF-TE—and connection setup can be initiated by the head-end of a connection (following a TE request from the NMS) and realized by an exchange of messages between adjacent nodes, namely using RSVP-TE.

The generalization required by GMPLS is not simple, however, since many technology-specific rules and parameters must be taken into account by the enhanced signaling protocols.

2.5.2 Enhancing MPLS

Let us briefly outline the main enhancements introduced by GMPLS. A recommended more detailed overview can be found at [85].

- **Interfaces.** GMPLS extends MPLS to include six types of interfaces (Fig. 2.7) used by Label Switching Router (LSR)s:

  - Packet switch capable (PSC)
  - Layer 2 switch capable (L2SC): forwards data upon layer 2 headers (ATM, ethernet or frame relay)

---

[3] http://www.ietf.org/html.charters/ccamp-charter.html

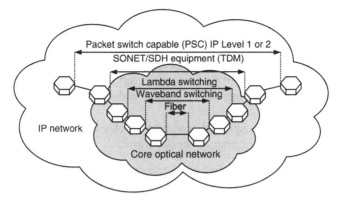

Fig. 2.7 GMPLS interfaces

- TDM: forwards data according to its time slot in a TDM signal, usually present in digital cross connects or in SONET/SDH add drop multiplexers (ADM).
- Lambda switch capable (LSC): forwarding process is based on the input wavelength of data like in optical cross-connect (OXC).
- Waveband switch capable (WSC): wavebands are forwarded with this kind of interface.
- Fiber switch capable (FSC): the input fiber determines the output fiber or fiber bundle. Interface switching capability descriptors are advertised via the link-state routing protocol.

• **Routing.** GMPLS implies making TDM and optical networks aware of IP routing protocols enhanced for traffic engineering, such as OSPF-TE and intermediate system to intermediate system (IS-IS)-TE, to convey information—namely available link capacity, termination capabilities and protection properties—that can be used by circuit provisioning protocols such as RSVP-TE. An LSP can become a TE link, not necessarily between adjacent nodes, and it is not required to establish a routing adjacency between at both ends of the LSP. Only a forwarding adjacency (FA) between both routers is established—the LSP is known as an FA-LSP—and announced by the routing protocol, the only premise being that both head and tail-end label switching router (LSRs) are of the same type. Hence, several specific types of FA are feasible: FA-packet switch capable (PSC), FA-layer 2 switch capable (L2SC), FA-TDM, and FA-lambda switch capable (LSC), and used in a hierarchical way. For instance, an FA-LSC would aggregate many FA-PSC from the set of PSC nodes whose LSPs share the same lambda. Link bundling is also supported, i.e., a TE link can actually be a "link bundle" and it is announced as such, summarizing the information of its component links. Component links can be uniquely identified by tuples <node ID, link bundle, link identifier>. This is called "unnumbered link" support since no explicit subnet is built per individual link or link bundle (Fig. 2.7).

Other information conveyed by routing protocols for GMPLS is the shared-risk link group (SRLG) and the "link protection type." The SRLG attribute—a 32 bit number unique in the domain—is used to compute strictly disjoint paths for protection purposes. The link protection type information is used by TE algorithms to search for paths with a target protection level. The protection types defined are extra traffic, unprotected, shared, dedicated 1:1, dedicated 1+1, and enhanced.

- **Signaling.** In order to support the new interface classes, a number of changes on signaling are required. The most relevant follow:

  - *Hierarchical LSPs*: Signaling must support LSP nesting even with unnumbered links. The LSP hierarchy has been developed to improve the scalability of GMPLS by allowing LSPs to be aggregated into a hierarchy of such LSPs [128]. An LSP may be advertised as a TE link for use within the same instance of the control plane as was used to set up the LSP.
  - *Bidirectional LSPs*: TDM circuits are bidirectional. GMPLS enables the specification of bidirectional LSPs to improve setup latency and path consistency.
  - *Labels*: A new label format is introduced—"generalized labels"—to enable the identification of time slots, wavelengths in a waveband, fibers in a bundle, and the MPLS label. Generalized label requests specify the technology-specific LSP type being requested. For example, it is possible to switch wavebands (a set of contiguous wavelengths) and the generalized label specifies the range of labels associated to the first and last wavelengths.
  - *Label use*: Unlike MPLS, GMPLS permits an upstream node to suggest a label to the downstream node in order to advance the change of state in the switch (this optimization is especially relevant in optical micro electro-mechanical systems (MEMS) switches before the label mapping is received from downstream (downstream label assignment is compulsory in MPLS). Moreover, a "label set" can be used to constrain the label range that can be used for LSPs between two peers. This is especially useful at the wavelength level where multiple physical constraints exist for switching, such as a maximum number of wavelength conversions, switchable wavelength sets, etc. The label set can also be used in the notification of label errors.
  - *Control/data plane separation*: Specific changes are also required due to control/data plane separation in GMPLS. Examples are the proper identification of controlled data channels and fault handling of control channel and nodes. GMPLS also proposes a new RSVP-TE notify message suitable to notify errors to nonadjacent nodes.
  - *Link management protocol (LMP)*: A new link-control protocol has been proposed to manage TE links between neighboring nodes over the separate control channel. Link provisioning, bundling, protection, fault isolation, link management, connectivity verification, etc. are functions assigned to this protocol that recall the level 2 functions of signaling system number 7 in SDH networks.

2.5.3 *MPLS vs GMPLS*

As reviewed, the generalization of MPLS to support optical and circuit-switched networks is not simple. GMPLS is an attempt to bring in a simple IP-based control solution to dynamically drive this sort of network, which will still be managed by centralized TE tools for some years. This will be the first step before seamless IP-driven hybrid packet-switched MPLS LSPs tunneled over circuit-switched GMPLS LSPs becomes commonplace. The advantages derived from the unification of worlds under the generic label-switching path concept (in terms of interoperability, planning, management, etc.) are a guarantee for a sustained convergence.

To summarize, the essential differences between MPLS and GMPLS are listed in Table 2.1.

Table 2.1 MPLS vs GMPLS

	MPLS	GMPLS
Data and control planes	Same channel	Dedicated signaling channel(s)
Type of interfaces	Packet (PSC) and cell/frame (L2SC)	PSC, L2SC, TDM, LSC, FSC
LSP start/end	At PSC/L2SC LSR	On the same type of interfaces
LSP uni/bidirectional	Unidirectional	Bidirectional
Label format	Unique	Depends on interface type: generalized label concept
Label processing	Used in data plane for packet forwarding and in control plane for LSP setup	Only used in the control plane in TDM, LSC, FSC
Label restrictions	No constraints to label allocation and no label suggestion to downstream nodes	Upstream can restrict labels used in path and suggests labels
Bandwidth allocation	Continuous	Discrete: lambda (OXC), STS-n, VT-n (SONET),…, VC (SDH). Encoded in RSVP-TE objects
Signaling awareness of physical layer	Labeled packets presumed	Media-specific signaling
Number of parallel links	A few, many labels per link	Hundreds. Link bundling, common labels
Fault notification	In-band	In-band (failure in control plane) and out-of-band (data plane failure). New RSVP-TE notify messages allow failure notification related to LSPs to a targeted nonadjacent node
LSP protection information	Not conveyed	Indicates LSP link protection type. Link protection capabilities are advertised via routing

2.6 ASON and GMPLS Interworking

GMPLS has been defined by IETF and therefore it is strongly associated with IP-based data networks. Indeed, GMPLS inherits IP protocols and concepts and it is the natural evolution from MPLS technology, which was designed to improve the efficiency of the data networks. With GMPLS, MPLS has been generalized and extended to cover circuit-oriented optical switching technologies.

On the contrary, the ITU-T community is characterized by a traditional telecommunications networks background. As a consequence, the ASON concept is based on a network view based on legacy transport networks, such as SONET/SDH and ATM.

This implies some differences on network views, which in turn are translated in the GMPLS and ASON definitions. As an example, all the nodes and links of the GMPLS network share the same IP address space and information (e.g., routing, link state, etc.) is shared between nodes (client and transport nodes). Indeed, GMPLS implies a trusted environment, which derives to the so-called peer network model. In this case, the topology as well as other network information is shared among all network elements across the layers by an integrated control plane.

On the contrary, with the ASON concept, the UNI interface is not a trusted reference point, and therefore routing and addressing information pertaining to the interior of the network is hidden to the client network, which belongs to a different address space. Such an ASON scenario corresponds to the so-called *overlay model*, which implies that there is no network information exchanges between the layers, since the routing in each layer is done separately.

While the peer model may be appropriate when the transport and client networks are operated by a single administrative entity, the overlay model is more suitable in case the networks are managed by different entities.

As a consequence, in case end-to-end connections must be created across different and heterogeneous control domains (both GMPLS and ASON), some interworking issues arise that need to be properly addressed.

The OIF has defined the OIF UNI 1.0 R2 [174, 175] and OIF UNI 2.0 [176, 177] and the OIF external network–network interface (E-NNI) [171] for ASON architecture, while the IETF has defined the GMPLS protocol architecture for peer network models.

The OIF interdomain interfaces support SONET/SDH, optical transport network (OTN)/optical transport hierarchy (OTH), and ethernet services while GMPLS manages also the request for full lambda services (LSC switching). The interoperability between ASON and GMPLS domains in terms of LSC switching can be solved requesting TDM services at the edges of each domain. In this way, no proprietary extensions to current OIF interfaces definition have to be added.

Both OIF and IETF interfaces are based on GMPLS protocols (RSVP-TE for signaling and OSPF-TE for routing, respectively) to create LSPs with various switching capabilities. However, OIF interfaces include the extensions required by the ITU-T ASON architecture.

Such interworking issues are related with both signaling and routing. A first way to cope with them is to use the same interfaces at the edge nodes, but in this case, ASON/GMPLS gateways at border nodes have to be used, such as in [178].

From the signaling point of view, the main difference, among others, between ASON and GMPLS signaling, resides in the single and multisession connection approaches. While GMPLS use the single-session connection approach, ASON and OIF use the multisession approach. The former implies a single signaling (RSVP) session, which is defined by the source and the destination addresses as well as the LSP identifier which have a global significance. In the case of ASON model, if an end-to-end call/connection has to cross different control domains, the call/connection segments concept is defined. The end-to-end connection is therefore the resulting concatenation of call/connection segments. Each connection segment has its local identifier and use, as source and destination session addresses the connection segments endpoints. Each UNI connection endpoint is identified by the so-called transport network assigned (TNA) address, which is carried by the signaling messages to globally identity the connection endpoint. The generalized UNI object has been defined to this extent.

Some efforts have been done to dealt with the interworking network scenarios. IETF in [187] addresses the functional requirements required to support ASON networks that may lead to additional extensions to GMPLS signaling to support these capabilities, while OIF is working on the signaling protocol interworking of ASON and GMPLS network domains [173].

From the routing point of view, the ITU-T G.8080 [107] and G.7715 [103] specify the routing requirements (architecture and protocols) for ASON-compliant control planes. The basic functionalities, among others, are the network partitioning in the routing area (RA) and the multilevel routing hierarchy.

For interoperability purposes, IETF defined the routing requirements for the GMPLS protocols to support the capabilities and functionalities of ASON control planes [21] and [188]; some new extensions to OSPF-TE routing protocol are being proposed while OIF is working on OSPF-TE extensions to cope with the ASON requirements [172]. Nevertheless, some differences still exist in the definition of these extensions.

2.7 Routing and Wavelength Assignment Problem

Unlike traditional IP networks where the routing process only involves a physical path selection, in *wavelength-routed optical WDM networks* the routing process not only involves a physical path selection process (i.e., finding a route from the source to the destination nodes) but also a wavelength assignment process (i.e., assigning a wavelength—or wavelengths—to the selected route), named the *RWA problem*. The RWA problem is often tackled by division into two different subproblems, the routing subproblem and the wavelength assignment subproblem. In this environment, it is very important to take into account the networks under wavelength

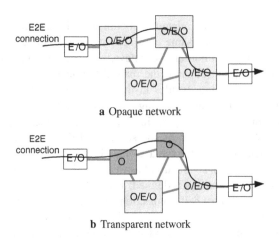

Fig. 2.8 Optical networks classification

continuity constraint, in which ligthpaths are set up for connection requests between node pairs, and a single path must be assigned to the same wavelength in all the nodes belonging to the selected route. If no wavelength is available for this path, then the connection request is blocked. Therefore, the networks can be classified in three basic approaches that can be found in the literature: *opaque, transparent, and semitransparent networks*. Opaque optical transport networks convert the signal from optical to electrical at each node port, that is, each link is optically isolated by transponders doing O/E/O conversions (Fig. 2.8a). Thus, the signal is switched electrically in each node and it is only maintained optically between adjacent nodes. The routing algorithms needed to compute the route and allocate the resources are relatively simple because all the resources on a given path are equivalent from the point of view of its functions. In fact, the routing algorithm used in classical transport networks (i.e., SDH) can be applied in opaque networks.

On the other hand, transparent optical networks do not convert the optical signal to electrical in the intermediate nodes of the end-to-end path (Fig. 2.8b). Thus, in the absence of wavelength converters, a lightpath must occupy the same wavelength on all the fiber links through which it traverses. In these networks the RWA algorithms must take into consideration that the transmission of the signal on the fiber has to follow certain restrictions due to technological constraints. The wavelength continuity constraint could result in rejection of a connection even though the required capacity is available on all the links of the path but not on the same wavelength. Because the optical signal is subject to impairments, a limit exists in the maximum distance reachable by an optical signal on a transparent network. Therefore, it is necessary to install regenerators/converters in the intermediate nodes breaking up the optical continuity. Networks with these features are known as *semitransparent networks*, and the routing algorithms have to take into both the choice of a lambda among the ones available and the placement of a regenerator/converters, when it is necessary.

This section briefly examines each approach from the point of view of RWA considering both the transparent optical networks and the wavelength interchangeable (WI) networks with wavelength conversion capability.

2.7.1 RWA in Transparent Networks with Static Traffic

With static traffic, the entire set of connection requests is previously known, and the static RWA problem of setting up these connection requests is named the static lightpath establishment (SLE) problem. The objective is then to minimize the network resources such as wavelengths or fibers needed for establishing these connection requests; or the objective is to maximize the number of established connections among the entire set for a given number of resources, wavelengths, and fibers. The SLE problem can be formulated as a mixed-integer linear program (MILP) [209], which is nondeterministic-polynomial (NP) complete. There are different approaches to solving the SLE problem; genetic algorithms or simulated annealing [284] can be applied to obtain locally optimal solutions. In general, the SLE problem is made more tractable by dividing into two subproblems, the routing subproblem and the wavelength assignment subproblem. For example, in [8] the authors propose using linear programming (LP) relaxation techniques followed by rounding to solve the routing subproblem, and graph coloring to assign the wavelengths once the route has been assigned.

The SLE problem is often also referred to as the *virtual topology problem* [54, 210].

2.7.2 RWA in Transparent Networks with Dynamic Traffic

In a dynamic traffic scenario the connections are requested in some random fashion, and the lightpath has to be set up as needed. Source-based routing is one of the recommendations stated in the ASON specifications [107]. According to source-based routing, routes are dynamically computed in the source nodes based on the routing information contained in their network state databases. There are many contributions in the literature that address the dynamic RWA problem and propose some algorithms dealing with both routing selection and the wavelength assignment subproblems.

2.7.2.1 The Routing Subproblem

Concerning to the routing subproblem, the routing algorithms can be put in two different classes: offline (fixed) and online (adaptive). In offline routing the algorithm is executed offline and the precomputed route(s) for every source-destination node pair are stored for later use. An example is the shortest path (SP) algorithm. The main drawback of the SP algorithm is the lack of network load balance since the selected route between a fixed pair of nodes will always be the same regardless the traffic load. In [87] the authors propose the fixed-alternate routing algorithm, which provides the network with more than one route for each pair of nodes. Unfortunately, offline routing does not consider the current network state when it computes routes, a situation that significantly impacts on the global network performance. Instead, online (or adaptive) routing relies on the network state information when it computes routes. These adaptive algorithms are executed at the time the connection request arrives. The route can be calculated online or the routes can be precomputed (offline), and the online algorithm selects one of them according to the current network state information.

An example of these dynamic algorithms is least-loaded routing (LLR) [33], where the selected route is the least congested among a set of precomputed routes, that is, the route with more available wavelengths. Congestion in a route is the congestion of the most congested link on the route, that is, the link with less available wavelengths. Two variants of the LLR algorithm are proposed in [140]. The first algorithm is called fixed-paths least-congestion (FPLC) and is basically the same as the LLR but limits the number of precomputed routes to the two shortest and to a link disjoint. The use of link disjoint routes is very typical in many RWA algorithms, mainly because the algorithm will select among parallel routes, and, furthermore, if one route fails the connection can be rerouted to another route. The authors in [140] argue that the use of more than two routes does not significantly improve the performance. The second proposed algorithm in [140] is the FPLC-N(k); in this case, instead of searching all links of the precomputed routes for the availability of the wavelengths, only the first k links on each route are searched. This solution seeks a trade-off between low control overhead and low blocking probability.

On the other hand the algorithms proposed in [253] compute dynamically the route instead of selecting it among a fixed set of precomputed routes. These algorithms are the least congested shortest hop routing (LCSHR) and the shortest hop least congested routing (SHLCR). In the first one, LCSHR, the priority is to utilize efficiently the routes, and it selects the least congested route among all the shortest hop routes currently available. In the second, SHLCR, the priority is to maintain efficiently the load in the network, and it selects the shortest hop route among all the least congested routes.

2.7.2.2 The Wavelength Assignment Subproblem

The reviewed algorithms address the routing subproblem, but as mentioned previously the RWA problem is often divided in order to simplify, into the routing subproblem and the wavelength assignment subproblem. The wavelength assignment process can also be used for static traffic or for dynamic traffic. Usually the static wavelength assignment is solved by means of graph-coloring [158]. On the other hand, there are several heuristic algorithms proposed in the literature dealing with the dynamic assignment problem, such as random, first-fit (FF), least-used (LU), most-used (MU) [242], min-product (MP) [115], least-loaded (LL) [119], max-sum (MS) [242], relative capacity loss (RCL) [283], protecting threshold (THr) [18], wavelength reservation (Rsv) [18] and distributed RCL (DRCL) [98].

The random scheme assigns randomly a wavelength among all the available wavelengths on the route. The FF scheme numbered all the possible wavelengths. The wavelength selected is that with the lowest number among those available on the route. The LU scheme selects the wavelength that is the least used in the network. The MU, the opposite of LU, attempts to assign the most used wavelength in the network. This is done in order to pack the connections in fewer wavelengths. The MP is for multifiber networks, where the links between nodes consists in several fibers, and then there are several wavelengths of each color. It tries to minimize the number of needed fibers in the network. First, for each wavelength the product of the assigned (or occupied) fibers on each link of the route is taken. Then, the wavelength selected is the one with the lower number among the wavelengths that minimize that product. In a single-fiber network the number of possible assigned fibers in each link of the route can only be 0 (if the wavelength is free) or 1 (if it is assigned). So, the product for the wavelengths that are available in the route will be 0, and the MP becomes the FF.

The LL selects the wavelength with more capacity (more unassigned fibers) in the most loaded link of the route. Like the MP, the LL scheme is designed for multifiber networks and it also becomes the FF in single networks.

The MS scheme is designed for both single and multifiber networks. It considers all the possible lightpaths (route and wavelength) between a source and destination node. It selects the wavelength that maximizes the sum of remaining capacities (free fibers, or not assigned) of all the lightpaths if that wavelength is assigned. That is, the max-sum scheme selects the wavelength that minimizes the capacity loss due to set up a lightpath.

Similar to the MS the RCL scheme decision is based on selecting that wavelength which minimizes the relative capacity loss due to set up a lightpath with this wavelength.

The schemes Rsv and THr seek to protect long routes instead of minimizing the blocking probability. Applying them, the long routes will not suffer high blocking probabilities, thus achieving a greater degree of fairness. The complete fairness is achieved when the blocking probability is independent of the source, destination nodes, and number of hops of the route. That is, all the routes suffer the same blocking probability, independent of the length. The Rsv scheme reserves wavelength in links to be used only by long routes that traverse that link. In the case of THr, a wavelength is assigned to connections of single-hop only if there is a minimum value (threshold) of free wavelengths.

A variant of the RCL is the DRCL which is applied for online calculation of routes while RCL is applied for fixed routes. It is necessary to note that most of the routing algorithms reviewed above are combined with some of the previous wavelength assignment algorithms. Usually first the routing algorithm selects a route and then the wavelength algorithm selects a wavelength among those available for such a route. Just as an example, the routing algorithms LCSHR and SHLCR [253] are combined with the FF and MU schemes of wavelength assignment to evaluate the blocking probability produced by such combinations.

There are other techniques, such as unconstrained routing [157], where first the wavelength is assigned and then the route is selected. First the wavelengths are ordered according to their use, the MU wavelength is selected, and then the shortest route on this wavelength is dynamically computed.

2.7.3 RWA in Wavelength Interchangeable Networks

In order to improve network performance the wavelength continuity constraint can be eliminated by introducing wavelength converters. Wavelength routed networks with wavelength conversion are known as *wavelength-interchangeable* (WI) *networks*. In such networks the OXCs are equipped with wavelength converters so that a lightpath can be set up using different wavelengths on different links along the route. Widely shown in the literature are the positive effects in network performance because of the addition wavelength conversion capabilities (see for example [129, 207]).

If all the OXCs of the network are equipped with wavelength converters the situation is referred as *full wavelength conversion*. When full conversion is available the WDM network is equivalent to a circuit-switched network. Unfortunately, wavelength converters are still very expensive. If only a percentage of the OXC has wavelength converters then it is a *sparse wavelength conversion network*. There are many proposals to allow the network to include wavelength conversion capabilities which also minimize the economical cost by allowing sparse wavelength conversion.

Many of the reviewed RWA algorithms for transparent networks do not consider explicitly the length of the routes in the route selection. In these transparent networks usually the routes with more available wavelengths are the shortest, since the probability of a long route with a lot of available wavelengths is small. However, this property is carried out only weakly in WI networks. For this reason, usual RWA algorithms for WI networks take into account explicitly the length of the route in its decision.

In [40, 137] the authors present an RWA algorithm for networks with sparse wavelength conversion, the weighted least-congestion routing, first-fit (WLCR-FF), in conjunction with a simple greedy wavelength converter placement algorithm. The WLCR-FF algorithm selects the route maximizing the weight F/h among a set of precomputed shortest and link disjoint routes. F accounts for the availability of the route, and for transparent networks it is the number of common wavelengths on all the links of the route. For WI networks with full wavelength conversion, F is the smallest value of available wavelengths among the links of the route. And finally, for sparse wavelength conversion, F is the smallest value of available wavelengths among all the segments of the route between wavelength converters.

Moreover, h is the length of the route in number of hops. Once the route is selected the first-fit algorithm is applied in every one of the segments of the route to select the wavelengths.

2.8 Summary and Conclusions

This chapter introduces the problem of transporting today's ubiquitous IP traffic into optical WDM transmission. The ever-growing traffic demand, still present at the end of twentieth and the beginning of twenty-first century despite technological breakdown, motivates the migration toward efficient, flexible, and reliable network architectures. In this perspective, the key objective is the introduction of some level of intelligence in the network devices. This introduction should be gradual and not destructive and in this chapter we have discussed the state of the art and its short-term deployment.

We have presented the current gradual migration from legacy SONET/SDH networks to the next generation infrastructures equipped with novel VCAT and LCAS functionalities. On one hand, VCAT enables fine bandwidth allocation by grouping virtual containers in virtual concatenation groups. On the other hand, LCAS introduces some degree of flexibility providing the possibility to increase/decrease the bandwidth of the virtual concatenation groups. Moreover, the standardization of the GFP encapsulation allows transporting packet data directly over SONET/SDH, skipping intermediate layers like ATM and HDLC.

The deployment of NG-SONET/SDH equipment only brings very short term advantages to network providers, while a further, more enhanced, step is required to better cope with the current needs. The solution is the implementation of a control plane performing call and connection control function in real time. We have presented the two control planes currently under standardization process, namely ASON and GMPLS. Although ASON and GMPLS have been made to be complementary pieces of work, some differences can be appreciated and are discussed in this chapter. It is clear that these control planes must converge toward a common scenario, and, indeed, one of the current major activities concentrating ITU-T, IETF and OIF bodies is the definition of methods and potential solutions for protocol interworking between ASON and GMPLS network domains.

This chapter concludes with an overview of the RWA solutions for different kinds of networks and traffic patterns.

Chapter 3
Optical Packet Switching

**Carla Raffaelli, Slavisa Aleksic, Franco Callegati, Walter Cerroni,
Guido Maier, Achille Pattavina, and Michele Savi**

3.1 Issues Concerning Optical Packet Switching (OPS)

This chapter provides an outline of the main concepts and issues related to optical packet switching (OPS). The basic network functions required by this paradigm are discussed and references to past and current research on the topic are provided. Optical packet switching is a transport technique that assumes information to be organized in packets formed by a payload and a header both encoded as optical signals. The payload is transferred through the network without any optical to electronic conversion. The header is processed in the early phase in the electronic domain. Optical packet switching may be considered as a long-term and more flexible alternative to the circuit-switched optical networks currently being deployed by operators. This innovative paradigm aims at optimizing the utilization of the dense wavelength division multiplexing (DWDM) channels by means of fast and highly dynamic resource allocation, overcoming the inefficiency typical of the circuit transfer modes. Traditionally, packet transfer modes have proved to be very flexible by nature, with respect to bandwidth exploitation. In fact, link capacity is shared in time by means of statistical multiplexing, while contentions occurring at each node are solved by storing packets as long as the required resources become available again. Therefore, network links are in general used more efficiently in OPS than in circuit-switching.

3.1.1 Background

The implementation of packet switching techniques in the optical domain is a research topic that has been investigated all through the last decade [57, 97, 273], with

C. Raffaelli (✉)
Department of Electronics, Computer Science and Systems, Università di Bologna, Italy
e-mail: craffaelli@deis.unibo.it

J. Aracil and F. Callegati (eds.), *Enabling Optical Internet with Advanced Network Technologies*, Computer Communications and Networks,
DOI 10.1007/978-1-84882-278-8_3, © Springer-Verlag London Limited 2009

several projects focused on it, for example, ACTS-KEOPS [83] and IST-DAVID [48]. The original aim was to build transparent photonic network equipment, also known as *optical packet switches/routers*, capable of carrying transition control protocol (TCP) and other data-centric traffic at huge bit-rates. Since electronics-based devices may be too slow to perform the required ultra-fast switching operations, the basic idea is to exploit the bandwidth made available by optical components while reducing the electro-optical conversions as much as possible and achieving a better interfacing with DWDM transmission systems. The adoption of such *all-optical* switching solutions also provides the significant capability to carry information in a *transparent* way, which means that the optical packet is considered as a sort of "data container" switched independently of the protocol, framing structure and, up to a given extent, bit-rate used.

3.1.2 Network Scenario

An example of photonic packet-switched network with mesh topology is shown in Fig. 3.1. Legacy packet-oriented networks (e.g., based on IP, ATM, or gigabit ethernet protocols) are "clients" of the optical core network and supply heterogeneous datagrams/cells/frames to it through the ingress *edge systems*, which are responsible for building optical packets. In particular, each ingress node has to collect incoming data units and arrange them into optical packets, according to the specific format adopted by the network. While performing this operation, this nodes may have to aggregate small incoming data units or split long ones in order to fit them properly into the optical container. Furthermore, the edge system is also in charge of creating a packet header and adding control information to it, needed to accomplish a correct routing inside the core network.

Once a packet has entered the optical domain, it is transparently switched by the optical routers according to a statistical multiplexing technique:

1. Each node processes the packet header and retrieves routing information, as, for example, the destination address or the virtual circuit identifier.

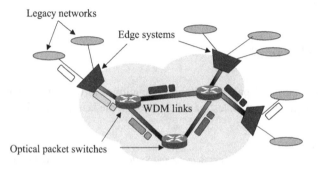

Fig. 3.1 An Optical packet-switched network (OPN)

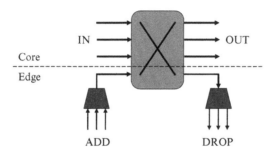

Fig. 3.2 An OPS with add/drop functionalities

2. Then it executes a routing table look-up and finds out which output port must be used to route the packet toward the destination.
3. If the output port is not immediately available, a contention resolution scheme is applied, for example, by buffering the packet.
4. Eventually the packet is either transmitted to the next node or, in case the resources used for contention resolution are insufficient, it is dropped.

The routing table used by each node may be created by means of standard routing protocols, adapted to the optical scenario, or new ad hoc protocols and algorithms may be devised. In any case, routing table entries must specify the appropriate output port, which in DWDM networks means either the output fiber only, when all wavelengths on the same fiber are considered equivalent for routing purposes, or both fiber and wavelength, when different wavelengths are considered different paths by the routing algorithm. However, in general, the same optical packet may change wavelength from node to node.

As soon as the packet has reached the proper egress edge node, its data content is translated back to the original format and delivered to the destination legacy network. Here some reassembling operations may be needed. In Fig. 3.1 edge nodes are clearly distinguished from core nodes. However, it may happen that a given node is an ingress or egress system for some packets, while it is just an intermediate node for other ones, i.e., some core nodes may also have incoming/outgoing traffic from/to client layers. Therefore, a generic optical packet router should be able to perform switching actions for crossing packets as well as add/drop functions for incoming/outgoing traffic, as sketched in Fig. 3.2.

3.1.3 Packet Format

A key issue in OPS is the optical packet format that should be chosen, taking into account the limits of the optical technology on one side and traffic characteristics as well as transparency requirements on the other. A typical optical packet format is shown in Fig. 3.3.

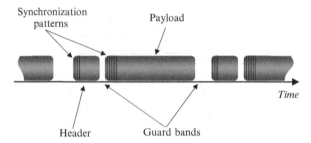

Fig. 3.3 A typical optical packet format

Figure 3.3 refers to the case of *in-band signaling*, where control information is carried by a *header* transmitted on the same wavelength as the *payload*. A different approach, adopted for example by optical burst switching (OBS) (Chapter 4), considers *out-of-band signaling* with headers and payloads being transmitted on different channels. In this case, synchronization issues between control and data channels may arise.

3.1.4 Multiplexing Schemes

Different multiplexing schemes can be adopted for optical packet forwarding. Asynchronous multiplexing means that optical packets assembled at the edge can be injected in the optical network at any point on the time axis and can have in principle any length or duration, possibly different from packet to packet.

Synchronous multiplexing assumes on the other hand that the time on the optical network is slotted and packets are transferred within defined intervals in time. Typically this solution turns into optical payloads of the same length or lengths that are multiples of a unit length (train of packets). Fixed and variable length packets have significant impact on network implementation and performance.

The performance of a delay line buffer when dealing with variable length packets is strongly influenced by the ratio between the average packet length and the unit of the delay lines [22]. This problem can be overcome by applying synchronous operation and choosing the delay unit equal to a multiple of the slot time.

In practice, as shown in Fig. 3.4, four alternatives can be considered.

1. **Asynchronous variable length packet (AVLP).** Incoming datagrams are put into the optical payload "as they are" and each packet may be received, switched, and transmitted at any time (Fig. 3.4b).
2. **Asynchronous fixed length packet (AFLP).** Incoming datagrams are put into one or more optical packets of a given size, which may be received, switched, and transmitted at any time. Insertion of some padding to fill up the optical payload may be necessary (Fig. 3.4c).
3. **Synchronous variable length packet (SVLP).** Packets may have variable sizes as long as they are whole multiples of the time slot. As in the previous case, the

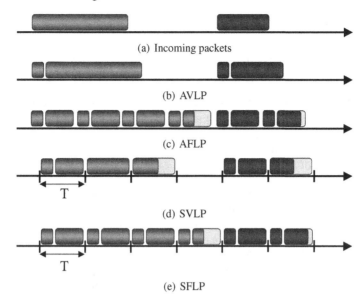

Fig. 3.4 Data incoming from client layers can be placed in different optical packet formats

client burst may fit a single slot or span over multiple slots, except that different slots are now treated as a whole *train of slots* and then processed and sent sequentially, no slot belonging to other packets being allowed to be inserted between them. This choice implies the possibility of using a single header, placed in the first slot, for the whole packet (Fig. 3.4d).

4. **Synchronous fixed length packet (SFLP).** All packets must have the same duration and each packet is transmitted in a single time slot. In this case the client burst either may be short enough to be carried by a single packet or it has to be segmented into several packets, which will be treated as independent entities, each with its own header. In both cases, some padding may be required to complete the (last) packet. Reordering and reassembling processes must be performed when the packet leaves the network in order to restore original bursts (Fig. 3.4e).

The main advantage of synchronous variable length packet (SVLP) is that the processing in the optical nodes is reduced to the minimum. It is well known that header processing and forwarding decisions are critical issues in an optical packet router because of the very high speed links and the related very high packet arrival rate [24]. With SVLP the routing information is inserted only in the first slot of the train and the whole train is then processed according to this information. The mean load on the control logic of the switch is thus reduced by a factor that is roughly proportional to the average number of packets per train. Also the overhead due to header information is reduced by a similar factor, since less slots carry the control information of the header. Moreover, there is no need for packet reordering and reassembling at the edges.

3.1.5 Overhead and Control

Adopting the synchronous multiplexing scheme illustrated previously, three kinds of overhead are introduced by the encapsulation of client data into optical packets:

- *Header overhead*, due to the insertion of the header before each optical packet.
- *Guard bands overhead*, due to the presence of guard bands between time slots and between header and payload.
- *Padding overhead*, due to the padding required to fit variable length data units into a number of fixed size slots.

In this section the effects of the padding overhead on the network load are analyzed, while the overhead due to headers and guard bands is neglected. This approximation is reasonable as long as we assume that the header and the guard bands are much smaller than the slot duration, which is mandatory in order to have an efficient utilization of the bandwidth.

The overhead evaluation is an important issue that usually has not been considered in previous studies on slotted optical networks. Often the client traffic is natively made by variable length packets, as is the case with IP, by far the most significant client of a backbone network, at least for the foreseeable future. Internet protocol datagrams may be transmitted on the optical network as they are or, more likely, groomed into longer batches, but the basic data block to be transmitted still has variable length. In order to make such variable length data units fit into slots, the optical backbone network must *round them up* to an integer number of slots (padding). Therefore any burst carried by the optical backbone will be in general longer than its original size, with a consequent increase of the overall network load. Such an increase is, of course, directly related to the slot size.

Control processing is one of the main tasks to support packet forwarding in optical packet networks. Electronic processing has been adopted in the first examples of optical packet switches. The electronic packet processing is a severe limitation to node throughput and must be kept as simple as possible. Optical signal processing can help in routing packets directly in the optical domain [117]. The idea is to merge the optical packet concept with the GMPLS paradigm and encode labels by suitable codes. The fabrication of encoders/decoders that perform label generation and processing has been recently demonstrated and promises to meet the processing constraints of optical packet switches [262].

3.1.6 Contention Resolution

One of the main and still unresolved issues with optical packet switches is the contention resolution that arises when packets compete for the same fiber and wavelength at the same time. Space, time, and wavelength domains are the three options typically applied for contention resolution. While in electronic packet switches contention is managed in the time domain through random access memories used as buffers, in the optical domain this approach has limited applicability since fiber delay lines offer only discrete and limited delay values while they are contributing to further signal quality degradation. On the other hand, contention resolution can be performed in the wavelength domain taking advantage of wavelength conversion [46].

Since tunable wavelength converters (TWC) are expensive components [145], switch architectures where tunable wavelength converters (TWC)s are shared between the fibers or the wavelengths in a node have been proposed [4, 61].

3.1.7 Enabling Technology

A major challenge in building optical packet switched networks (OPNs) is the difficulty in implementing all-optical packet switching nodes, i.e., optical routers. The main limitation with state of the art technology is the difficulty of building reasonably large optical buffers to meet quality of service (QoS) requirements. Another issue that needs to be faced by an OPN designer is that of providing switching fabric that is able to switch on per packet basis. To ensure efficient use of the switching fabric, the switching time should be small compared with the packet length. Thus, for short packets (e.g., ATM cells) at say 10 Gbps the switching time in a high capacity router needs to be in the order of 1 ns or less. In principle, all-optical (i.e., optically controlled) header processing and switching is possible in optical packet switching [19, 34, 263]. However, it is very unlikely that this functionality will ever be performed in optical domain in medium- or large-size routers because management functions in routers, such as address lookup [34], require intensive computing. Therefore, we strongly believe that control functions will be given up to the electrical domain.

Special attention will be paid in the near future to novel types of optical buffers that can open up a new era for all-optical packet switching.

3.1.8 Inter-working with Legacy Networks

Optical packet switched networks can act as long haul interconnection networks for metropolitan area networks supporting TCP/IP end-to-end applications [116]. The traffic coming from electrical networks is suitably managed at the OPN access before being sent to the optical backbone [180]. An optical packet generating procedure, forthwith referred as optical packet assembly mechanism (O-PAM) is required, which mainly depends on the characteristics of the optical payload. The O-PAM functions are typically performed at the edge routers where incoming traffic is collected in order to build optical packets equipped with additional header information needed to take the correct forwarding decision within the core optical switches [180]. More specifically, the inter working unit (IWU) is the entity responsible for performing the optical packet assembly functions taking into account different pieces of information, such as IP destination address and the QoS requirements [26]. It has been proved in previous studies [78,205] that this process impacts on overall connection performance in terms of additional transfer delay, depending on the design choices. The result is represented by a harmful drop in the application throughput, and in order to suitably upper bound this delay an assembly time-out is typically introduced. Moreover, the greater the number of segments of the same congestion window carried in the optical packet, the more accentuated becomes the favorable effect of correlated deliveries of TCP segments. On the other hand, with high packet loss rate the drop of a single optical packet results in several segments being lost [78].

3.2 Header Coding Techniques

In general, signaling techniques for optical networks can be classified into in-band signaling and out-of-band signaling. Usually, in-band signaling is the case of both the control information and user data being transmitted over the same channel. Out-of-band signaling uses a separate channel or even a separate transmission medium for the exchange of the control information.

In packet-switched photonic networks, medium access control information (usually transmitted in the packet's header) has to be attached to every data packet (referred to as the *packet's payload*) in order to route an optical packet through the network from a source node to a specific destination node.

There are several methods for coding the header onto the optical medium. These methods can be classified into three basic categories, namely *time domain coding (TDC), frequency domain coding (FDC),* and *code domain coding (CDC)* (see Fig. 3.5).

Time domain coding is the most utilized method in telecommunication networks [44, 77, 130, 179], where the header is transmitted at the same wavelength as the payload. Here, the same modulation format (mostly ON–OFF keying (OOK)) is used for both data and control signals. Header and payload sections of a packet are transmitted consecutively in a serial manner. In *optical pulse interval (OPI)* signaling, the data rates of the header and the payload sections are the same. Alternatively, if the header is transmitted at a lower bit rate than the payload, it is then called *mixed rate (MR)* signaling.

In FDC the header is transmitted on a frequency band separated from the frequency on which the payload is transmitted. Here, the payload and header can be transmitted in parallel.

Using the *optical sub carrier multiplexing (SCM)* technique, the payload and the header are encoded as radio frequency (RF) sidebands on the optical carrier, each at a distinct sideband frequency [141, 152, 268]. In the network nodes, header information is separated from the payload by electrically filtering the sidebands from the

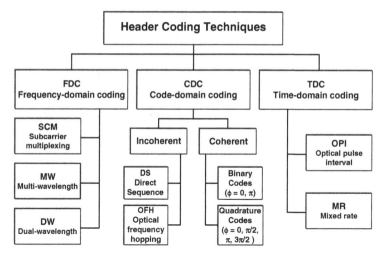

Fig. 3.5 Header coding techniques

optical carrier (see Fig. 3.8). The recovered control information can be processed electronically in the header processing unit.

In the *multi-wavelength (MW)* approach, control information is transmitted in a parallel manner on N wavelengths. The time-skew between header bits on different wavelengths caused by the group velocity dispersion (GVD) can seriously limit the achievable transmission distance in MW coding. Since the bit-parallel MW coding requires a large number of wavelengths, a large number of transceivers have to be deployed at each node. This makes the system more expensive and restricted in terms of transmission length. *Dual-wavelength (DW)* coding is similar to the SCM approach, with the slight difference that instead of two RF sidebands, two separate wavelength channels are dedicated to carry the payload and the control information. That is, the control information is transmitted on a separate wavelength channel in parallel with the payload.

Code domain coding is well-suited for easy and fast all-optical detection of high-speed labels that can represent the nodes' destination addresses [5, 125, 169]. The code sequences can be easily assigned to the destination addresses in a network. Consequently, the header processing can be fully accomplished optically in an OCDM decoder only by the detection of the autocorrelation peak. In general, there are two types of CDC techniques, namely *incoherent* and *coherent* CDC.

Incoherent techniques comprise *direct sequence (DS)* coding and *optical frequency hopping (OFH)*. The first one uses the OOK pulse code sequences, where control information is coded in the time domain using sequences of short pulses called chips [198, 224]. The second one is a frequency or a time-frequency domain approach, where short-duration wide-band pulses are encoded/decoded using specially designed optical filters, e.g., chirped Moiré gratings [35] or a cascade of filters (an array of uniform fiber Bragg gratings) [64]. OFH-CDC uses unipolar codes, where the ith pulse is coded in the frequency domain according to a set of discrete frequencies $S_f = \{f_1, f_2, \ldots, f_q\}$ placed around the carrier frequency f_c:

$$f_i = h_p(i) \frac{B_0}{q}, \quad i = 1, 2, \ldots, N_s, \quad 1 \le h_p(i) \le q, \tag{3.2}$$

where B_0 denotes the available frequency bandwidth, $h_p(i)$ is the placement operator indicating the placement of discrete frequencies from the set S_f over time slots, q represents the number of available frequencies, and N_s is the number of time slots in an OFH system.

Coherent CDC techniques provide a larger ratio of the central autocorrelation peak to the side lobes resulting in a better code detection [264]. Here, the control information is coded not only in time, magnitude, or frequency but also the phase of the optical signal is modulated. If the phase is changed in discrete manner using two values ($\phi = \pi$ or $\phi = 0$), the coding is named *binary coherent* coding, while codes incorporating a change of carrier phase between four values ($\phi = 0, \pi/2, 3\pi/2$ or π) are called *quadrature coherent* codes [135].

3.2.1 Time-Domain Coding

3.2.1.1 Optical Pulse Interval

Optical pulse interval is the most used method in communication networks. In systems where data are processed electronically, the use of this method is reasonable because it can simplify significantly the implementation of the header processing unit.

At high bit rates, OPI can only be realized by employing all-optical signal processing (Fig. 3.6). The implementation of an all-optical header processor in the time domain is still difficult and usually restricted in terms of supported header lengths. However, this technique can significantly reduce node latency and header-processing time.

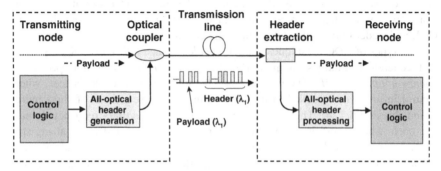

Fig. 3.6 Optical pulse interval (OPI) signaling

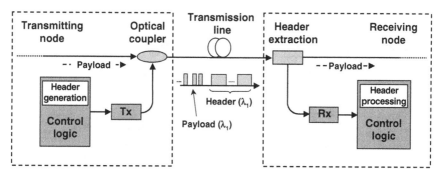

Fig. 3.7 Mixed-rate (MR) signaling

3.2.1.2 Mixed Rate

Even in very high bit rate systems, header processing can be implemented fully electronically if the header bit rate is chosen to be lower than the bit rate of the payload. The payload is processed only by the receiving node, while the header has to be processed by all transit nodes in the network. As it can be seen from Fig. 3.7, the header is first generated at the transmitting node, then converted into the optical domain by the optical transmitter (Tx), and finally transmitted by the transmission line in the front of the payload. At the receiving (or a transit) node, the low bit rate header is received by the optical receiver (Rx) and processed electronically.

Mixed rate (MR) signaling makes the nodes cheaper and easier to realize. Since the header processing is implemented in electronics, very complex medium access control (MAC) protocol functionalities, which require a complex header structure, can be implemented. Moreover, optical transparency can also be achieved by bit rate variable payloads and a header at a fixed lower bit rate. However, due to the low bit rate of the header, signaling overhead and node latency are mostly large.

3.2.2 Frequency-Domain Coding

3.2.2.1 Optical Sub-Carrier Multiplexing

Optical subcarrier multiplexing (SCM) technique is efficient in terms of optical spectrum utilization at the expense of bit rate. The payload bit rate is constrained to be lower than the subcarrier frequency, while the payload and header data rates dictate the separation of the sidebands. In SCM signaling the subcarrier header recovery is based upon optical and microwave direct detection. A significant advantage of SCM is that microwave devices such as microwave oscillators, filters, and mixers are usually cheaper and more mature than optical devices. The header data rate can be lower than the payload rate. Thus, the header recognition unit only needs to operate over the narrow electronic bandwidth of the control channel.

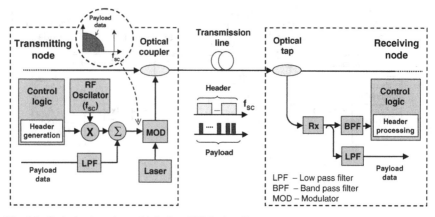

Fig. 3.8 Optical subcarrier multiplexing (SCM) signaling

At the transmitting node, the packet header modulated on a subcarrier frequency (f_{sc}) is impressed together with the payload onto an optical carrier using an optical modulator as shown in Fig. 3.8. When packets arrive at the receiving node, a small fraction of the optical power is tapped off for SCM header detection and processing. The packet header is easily extracted by filtering the signal after receiver in a band pass filter (BPF) with center frequency f_{sc}, then demodulated, and finally processed electronically in the header processing unit.

The main limitation for SCM in high speed all-optical networks is the necessity for the electronic processing of header and payload. At a receiving (or a transiting) node, the payload and header has to be separated electronically in order to access the header information. Thereby, the data rate of the payload is limited by the electronics bottleneck. Moreover, due to the fact that both header and payload are transmitted on the same optical carrier, the transmitter needs to supply sufficient power levels to both signals. In other words, the optical power going into each signal is reduced, thereby inducing an additional power penalty and increasing the bit error rate of the transmission.

3.2.2.2 Bit-Parallel Multi-wavelength

Control information can also be transmitted in a bit-parallel manner on N wavelengths as shown in Fig. 3.9. Each of the N parallel bits of control information is used to modulate an optical source at a different wavelength. The wavelengths are then multiplexed in a WDM multiplexer and launched into the fiber. A receiving (or a transiting) node recovers the control information using a WDM demultiplexer and N receivers. The N-bit parallel electrical signal is then processed by the control logic that generates control signals for the photonic packet switch. Note that the header and the payload can be transmitted either at the same time in a parallel manner as shown in Fig. 3.9 or sequentially, i.e., in separated time slots.

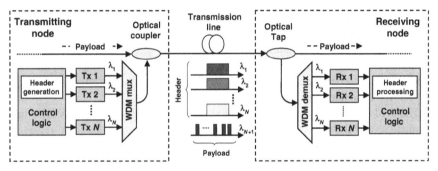

Fig. 3.9 Bit-parallel multiwavelength (MW) signaling

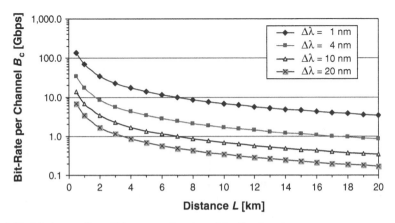

Fig. 3.10 Maximum allowed bit rate as a function of the fiber length

The major problem in bit-parallel MW systems is the time skew among bit-parallel signals transmitted at different wavelength channels. This bit skew is caused mainly by the group delay dispersion of the optical fiber, i.e., by the chromatic dispersion.

The maximum bit skew of an N-bit parallel control signal transmitted on N wavelengths in the total spectral range $\Delta\lambda = [\lambda_1, \lambda_N]$ over distance L is given by [3]

$$\Delta\tau_g = L \cdot \Delta\lambda \cdot D(\lambda_c). \tag{3.3}$$

Here it is assumed that there are N equally spaced wavelength channels within $\Delta\lambda$ with a central channel at λ_c, where $\lambda_c \gg \Delta\lambda$.

Figure 3.10 shows the maximum achievable bit rate as a function of the standard single mode fiber (SSMF) length relating to different values of $\Delta\lambda$. The maximum achievable bit rate per wavelength channel is defined by the maximum allowed *bit skew* equal to the bit-period, i.e., $B_c = 1/\Delta\tau_g$. The central wavelength is chosen to be at $\lambda_c = 1.54\,\mu\text{m}$ and the dispersion coefficient at this point $D = 14.7\,\text{ps/(nm·km)}$.

It can be seen that for a total system bandwidth of $\Delta\lambda = 1$ nm (≈ 125 GHz at 1.5 μm wavelength), in which two wavelength channels can be placed, less than 10 Gbps is allowed for distances up to 7 km, while 2.5 Gbps bit-parallel signal can be transmitted over 20 km. If more than 10 wavelengths are required, the total bandwidth has to be at least 10 nm, which means a maximum allowed span length of 3 km for a channel bit rate of 2.5 Gbps.

The hard restrictions caused by the bit skew make the bit-parallel MW signaling impractical and difficult to implement. Moreover, N transmitters and N receivers are required at each node making the implementation relatively expensive. However, since the control information can be transmitted in a parallel manner, no parallel-to-serial and serial-to-parallel conversions are needed and the bit rate per channel can be kept low because the aggregate bit rate is $B_a = N \cdot B_c$.

Recently, a number of bit skew compensation techniques have been proposed. A significant improvement has been achieved by the use of a dispersion shifted filters (DSF) in order to minimize the chromatic dispersion near 1.55 μm wavelength. Using this method, a transmission experiment with $\Delta\lambda = 15$ nm and a channel bit rate of 1 Gbps over 25.2 km of the Corning DSF have been reported [14]. However, influence of nonlinear effects such as four wave mixing (FWM) and cross phase modulation (XPM) on the bit-parallel MW transmission increases by the use of DSF. Introducing shepherding pulses can additionally improve the transmission capabilities of bit-parallel MW systems [15]. This shepherding effect is based on XPM occurring when high power shepherd pulses on one wavelength copropagate together with low-power data pulses in a bit-parallel MW system, thereby reshaping (compressing) the data pulses and concurrently enhancing the time alignment along the fiber.

In the reference [285], a bit-parallel non-return zero (NRZ) WDM transmission over 27.5 km of DSF has been demonstrated by sampling the bit-parallel WDM data at the receiver, thereby synchronizing them before demultiplexing. The experimental data rate was about 2.5 Gbps with a total system bandwidth of 24 nm. A bit-parallel MW transmission experiment has been demonstrated over 30 km of dispersion-managed fiber (DMF) with four channels at 10 Gbps and a total system bandwidth of $\Delta\lambda = 4.74$ nm using an optical bit skew compensator (OBSC) located at the receiver and based on a circulator and chirped fiber gratings [225]. Moreover, seven WDM bit-parallel channels have been transmitted with a total spectral range of $\Delta\lambda = 15$ nm over 2.5 km precompensated SSMF with less than 3 ps bit skew corresponding to possible channel rate beyond 100 Gbps [226]. The recent experimental demonstrations are summarized in Table 3.1.

Table 3.1 Experimental demonstrations of broadband transmission using bit-parallel WDM

Data rate per ch. B_c	No. of ch.	Tot. spectr. range λ	Distance L	Compensation method	Ref.
1 Gbps	12	15 nm	25.5 km	DSF	[14]
2.5 Gbps	3	24 nm	27.5 km	DSF + sampling	[285]
10 Gbps	4	4.47 nm	30 km	DMF + OBSC	[225]
>100 Gbps	7	15 nm	2.5 km	DCF + SSMF	[226]

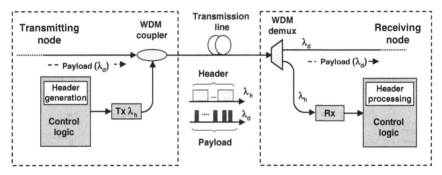

Fig. 3.11 Dual-wavelength (DW) signaling

3.2.2.3 Dual-Wavelength

A dual-wavelength approach could be a good choice because of its relatively simple and less expensive implementation. For this purpose, an additional transmitter/receiver pair in combination with a WDM mux/demux have to be used in the node (see Fig. 3.11).

To transmit the packet header, a separate wavelength λ_h is used, which can be easily separated at the receiving node using a WDM demultiplexer. Here, the header can be transmitted in parallel with the payload. Consequently, the header-processing latency can be minimized even for a lower header bit rate. A lower header bit rate implies an easier implementation of the header processing unit in electronics, thereby making the node realization cheaper. Unlike the SCM, dual-wavelength coding sets no limits to the payload bit rate. Moreover, the cross-talk between the header and data signals can be reduced by choosing an optimal wavelength spacing between λ_d and λ_h.

3.2.3 Code-Domain Coding

A code domain coding (CDC) technique can be implemented directly in the optical domain if the nodes' destination addresses are assigned to a set of code sequences. The code sequences can also represent the packet labels in a label-switched all-optical network. The code sequences are detected in optical code division multiplexing (OCDM) decoders using the optical code correlation. The correlation properties of the codes used in the network should enable an error-free label detection.

The generic diagram of the transmitter/receiver pair incorporating CDC technique is shown in Fig. 3.12. At the transmitter side, a short pulse is fed into an encoder to generate an OCDM label consisting of l-chips that is transmitted in the packet header. An OCDM decoder with matched filter geometry is employed in the receiving node to detect the appropriate label. If the incoming label matches the

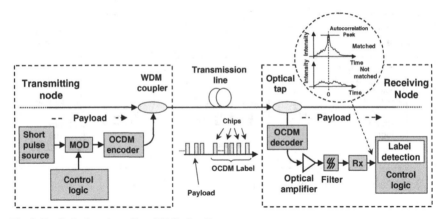

Fig. 3.12 Code-domain coding (CDC) signaling

local address, the autocorrelation peak is detected at the output of the decoder. Thus, CDC could be an easy and efficient way to realize all-optical label processing for high-speed packet-switched networks.

3.2.3.1 Direct Sequence Code-Domain Coding

In incoherent CDC techniques the phase of the light pulses is not modulated. The correlation procedure incorporates incoherent direct detection based on power summation of optical pulses. Direct sequence code domain coding (DS-CDC) is a simple incoherent coding method originating from spread spectrum communications. There are three possible correlator structures, namely all-parallel, all-serial, or a combination of these two.

The all-parallel structure depicted in Fig. 3.13a comprise a $1 \times W$ optical splitter, W optical delay lines, and a $W \times 1$ power combiner, where W is the weight of the implemented code [118]. It allows generation of any code sequence by selecting a proper combination of activated delay line paths. However, due to the large power loss in the splitter and the combiner, the parallel configuration is less suitable for the implementation of large codes. That is to say, the encoding and decoding process of a prime code sequence with the weight W leads to a minimum power loss in the coder and decoder circuits by a factor of $2 \cdot W$ if the all-parallel structure is used. Furthermore, the autocorrelation peak in direct sequence code domain coding (DS-CDC) is only W, while the ratio of the central autocorrelation peak to side lobes is $(W - 1)$.

The all-serial structure (Fig. 3.13b) has lower optical power loss than the parallel one [131]. It consists of $(n + 1)$ two-by-two optical couplers and n optical delay lines for generating or correlating any code word with weight $W = 2^n$. Therefore, the serial configuration is suitable for implementing large 2^n prime codes.

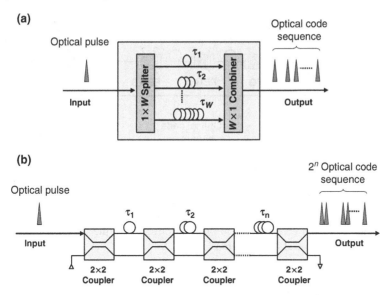

Fig. 3.13 Direct sequence code-domain coding (DS-CDC) encoder configurations, (**a**) all-parallel and (**b**) all-serial structure

Finally, using a combination of the serial and parallel structures, an incoherent asynchronous OCDM en-/decoder implementing Gold codes can be realized [250]. By the use of additional precoding and balanced detection, this configuration has shown superior performance over the prime code approach in the case of a large number of nodes.

3.2.3.2   Optical Frequency Hopping Code-Domain Coding

Two-dimensional coding can also be used to transmit the control information. That is, the header bits (or labels) can be coded in both time and frequency domain. Optical frequency hopping is one of the techniques that employ two-dimensional coding. For this purpose, an array of fiber bragg gratings (FBG) can be used, where the FBG center frequencies correspond to a number of contiguous frequency slots defined in Eq. (3.2.)

As shown in Fig. 3.14, a broadband pulse is used to generate a pulse sequence with a defined time–frequency pattern. The particular code sequence is determined by choosing an appropriate arrangement of FBGs in the encoder. At the output of the encoder, the code sequence consists of W optical pulses with different wavelengths. The OFH decoder has the same structure as the encoder, but with the slight difference that the FBGs are inversely arranged.

Because of the fact that the optical pulses with different frequencies have to be transmitted over a long single-mode fiber, the change of the relative positions among these pulses due to the difference of group velocities will cause additional limitations on the achievable transmission length. Therefore, a compensation scheme for

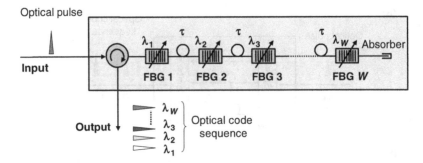

Fig. 3.14 Optical frequency hopping code-domain coding (OFH-CDC) encoder configuration (FBG: Fiber Bragg gratings)

group velocity has to be deployed in order to circumvent the walk-off effects and thus increase the allowed transmission length.

3.2.3.3 Coherent Code-Domain Coding

A better code detection than in DS-CDC systems can be achieved if additionally the phase of the optical pulses is modulated. The coherent CDC correlator can be built in a way similar to the incoherent DS-CDC correlators depicted in Fig. 3.13, with the difference that in each delay-line path an additional phase shifting element needs to be inserted.

Usually, the phase of the optical pulses (chips) is coded in a discrete manner, either binary ($\phi = \pi$ or 0 radians) or quaternary (four possible phase shifts $\phi = \pi, 3\pi/2, \pi/2$, or 0 radians). Here, the central autocorrelation peak is W^2 due to the stronger interference at the coupler, while the ratio of the central autocorrelation peak to side lobes is also larger than the ratio of DS-CDC—it amounts to $(W - 1)^2$ in this case.

Note that in coherent CDC systems, the coherence length of the light source has to be greater than the chip length. Moreover, the difficulties associated with the coherent transmission has to be taken into account.

3.3 Contention Resolution

Contentions occur when two or more packets need the same switching or transmission resource at the same time. If these contentions are not resolved, contending packets will be lost, contributing to an increased packet loss rate. Contention resolution techniques typically adopted by optical packet-switched networks exploit space, time and wavelength domains and will be explained in the following. There are also several approaches to alleviate packet loss due to contentions in OPS networks.

3.3.1 FDL Buffers

Time-based contention resolution techniques are among the most widely used in traditional packet-based networks. In electronic packet switching contention resolution in the time domain is based on a store-and-forward scheme, where contending packets are stored in a queue as long as the output port is available again. A number of different queuing schemes are available, with increasing complexity and performance, aimed at improving network throughput and providing QoS differentiation. Since the all-optical counterpart of a random access memory is not feasible, optical queuing may be realized with a number of fiber coils of given length used as delay lines: it takes some time for a packet injected inside a long fiber trunk to come out at the other side. Therefore, fiber delay lines may be used to delay packets as if they were placed for some time into a memory and then retrieved for transmission. Obviously, such an optical buffer is not completely equivalent to a conventional queue. The main difference is that, while a packet may be stored as long as needed into an electronic memory, it cannot stay within the optical buffer longer than an amount of time given by the propagation delay inside the delay line that is utilized. In case such delay is not long enough for the required resource to be available, either another contention resolution is performed or the packet is lost.

An optical buffer architecture that uses fiber delay lines is plotted in Fig. 3.15. The optical buffer is made of B fibers of different lengths, properly calibrated to cause different propagation delay including a "cut-through" fiber that, we may assume so short that it is traversed with no propagation delay. If we index the fiber in order of increasing length using $i \in [0 : B - 1]$, then the delay of each fiber is D_i with minimum delay $D_0 = 0$ and maximum delay D_{B-1}. In general it is assumed that all delays are multiple of the same delay unit D, so that $D_i = l_i D$ where l_i sets the length of the delay as a multiple of the delay unit. The delay unit d is also called *granularity* of the optical buffer in the literature. In general it is also assumed that any fiber of the buffer carries k wavelengths, therefore in a given instant at most k packets may experience the same delay.

In general terms D, the l_is and k are the parameters that are subject of the engineering problem of an optical buffer.

- D is crucial in determining the buffer performance and has to be dimensioned according to the packet length. The reasons for this will be discussed and appear evident in the following. In the synchronous fixed length packet (SFLP)

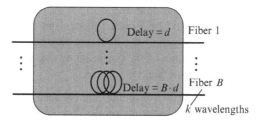

Fig. 3.15 Scheme of the optical buffer implementation

and SVLP with a slot size of T seconds, it is rather natural to choose $D = T$ even though, in principle, they are independent quantities, so that D can be greater than a time slot, for instance $d = 2T$, or even a noninteger multiple. It is known that the latter choice is nonoptimal and should be avoided [27]. In the case of an asynchronous and variable length packets D has to be dimensioned as a function of the average packet length.

- The delay distribution is also rather free choice for the network engineer and could in principle be optimized according to the traffic profile. Because of the difficulties in identifying an exact traffic profile and for the sake of simplicity usually it is assumed a distribution of delays as consecutive multiples of d, such that $l_i = i$ and $D_i = iD$. This is the so-called *degenerate* delay distribution while other, less uniform, choices are called *nondegenerate* [251].

- k basically sets up to what extent the delay lines of the buffer can be shared by several packets at the same time. It has to be dimensioned according to the probability that many packets has to be queued in similar conditions (same delay) and therefore to the size of the switching matrix and traffic distribution. In a switching matrix with M input channels and a uniform traffic distribution, in principle M packets may request the same output channel at the same time and therefore $k \geq M$.

Both D and k are very important in determining the packet loss probability at the optical buffer. Unfortunately, general formula for their dimensioning are not available and not easy to find in general due to strong dependence on the traffic profile and the amount of correlation phenomena into play. Formulas are available for specific cases and a good understanding of the design principle can still be achieved by computer simulation.

In the last part of this section we discuss the importance of D and show why it is so strongly related to the packet length. For the sake of simplicity we will assume an output queuing switching matrix with FIFO queues and no priority. Let us imagine that a packet arrives at time t and finds its required output channels busy, and going to be free at t_f. In an electronic router the packet would be queued and retrieved from the queue at t_f. On the contrary the packet is going to be delayed by an amount

$$\Delta = \left\lceil \frac{t_f - t}{D} \right\rceil D, \tag{3.4}$$

where $\lceil x \rceil$ indicates the smallest integer greater than or equal to x. In practice the packet will be sent to delay line i such that $i = \min[i : D_i = iD \geq |t_f - t|]$.

Any time $D_i \neq |t_f - t|$ for the time interval $\tau = \Delta - t_f + t \geq 0$ the output line is not used while there would be a packet to transmit as shown in Fig. 3.16. The interval τ is called *void* or *gap* in the literature and causes a vacation on the transmission channel. This vacation of the queue server can be seen as an artificial increase in the packet length, such that:

- ϑ is the *real length* of a packet ($\bar{\vartheta}$ its average); for instance, measuring the packets in time, it is the amount of bits in the packet divided by the link bit rate.

Fig. 3.16 Example of gap
and excess load for the AVLP
case

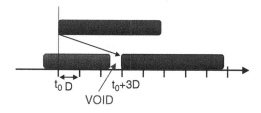

- ϑ_e is the *excess length* ($\bar{\vartheta}_e$ its average) defined as the amount of time the output link is busy because of that packet, even if for some time nothing is really transmitted.

This phenomenon happens likely depending more or less on the network scenario. In SFLP t_f is multiple of the time slot T and all packets are synchronous, therefore the choice $d = T$ is such that there is always i such that $D_i = |t_f - t|$ and $\tau = 0$. In the AVLP we have the opposite situation. Because of the asynchronous operation and of the variable length packets, whatever d is it almost never happens that $D_i = |t_f - t|$ and $\tau \neq 0$ basically for every packet that is queued. The SVP and AFLP fall in between these two extremes with more/less likelihood of having $\tau = 0$ or $\tau \neq 0$.

Assuming that the arrival process is independent of the state of the queue and that the lengths of consecutive packets are also independent, τ may take any value between 0 and D approximately with uniform probability. Therefore, its average is $\bar{\tau} = D/2$. Calling λ the average packet arrival rate, the load to a normal queue would be $\rho = \lambda \bar{\vartheta}$, while the optical buffer experiences an *excess load*:

$$\rho_e = \lambda \bar{\vartheta}_e \geq \rho. \tag{3.5}$$

Following what we just discussed, intuition suggests that, for fixed B, there must be a sort of optimal value for D because:

- If D is very small (in the limit going to 0) the time resolution of the FDL buffer increases but the buffering capacity also decreases (in the limit there is no buffering capacity if D approaches 0, in spite of the number of delay lines available); therefore the performance in terms of packet loss must improve with increasing D.
- If D is very large (in the limit going to infinity), the buffering capacity is large in the sense that long delays can be introduced, but the time resolution of the buffer is very small and the excess utilization is large (in the limit going to infinity with D), therefore the performance in terms of packet loss must improve with decreasing D.

In between these two situations we expect a sort of minimum of the packet loss, realizing the optimal trade-off between time resolution and amount of delay achievable. Results presented in the literature show that the optimal value of D is usually equal or almost equal to the average packet length. This problem was studied for

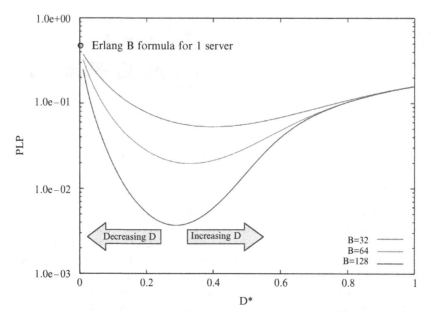

Fig. 3.17 AVLP: example of packet loss probability performance as a function of D (normalized to the average packet length) for Poisson arrival and exponential packet length, $F = 1$, $W = 1$, varying the traffic load as a parameter

the first time in [22], where a simple approximate analytical model to calculate the packet loss probability (PLP)as a function of D is derived for the asynchronous variable length packet (AVLP) case. Other works addressed the same problem in recent years. In [6] an exact model based on Markov chains is proposed again for the AVLP case. Reference [286] provides models for the asynchronous fixed length packet (AFLP) and SFLP cases. In [133] the case of SFLP and SVLP is considered.

An example of behavior of the packet loss probability as a function of D normalized to the average packet length is shown in Fig. 3.17 for the AVLP case. As expected Fig. 3.17 shows a typical concave behavior with a clear minimum. It is good that such minimum is rather flat, so that the optimization of D is not going to be very sensitive to the traffic profile. Errors in estimating the traffic profile of about 20–30% do not impair significantly the optimization.

3.3.2 Scheduling Algorithms

When the interfaces of a switching matrix are equipped with several output channels, for instance, multiple fibers and/or multiple wavelengths per fiber, contention resolution can be made more effective by means of a combined use of the time and fiber/wavelength domain. The ideally underlining this concept is that a packet may be transmitted on any channel (i.e., fiber/wavelength) that belongs to a given network link and therefore guarantees the same network path. In this way the routing of packets is kept consistent even though a packet may change transmission channel along its way through the network.

In this case more complex scheduling algorithms must be added to the switching matrix control functions that select the time/channel to transmit a packet with the aim to optimize the overall performance. Such algorithm were called in the literature *wavelength and delay selection algorithms* Wavelength and delay selection (WDS) or, more generally, *channel and delay selection* algorithm *(CDS)*. It is important to stress that resolution capabilities and acceptable performance in various scenarios are possible with very limited requirements in terms of queuing space. This is very important for feasible optical packet switching where the implementation of queuing is one of the major hardware constraints.

A proper definition of these algorithms allows a design of the switching procedures with no impact on the network architecture and on standard interworking protocols. The design of the algorithm is crucial to the performance and may depend on the architecture of the switching node as well as on the network scenario. As an example here we discuss CDS algorithms that are applicable to any switching architecture that logically keeps a virtual output queue per wavelength with AVLP network operation.

Let us assume the switching matrix is equipped per in/output interface with F fibers, W wavelengths per fiber, and B delays (including the zero-delay cut-through path). This output interface architecture provides a discrete set of access points to the future transmission time framework with a first-come-first-served scheduling.[1]

When a packet arrives at the switch, the typical behavior of the CDS algorithm is to scan all scheduling points and select one that is both available and optimal according to some criteria. In an ideal switching matrix, where information units can be freely switched in space and wavelength, the set of scheduling points for the transmission of a burst/packet arriving at time t is:

$$s(i, j, k) \in \mathcal{S} \qquad (3.6)$$

where

$$s(i, j, k) = (t_i, j, k) \qquad (3.7)$$

is a triplet of integer numbers with the following meaning: i is the index of the delay $t_i = t + id$, $j = 1, \ldots, W$ is the index of the wavelength, and $k = 1, \ldots, F$ of the fiber for burst/packet transmission. The number of elements (i.e., the cardinality) in $\mathcal{S}$ is $|\mathcal{S}| = B \cdot W \cdot F$.

However, depending on hardware and/or logical limitations, in real systems bursts/packets may be scheduled at $s(i, j, k) \in \mathcal{S}'$ where $\mathcal{S}' \subseteq \mathcal{S}$. The most evident case in which $\mathcal{S}' \neq \mathcal{S}$ is when the switching matrix is equipped with limited range wavelength converters, but this is not the only case in which it happens. For instance,

---

[1] The delay buffer is assumed *degenerate* consistent with the previous section.

in [29], S' is determined depending on the class of service of the bursts/packets, to provide some sort of quality of service differentiation, while in [25] some constraints on the choice of the delay are introduced in order to maintain the correct packet sequence.

For the time remainder of this section, in order to keep the discussion as simple as possible, we will proceed assuming that bursts/packets have full access to the scheduling points and therefore $S' = S$. In the following section we will discuss the relevance of limited range wavelength conversion.

The CDS algorithms are based on heuristics that differ in the definition of the optimal $s(i, j, k) \in S$. For instance, considering the time domain, two optimization alternatives are possible [28]:

- Delay-oriented CDS algorithm (D type), which tries to minimize the latency and therefore sends a burst/packet to the wavelength requiring the shortest delay.
- Gap-oriented CDS algorithm (G type), which tries to minimize the gaps between packets (i.e., to maximize the line utilization) and therefore sends bursts/packets to the wavelength providing the minimum gap.

Then a CDS algorithm may or may not try to fill as much as possible the gaps between packets with a technique known as void filling (VF) [248]. Therefore, CDS algorithms can be:

- D or G type without VF (noVF), in which the algorithm just explores the scheduling times after the last scheduled burst or packet on each wavelength.
- D or G type with VF, wherein it exploring all scheduling times, including those between other scheduled bursts/packets, to discover whether the newcomer may fit in.

Furthermore, the multi-fiber configuration allows one to reuse the same wavelengths on different fibers of the same output link, thus reducing the need for conversion. From this perspective, the CDS algorithm may adopt two alternative approaches [206]:

- *Optimize wavelength scheduling first, rely on time* (WT): The scheduler tries to transmit the packet to the output channel on the same wavelength as the input channel in order to avoid conversion as much as possible, and relies mainly on the time domain for contention resolution; in case no suitable wavelength is available, conversion is performed.
- *Optimize Time scheduling first, rely on wavelength* (TW): the scheduler tries to optimize the link utilization and relies on the wavelength domain (e.g., with a D type or G type scheduling).

An example of CDS scheduling with four choices for the algorithm is illustrated in Fig. 3.18. A packet has to be scheduled at an output interface where other bursts/packets have already been scheduled. The parameters of the example are $F = 2$, $W = 4$, and $B = 4$. Therefore $|S| = 32$ and $s(i, j, k)$ are the 32 possible scheduling instants from t_0 onwards. It happens that 20 out of 32 are currently busy (a transmission is already scheduled at that time) while 12 are still available

Fig. 3.18 Examples of CDS algorithms for the case $F = 2$, $W = 4$ and $B = 4$: (1) D type no VF, (2) G type no VF, (3) D type VF, (4) G type VF

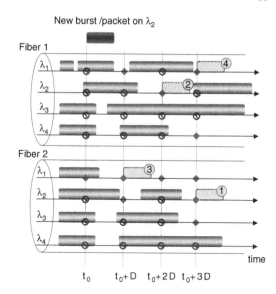

(outlined with the gray diamonds). The CDS algorithm is supposed to choose the *best* of these 12 scheduling possibilities. In case 1 the CDS goes for optimize wavelength conversion first (WT) with no void filling (noVF) choice, which leads to scheduling the incoming the burst/packet at time $t_0 + 3D$ on λ_2. The D or G choice does not matter in this case since this is the only scheduling point available for WT and no VF. If void filling is acceptable, then case 2 is preferable in case minimizing the delay (D-type) is more important than minimizing the gap (G-type). Otherwise, case 1 is still preferable. Cases 3 and 4 show that when optimizing wavelength conversion does not have priority and the CDS may optimize time scheduling regardless of wavelength conversion, the scheduling has many more options available. In particular case 3 is a better choice if the focus in on delay (D-type) while case 4 is a better choice if the focus is on the gap (G-type). In both cases and according to the related optimization perspective, the scheduling in more optimal in the TW than in the WT option, as usual, trading off performance for implementation complexity.

3.3.3 Wavelength Converters

When an algorithm utilizes the wavelength domain for contention resolution, in the case of asynchronous OPS, the contending packet is converted to an idle wavelength on the same fiber and immediately transmitted. In slotted OPS, one packet is transmitted on the wavelength the packets contended for, while the rest of the packets are converted to idle wavelengths on the same fiber, and transmitted in the same time slot. In order to realize such wavelength conversion in the optical domain, all-optical wavelength converters are required. Wavelength converters may be placed at each output wavelength, or in a pool shared by all output wavelengths. Furthermore, wavelength converters may either be full range converters, which means that they can convert to any output wavelength, or limited range wavelength converters, which means that they can convert to a subset of available wavelengths. In this section we will provide an overview of the performance of the different wavelength converter algorithms.

3.3.4 Deflection Routing

Space domain is used by the so-called *deflection routing* scheme [273]: When two or more packets contend for the same output, one of them is forwarded to it while the other ones are transmitted on different fibers, i.e., they take different network paths, which, eventually, will lead to the correct destination by alternative routes. Performance of the deflection routing scheme can be evaluated with a network-wide analysis.

3.4   Switch Architectures with Shared Wavelength Converters

Since tunable wavelength converters (TWC) are expensive components [145], switch architectures where TWCs are shared between the fibers or the wavelengths in a node have been proposed [4, 61]. A simple example of contention resolution in the wavelength domain is presented in Fig. 3.19. In Fig. 3.19a an ideal switch without conversion capability is presented. In this situation if two packets coming on different input fibers (IFs) h and s, but in the same wavelength, are directed to the same output fiber (OF) at the same time, one of them is lost due to wavelength

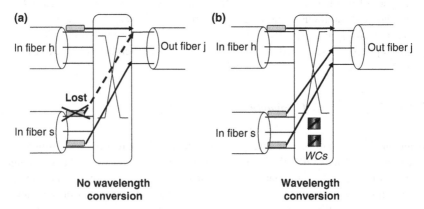

Fig. 3.19 Example of contention resolution in the wavelength domain. In (**a**) the switch is not equipped with wavelength converters and a packet is lost due to wavelength contention; in (**b**) the packets can be forwarded by exploiting wavelength conversion

contention. Instead, in Fig. 3.19b a switch equipped with wavelength converters is presented. In this case, if two packets on the same wavelength are directed to the same OF, one is sent without conversion as in the previous case, and the other is wavelength shifted to another free wavelength by exploiting a wavelength converter.

To exploit properly this simple technique to solve contention, the first idea was to equip the switch with a TWC for each input (or output) wavelength channel. As already mentioned, the main drawback is that TWCs are the most complex components to be implemented in optical technology. For this reason, different strategies to limit the number of TWCs employed in a node, by sharing them, have been proposed in the past [60, 61].

The main schemes to organize wavelength converters are:

- *Shared per output link.* A wavelength converter pool is provided for each output interface. All packets addressed to an output interface can benefit for one of the converters of the pool [203].
- *Shared per node.* A common wavelength converter pool is provided inside the switch and shared among all input and output interfaces. A packet from any input interface can benefit from wavelength conversion using any wavelength converter of this pool.

Both these schemes are suitable to be applied also with multi-fiber switch interfaces [160].

3.4.1 Shared-Per-Link Scheme

In shared-per-link (SPL) the TWCs are shared on the output interfaces, meaning that each output interface has a dedicated pool of TWCs shared by packets directed to that interface [203].

The SPL concept and the related ideal scheme are presented in Fig. 3.20. It represents a bufferless packet switch with wavelength converters shared per output interface (optical link). It consists of N input and N output fibers each carrying a WDM signal with M wavelengths. A nonblocking space switching matrix is provided to transfer packets arriving on any input wavelength/any fiber to any output wavelength/any fiber. Each output interface is equipped with $R \leq M$ full range tunable-input/tunable-output TWCs, and $M - R$ simple optical channels (OCs) without TWCs.

This switch configuration has the advantage of reducing the number of TWCs used and avoiding wavelength conversion if contention is absent. The special case $M = R$ has been studied in [183] for the synchronous environment. The WDM signal arriving to the switch from an input fiber is demultiplexed and synchronized. Packets on input channels are then transferred by the space switching matrix to the proper output interface according to the routing information. The principle to solve contention is as follows: The control unit assigns the packet to a free optical channel (OC) if the wavelength of the packet is not already assigned on that output

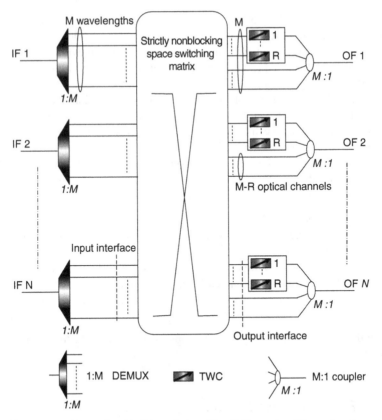

Fig. 3.20 SPL switching node with N input/output fiber (IFs) carrying M wavelengths each. The node is equipped with R TWCs on each output interface

interface. If there is not free OC, a TWC is used to send the packet even if it is not wavelength-shifted. If the wavelength on the output interface is busy, the packet is sent with wavelength conversion by exploiting a free TWC.

In fully equipped switch (equipped with one TWC per channel, for a total amount of NM), packet loss occurs only if all wavelengths on the destination fiber are busy [183]. Instead, with the proposed switch configuration two different situations cause packet loss: (i) the number of packets for the target output interface is greater than the number of wavelengths per fiber M (called *output blocking*), (ii) the number of packets that effectively need wavelength conversion is greater than R (loss due to lack of TWCs).

The basic all-optical elements for the implementation of this architecture have been described in [145, 222, 238]. They are typically based on optical components like MEMS or semiconductor optical amplifiers (SOAs), used as wavelength selectors, as well as optical filters and tunable wavelength converters [145, 238].

To perform the switching function a proper scheduling algorithm (SA) is needed to control the optical packet forwarding from the input to the output channels, done

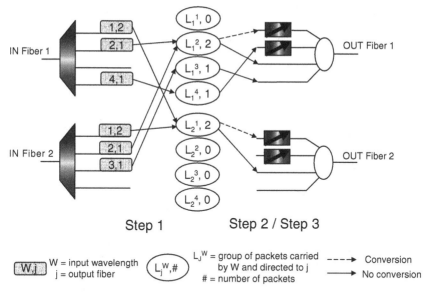

Fig. 3.21 Example of packet forwarding in a time slot with the proposed scheduling algorithm: $N = 2$ input/output fibers with $M = 4$ wavelengths each, 4 packet arrivals directed to output 1, and 2 packet arrivals for output 2

so applying contention resolution through wavelength conversion. The resulting packet loss probability depends on the capability of the algorithm to find a matching between the transfer requests and available output (and internal) resources. In [60] a scheduling algorithm that minimizes the packet loss probability is presented. This scheduling algorithm is applied to manage packet forwarding and is here briefly described. It consists of three phases sequentially executed in each time slot (see Fig. 3.21). In the first step, headers of the incoming packets are read and packets coming on the same wavelength W and directed to the same output fiber j are grouped in the set L_j^W. Packets on the same set contend for the same output channel; for this reason in the second phase one packet is randomly select from each set L_j^W and sent to the output fiber j without conversion. Such a packet can be sent on the output fiber by exploiting an OC (Fig. 3.21, packets from L_1^2, L_1^3, L_2^1) or a TWC, if no OCs are available (Fig. 3.21, the packet from L_1^4). In the third phase other packets randomly chosen are sent to the proper output fiber by exploiting wavelength conversion (Fig. 3.21, packets from L_1^2 and L_2^1), as long as there are available TWCs and there are free channels on OF. The remaining packets are lost.

3.4.2 Shared-Per-Node Scheme

In shared-per-node (SPN) concept the switching node is equipped with a single pool of TWCs that serves all input channels. In this way TWCs are shared among all incoming packets.

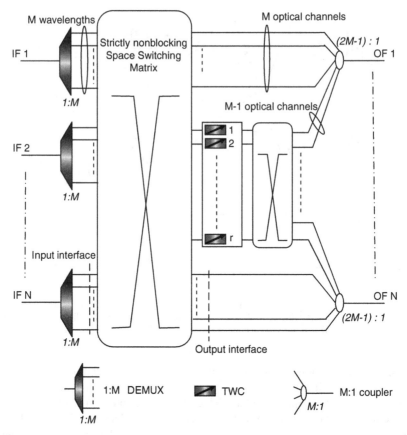

Fig. 3.22 Shared-per-node (SPN) switch architecture with N input and output fibers, M wavelengths per fiber and a limited number r of TWCs

The reference SPN switch scheme is shown in Fig. 3.22. It is equipped with N input/output interfaces, each carrying M wavelengths. Full range TWCs are grouped together in a single pool and shared among all input channels, so that an incoming packet can exploit whatever TWC. For this reason, also in this case tunable-input/tunable-output TWCs are needed. A fully equipped switch would require NM TWCs, one per channel, while in SPN, $r \leq NM$ TWCs are considered so packet loss can occur due to the lack of TWCs.

In each time slot, packets coming on different wavelengths in an input fiber are split and synchronized. A first attempt is made to forward incoming packets without wavelength conversion by exploiting the strictly nonblocking space switch. Otherwise the packet is sent to the TWC pool if a free TWC is found, and forwarded after wavelength conversion. Channels on output interfaces are multiplexed by means of couplers. At the ingress of each coupler a maximum of M packets, each carried by a different wavelength, is allowed. Excess packets are lost due to output contention.

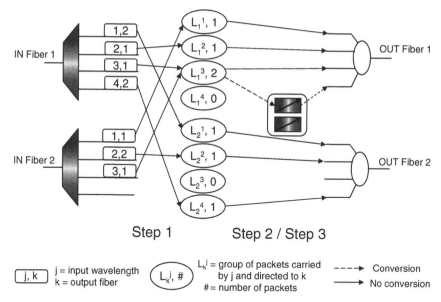

Fig. 3.23 Example of the scheduling algorithm in SPN architecture with $N = 2$ input/output fibers, $M = 4$ wavelengths per fiber, $r = 2$ TWCs

A scheduling algorithm composed by three phases sequentially executed to control packet forwarding in SPN switches has been proposed in [60]. This scheduling algorithm provides a lower bound of packet loss given that it allows forwarding the maximum number of packets in a time slot. An example of how the scheduling algorithm works is proposed in Fig. 3.23. In the first step, packets carried by wavelength j ($j = 1, \ldots, M$) and directed to output fiber k ($k = 1, \ldots, N$) are grouped (the corresponding group is called L_k^j). Packets in the same group contend for the same output channels, while packets on different groups are output contention-free. In the second step one packet from each group (randomly chosen) is sent without conversion, so the maximum number of packets is forwarded without conversion. These two steps are the same as in the scheduling algorithm for the SPL switch. In the third step the other packets are sent by exploiting wavelength conversion (the packet of L_1^3), until there are both free output channels and available TWCs in the pool.

3.4.3 Shared-Per-Wavelength Scheme

The reference shared-per-wavelength (SPW) scheme is presented in Fig. 3.24. It is equipped with N input fiber (IF)s/OFs, each carrying a WDM signal with M wavelengths. A multi-fiber version of this concept is presented in [62], meaning that multiple fibers are available on each input and output interface. Packets arriving at

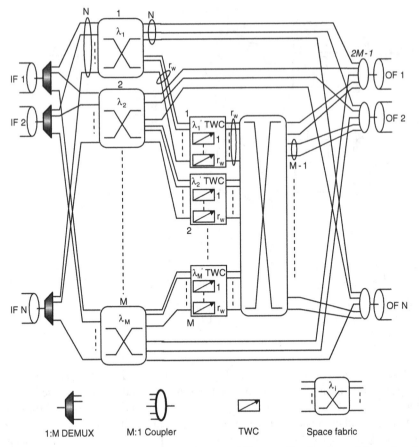

Fig. 3.24 SPW reference architecture with N input and N output fiber interfaces, M wavelengths per fiber, and r_w fixed-input/tunable-output wavelength converters shared-per-wavelength.

the switch on different fibers on the same wavelength share the same pool of wavelength converters. M different pools of r_w wavelength converters are considered, for a total amount of Mr_w. The wavelength converters in the same pool have the same input wavelength, so fixed-input/tunable-output TWCs are employed.

This kind of TWCs are expected to be simpler with respect to tunable-input/tunable-output ones, that makes the SPW architecture worth of interest. In addition, the SPW concept allows one to organize the switch in a less costly way, given that M small switching fabrics dedicated to each wavelength can be employed instead of a single large switching fabric needed in the SPN and SPL schemes [62].

A packet can be lost either for output contention (not enough wavelengths in the destination output interface are available to accommodate all the packets directed to it) or inability to convert the packet (related to the lack of TWCs).

A proper scheduling algorithm is needed to manage packet forwarding in an SPW switch. The scheduling algorithm proposed in [62] for the multi-fiber SPW switch can be used also for a mono-fiber switch and is here briefly recalled. This algorithm aims at maximizing the number of packets forwarded without conversion thus minimizing the number of wavelength conversion requests in a time slot. In this way, it provides a lower bound of packet loss probability and is, in this sense, optimal [62]. The scheduling algorithm is composed by three steps. Phase 1 is the initialization phase, where the variables used by the algorithm are initialized and the packets carried by the same wavelength and directed to the same output fiber are grouped together in the same set. Packets in the same set contend for the same output channel while packets belonging to different sets are channel contention free. For this reason, in phase 2 one and only one packet, randomly chosen, from each nonempty set is sent without conversion. In addition, in this phase the packets lost due to output contention are evaluated and discarded. Remaining packets, which are those not lost due to output contention and needing wavelength conversion, will contend in phase 3 for the available TWCs. In phase 3, up to r_w packets per wavelength, randomly selected, are sent to the TWC pool dedicated to that wavelength and forwarded by exploiting wavelength conversion. Remaining packets are those lost due to the lack of TWCs. It has been demonstrated in [62] that the computational complexity of phases 2 and 3 are $O(NM)$ and $O(NM + Mr_w)$ respectively, so the total complexity of the SA is $O(NM)$, given that $r_w < N$.

3.4.4 Analytical Model of the Packet Loss for SPN

In this section an analytical model for the SPN is described as an example for synchronous operation. Models for the other two schemes, the SPL and the SPW, can be found in [62, 203].

The proposed SPN model is based on the following general hypothesis:

- Independent Bernoulli arrivals on the input wavelengths with probability p in each time slot.
- Arrivals on input wavelengths addressed to output fibers with uniform probability $1/N$.

The Bernoulli assumption is general but reasonably accurate. In fact it has been shown that the assembly process can absorb much of the correlation existing in the incoming peripheral traffic, e.g., internet protocol traffic [213].

The model is developed taking into account the scheduling algorithm presented above. In the proposed model packet loss probability is evaluated following a tagged incoming packet carried by wavelength j and directed to output fiber k. Two events lead to packet loss:

- More than M packets are directed to output fiber k, M of them are sent and the tagged packet is not one of them. Packet loss probability associated with this event is indicated as P_u.

- More than r packets need conversion, r of them are sent to the proper output fibers by using TWCs and the tagged packet is not one of them. Packet loss probability related to this event is indicated as P_{bwc}.

The expression of the overall packet loss probability P_{loss} that takes the two above contributions into account is

$$P_{loss} = P_u + P_b \left(1 - \frac{P_u}{P_b}\right) P_{bwc}, \qquad (3.8)$$

where the second term is the joint probability of P_{bwc} and $P_b \left(1 - P_u/P_b\right)$. The latter represents the probability that the tagged packet effectively requires conversion (joint probability that the tagged packet is blocked on its wavelength, P_b, and at least one free wavelength on the output fiber k is available, $1 - P_u/P_b$).

The probability P_u that the tagged packet is blocked on the destination output fiber results in

$$P_u = \sum_{h=M+1}^{NM} \left(1 - \frac{M}{h}\right) \binom{NM-1}{h-1} \left(\frac{p}{N}\right)^{h-1} \left(1 - \frac{p}{N}\right)^{NM-h}, \qquad (3.9)$$

where the probability of h arrivals addressed to destination output fiber is expressed as the probability of $h - 1$ arrivals at the other $MN - 1$ input channels. Loss occurs when there are more than M arrivals and tagged packet is not among those chosen for transmission.

The probability P_b that the tagged packet is not forwarded into its wavelengths is given by

$$P_b = \sum_{h=2}^{N} \left(1 - \frac{1}{h}\right) \binom{N-1}{h-1} \left(\frac{p}{N}\right)^{h-1} \left(1 - \frac{p}{N}\right)^{N-h}. \qquad (3.10)$$

by considering that there are N input fibers and the wavelengths are replicated in each of them, it is possible to have up to N packet arrivals directed to the same output fiber and carried by the same wavelength.

As a consequence the load offered to the TWC block by a single wavelength is

$$A_{wc} = pP_b \left(1 - \frac{P_u}{P_b}\right). \qquad (3.11)$$

Packet loss probability in the TWC block occurs when there are more than r conversion requests in the same time slot. The assumption of NM independent Bernoulli arrivals at the TWC block in a time slot is made. As a matter of fact these arrivals are not independent and are negatively correlated since, for a switch with N input/output fibers, the total number of new packets arriving in each time slot at the same wavelength is no greater than N. As a consequence, each packet addressed to the output fiber g reduces the likelihood of packets destined for output fiber k, for $g \neq k$. In the extreme case, if N packets arrive during a time slot for a single OF g, no packet can arrive for any of the other OFs [55, 142]. In [55] the effects of this correlation are shown to apply only when the load per wavelength is high, otherwise they can be neglected. In this context the correlation can be omitted, because, when the load is high, the packet loss due to the lack of TWCs is shadowed by the contention on output fiber. Further, the effect of this negative correlation decreases when the switching size N increases. Under this hypothesis, the packet loss probability due to the lack of TWCs, P_{bwc}, is calculated as

$$P_{bwc} = \sum_{h=r+1}^{NM} \left(1 - \frac{r}{h}\right) \binom{NM-1}{h-1} (A_{wc})^{h-1} (1 - A_{wc})^{NM-h}. \qquad (3.12)$$

When $r = MN$ (fully equipped architecture), $P_{bwc} = 0$ and $P_{loss} = P_u$; the same as the full wavelength conversion case. When $r = 0$, instead, $P_{bwc} = 1$ and $P_{loss} = P_b$; in fact if one packet is blocked on its wavelength, it is lost because conversion is not possible. This model makes it possible to find the minimum number of TWCs leading to the same packet loss as in the full wavelength conversion case. Analytical (A) and simulation (S) results are compared in Fig. 3.25 which shows the packet loss probability (PLP) as a function of $\alpha = r/NM$, varying the load per wavelength p and the number of wavelengths per fiber M, for $N = 16$. Simulation results, obtained by applying the scheduling algorithm presented above (which maximizes switch throughput), considers a confidence interval at 95% less than or equal to 5% of average. Analytical and simulation results exhibit good matching. The packet loss decreases, as expected, when the number of wavelengths increases.

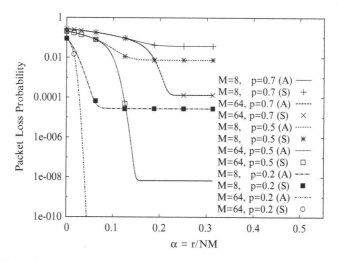

Fig. 3.25 Packet loss probability of the SPN switch architecture as a function of the normalized number of TWCs, α, varying the load per wavelength p in case $N = 16$, $M = 8$ and 64. (A) is for analysis and (S) is for simulation

3.4.5 Comparison Among SPL, SPN, SPW

In this section the three proposed schemes are compared in terms of performance (PLP) and complexity (number of main optical components).

The SPN scheme represents the perfect sharing, given that any TWCs are shared among any packets. In SPL the TWCs are partitioned among N fibers, and each TWC pool is shared by the packets directed to the same OF, that are on average M. Instead, in SPW the TWCs are partitioned among the M wavelengths. The TWC pool dedicated to a wavelength is shared by N input channels (those related to the that wavelength on the IFs). For this reason, the SPL scheme is more effective in solve contention when N is low and M is high. In fact in this case the TWCs are partitioned in few groups each shared by a relevant number of packets. On the contrary the SPW scheme performs better when N is high and M is low, for the same reason. This is confirmed by observing Figs. 3.26 and 3.27 where the PLP obtained with SPL, SPN, SPW schemes is plotted, for different values of load (p = 0.3, 0.5, and 0.8), in case 3.26 $N = 32$, $M = 8$, (Fig. 3.25) and $N = 8$, $M = 32$.

The PLP is plotted as a function of the total number of TWCs employed. In Fig. 3.26, where $N > M$, the PLP obtained with SPL switch is far from the one of the SPN switch, while the PLP obtained with SPW is nearer. In Fig. 3.27, the PLP of SPL is lower than the one of SPW switch, that is far from the one of SPN.

All the schemes lead to the same asymptotic value of PLP, related to the output blocking, but the minimum number of TWCs needed to reach this asymptote differ for SPN, SPL, and SPW. The number of TWCs needed is related to the switch dimensioning. For all switch dimensioning, the SPN requires the lower number of TWCs. The higher the N with respect to M, the higher the additional number of TWCs needed for SPL scheme with respect to SPN. Instead, in this situation the

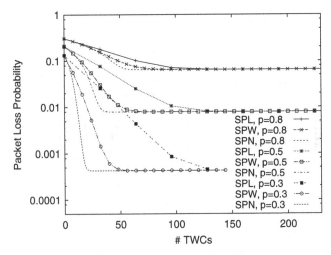

Fig. 3.26 Comparison of SPL, SPN, and SPW schemes, PLP as a function of the total number of TWCs varying load in case $N = 32$, $M = 8$

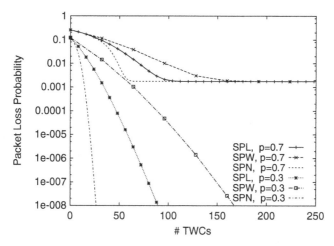

Fig. 3.27 Comparison of SPL, SPN, and SPW schemes, PLP as a function of the total number of TWCs varying load in case $N = 8$, $M = 32$

additional number for SPW scheme is lower. The opposite is obtained when N is low with respect to M.

Some considerations about the complexity of each scheme can be made. All schemes rely on strictly nonblocking space switching matrices with large size. The SPL scheme does not require any additional complexity with respect to the fully equipped architecture (equipped with one TWC for each output channel), while SPN and SPW schemes require additional complexity to reach the shared TWCs and to connect them to the output fibers. This additional complexity is proportional to the total number of TWCs. In particular, as can be seen from Figs. 3.26 and 3.27, the SPW scheme requires a higher number of TWCs with respect to the SPN, so its complexity in terms of optical components is higher. On the other hand, the SPW scheme takes advantage by employing fixed-input/tunable-output TWCs, which are simpler to be implemented than tunable-input ones. In particular, in this work the space switching fabrics are considered as implemented by means of semiconductor optical amplifiers (SOA)s used as optical gates. In fact SOAs used as gates present good properties, such as very low switching time (in the range of few nanoseconds) and high extinction ratio. The number of SOAs needed for a switching fabric is given by the number of crossing points of the fabric. By observing Fig. 3.20 it can be deduced that the size of the switching fabric is $NM \times NM$ so the complexity in terms of SOAs of the SPL scheme results in

$$N_{SOA}^{SPL} = (NM)^2. \tag{3.13}$$

From Fig. 3.22 the size of the two switching fabrics needed in the SPN scheme results in $NM \times (NM + r)$ and $r \times N(M - 1)$, respectively, so the total number of SOAs is

$$N_{SOA}^{SPN} = NM(NM + r) + rN(M - 1) = (NM)^2 + rN(2M - 1). \tag{3.14}$$

Finally by observing Fig. 3.24, the SPW scheme needs M switching fabrics with size $N \times (N + r_w)$ and an additional fabric with size $Mr_w \times N(M - 1)$ so the number of SOAs is:

$$N_{SOA}^{SPW} = MN(N + r_W) + Mr_{wN}(M - 1) = M(N^2 + NMr_w). \qquad (3.15)$$

To reduce the complexity, practical implementations where strictly nonblocking matrices are replaced by simpler switching fabrics have to be defined.

The implementation of optical packet switches can be based on multistage solutions in order to overcome physical constraints or to save optical components. As an example some switching fabrics have been demonstrated to be feasible with a limited number of input and output interfaces. Thus, larger fabrics solutions based on Clos organization of switching elements have been proposed [202]. When switching schemes based on wavelength conversion are considered the number of optical components increases significantly. As a consequence, multistage solutions that reduce the overall switch complexity have been proposed [204].

3.5 Buffered Switch Architectures

Given the general principles explained in Sections 3.3.1 and 3.3.2 the implementation of an optical buffer depends on the switching matrix and several architectures can be found in the literature. Optical buffers can be classified depending on their placement in the matrix as:

- *Feed-forward:* The FDLs are part of the switching path and connected to the inputs/outputs of the switching matrix, thus each packet has to pass through the buffer, typically only once.
- *Feedback buffers:* The FDLs are connected to some of the space switch outputs and the buffer outputs are connected back to some of the input ports of the space switch, such that buffered packets re-enter the switching matrix and have another chance to be switched to the requested output.

Similar to the switching matrix the FDL buffers can be:

- *Single stage:* Built by using a single set of FDLs.
- *Multi-stage:* Built by cascading several sets of FDLs, typically of different lengths and interconnected with optical space switches.

Finally FDLs can be shared by different traffic flows, very similar to what we have already presented for the wavelength converters:

- *Shared per channel:* One set of FDLs and related space switches per output channel (wavelength/fiber).
- *Shared per link:* One set of FDLs and related space switches per output link such that it is shared by all packets to be transmitted on any channel of that link.
- *Shared per node:* One set of FDLs and related space switches per node such that it is shared by all packets traversing the node.

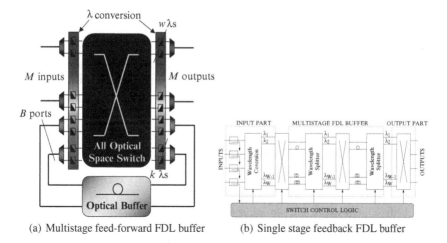

(a) Multistage feed-forward FDL buffer   (b) Single stage feedback FDL buffer

Fig. 3.28 Examples of FDL buffer architectures

Examples of a feedback [48] and feed-forward [30] architecture are presented in Fig. 3.28. In both cases the buffer is shared per node, the buffer in 3.26a is a multi-stage buffer and that of 3.26b is a single stage buffer. These figures are just examples, obviously all possible architectural combinations are possible, bringing to different complexity trade-offs in terms of components used.

One last issue is related to the distribution of delays. We have already mentioned the degenerate/nondegenerate alternative in Section 3.3.1, implicitly assuming that the delay lines of a buffer are of different length, thus realizing a set of different delays. This is not mandatory of course and a delay line buffer may be built with replicated delays. This is possible either by means of several fiber delay line (FDLs) of the same length or by operating the FDL in WDM. Replication of delays may be of particular importance in switch configuration where the optical buffer is shared by many (or even all) traffic flows. In this case it is likely that more than one packet may need the same delay and therefore having many is of use.

With the aim to answer to the need of optical industry to design optical packet switches that employ available components, hybrid switch architectures can be considered [182]. Contention resolution in the time domain is obtained by means of electronic buffers after optical to electronic conversion. Different queuing policies can be applied to optimize time transparency.

3.5.1 QoS Support

Quality of service support is an important function of next generation packet networks to support multi-service functions. Due to the lack of random access memory in optical packet switches, complex queue management must be avoided. Typically, threshold-based or resource reservation schemes are applied to achieve some level of service differentiation [29, 30]. Different schemes have been investigated and compared to show the effectiveness of wavelength and time exploitation [68]. In hybrid switch architectures with electronic buffers QoS mechanisms operate to optimize the traffic sharing among all optical paths and hybrid paths inside the switch to meet service requirements.

3.5.2 Performance of Channel Scheduling Algorithms in Practical Implementations

In real life contention resolution impacts on the cost of the switching matrix. This is particularly true in implementing an optical buffer. FDLs cause delay and an excessively long delay line could impair the optical signal level to the extent that additional regeneration may be required. Moreover, switching packets to the delay lines require optical space switches and changing transmission channel also requires space switching and/or wavelength conversion. In general the optical buffer will cost in terms of hardware implementation and in impairment of the signal quality.

It is common in the literature to find works that describe specific buffering architectures and discuss the related performance/complexity. On the other hand limited works exist that try to compare different solutions and that provide guidelines for the choice of one possible architectural solution or another. In this section we address such an issue, with particular reference to the comparison of CDS algorithms and of their respective implementations.

The case study is that of a single stage FDL buffer that is shared per link. The output interface is equipped with F fibers each carrying W wavelengths and packets can be sent to any outgoing channel. As explained before, this is a typical CDS case. Wavelength conversion is necessary if $W > 1$ and this is the first implementation issue to be addressed.

TWC are used to feed packets to the proper channel so that a packet entering the switch on λ_{in} may leave it on $\lambda_{out} \neq \lambda_{in}$. If λ_{out} can be any wavelength, regardless of λ_{in}, we call this *full wavelength conversion (FWC)*. If λ_{out} is somewhat limited we call this *limited wavelength conversion (LWC)*. Generally speaking, we expect full range converters to be more complex and expensive than limited range converters. In addition, the computation of the CDS algorithm becomes more complex when a large number of wavelengths has to be considered, up to the point that it may turn into a system bottleneck [24]. Therefore, by limiting the range of the converters, the implementation of the switching matrix is made simpler both from the hardware and the scheduling point of view. In this perspective, limited-range wavelength conversion (LWC) is studied as a trade-off between flexibility and cost.

Moreover, the number of converters is usually limited. If R converters were available, it may happen that some stage, in order to successfully schedule a burst/packet, one would need a wavelength conversion. However this could not be accomplished when/if all R converters were used by other bursts/packets already.

In general the CDS algorithm has now restrictions on the scheduling of a packet. Given all the scheduling points $s(i, j, k) \in \mathscr{S}$, it may be just a subset $\mathscr{S}' \subset \mathscr{S}$ of them is available because of conversion capabilities limitation.

3.5.2.1 Wavelength Conversion Constraints

Wavelength converters providing a limited range of conversions may be utilized in different ways that impact the conversion capabilities [277]. In general we can say that the pool of W wavelengths available on each of the F fibers is divided in wavebands of L wavelengths and conversion may happen only within the same waveband. As such a given λ_{in} can only be converted to a set of λ_{out} whose size is $L < W$ wavelengths.[2]

Depending on different implementations of the wavelength converters the "reachable" wavelength set may not be the same, as in the following two alternative cases:

- *Nonoverlapping (fixed) wavebands (FB):* W/L wavebands are defined on each fiber, each being a set of L adjacent and nonoverlapping wavelengths. The nth waveband includes wavelengths in the set

$$b_n = [(n-1)L + 1, (n-1)L + 2, \ldots, nL]$$

with $1 \leq n \leq W/L$. If a packet arrives on $w_{in} \in b_n$, the CDS algorithm can convert this packet only to a $w_{out} \in b_n$ on any fiber in the output link.
- *Overlapping (variable) wavebands (VB):* All wavelengths are considered in a circular sequential list and to each w_{in} corresponds a waveband on which w_{in} occupies a central-right position. If $w_{in} = j$ then the corresponding waveband is the set of wavelengths

$$b_j = [j - L/2, \ldots, j - 1, j, \ldots, j + L/2 - 1],$$

where the operations on the indexes are modulo W. If a packet arrives on w_{in} it can be converted to a w_{out} that belongs to the waveband on which w_{in} is in the central-right position.

As an example for $F = 1$, $W = 8$, $L = 4$, and $B = 2$, the scheduling space for FWC is $\mathscr{S}$ such that $|\mathscr{S}| = 16$. For LWC the scheduling space for a packet entering, for instance, on $\lambda_{in} = 2$ is $S' \subset S$. In the case of FB-LWC assume the subbands are $W_1 = \{1, 2, 3, 4\}$ and $W_2 = \{5, 6, 7, 8\}$; then the subset of scheduling points is $s(i, j, k) \in S | 1 \leq j \leq 4$, and $|S'| = 8$ and not 16.

This is true if there is a wavelength converter available. If there are not free wavelength converters available the scheduling space is further reduced and becomes $s(i, j, k) \in S | j = 2$ and $|S'| = 2$.

---

[2] For the sake of simplicity, in this work we always consider W to be a multiple of L.

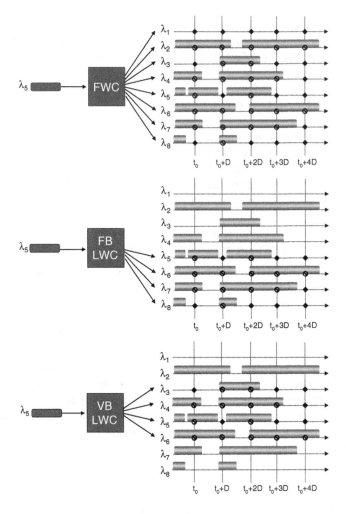

Fig. 3.29 Wavelength conversion alternatives, when $W = 8$, $L = 4$ and $w_{in} = 5$

The differences between FWC, FB-LWC, and VB-LWC, are clarified in the example of Fig. 3.29, showing the allowed conversions when $W = 8$, $L = 4$, and $w_{in} = 5$.

3.5.2.2 Key Parameters for Contention Resolution

The discussion in the first part of this section and in Section 3.3.2 shows that there are a number of parameters to be accounted for when designing the optical buffer, namely:

• The number of fibers F per output link

- The number of wavelengths W per fiber
- The wavelength conversion capability, in terms of the number of wavelengths L per conversion waveband
- The number of available wavelength converters R per output interface, assuming converters are shared per output
- The nature of wavelength conversion, either FB or VB
- The number of delays B and the delay unit D
- The kind of CDS scheduling algorithm, either WT or TW, either D or G type, with or without void filling

These parameters determine the cardinality of the scheduling space, that is a sort of measure of the "cost" of the CDS algorithm, since it is correlated to the complexity and amount of devices needed to implement the switching matrix. Therefore, we argue that CDS algorithms should be compared for same values of $|\mathcal{S}'|$ and R. This leaves a lot of freedom to the engineer that has to dimension the B, W or L, F etc. parameters, facing several trade-offs:

1. *Time vs. channel multiplexing*: Is it better to have more delays or more channels (i.e., wavelengths and fibers) on the output links?
2. *Space vs. wavelength multiplexing*: Is it better to have more fibers or more wavelengths on the output link?
3. *Number or complexity of the wavelength converters*: Is it better to have many converters of limited complexity (LWC) or a few more complex converters (FWC)?

Research results available about the aforementioned issue show that, given the dimension of the scheduling space it is more profitable to invest in channels rather than in delays, as long as long as at least one delay is provided. As shown in Fig. 3.30a the $B = 1$ (0 delays only cut-through) choice is by far not optimal, while the choice of $B = 2$ outperforms significantly the other cases. Moreover LWC is not necessarily worse than FWC, as intuition would suggest. The example in Fig. 3.30b shows that a little increase in delays may well compensate the limited range conversion and

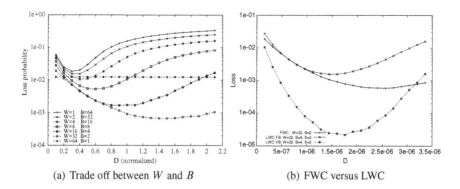

(a) Trade off between W and B (b) FWC versus LWC

Fig. 3.30 PLP as a function of D for a switch with $F = 1$ and CDS algorithms working on a scheduling set having cardinality $|\mathcal{S}| = 64$: (**a**) FWC, trade-off between W and B, better investing on wavelength rather than delays, (**b**) LWC may be better of FWC with the same scheduling space

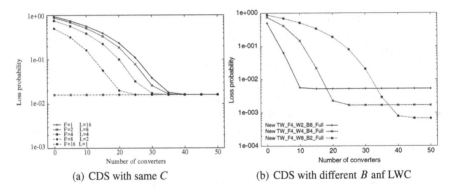

(a) CDS with same C (b) CDS with different B anf LWC

Fig. 3.31 PLP as a function R: (**a**) sensitivity of the PLP to the number of fibers and wavelength given the same total number of channels; (**b**) PLP as a function of R for CDS algorithms with same scheduling space but different ratios of B and W

may also improve the overall performance. The CDS used for these examples is delay-based without void-filling.

In Fig. 3.31 the PLP is plotted against the number of converters R. The PLP is very sensitive to the number of converters for small values of R, then it becomes insensitive to this parameters once it is large enough. This suggests that a minimum number of converters R is necessary to provide optimal performance and this minimum has to be chosen carefully once the other parameters are known. Obviously given the number of channels C an implementation of the output interface with more fibers with less wavelength per fiber requires fewer converters because the same wavelength is available F times at the interface. Finally Fig. 3.31 also shows that the PLP is sensitive to C but not to F and L alone once the proper value of R is reached. In conclusion a large number of fibers with less wavelengths per fiber requires fewer converters and more space switching, therefore if the number of converters is crucial it is better to bet on fibers rather than on λs.

3.6 AWG-Based Space Switching Architectures

The general architecture of the optical transport network is assumed to consist of M *optical packet-switching nodes*, each denoted by an optical address made of $m = \log_2\lceil M \rceil$ bits, which are linked together in a meshlike topology. A number of *edge systems* (ES) interfaces the optical transport network with IP legacy (electronic) networks.

The transport network operation is *asynchronous*; that is, packets can be received by nodes at any instant, with no time alignment. The internal operation of the optical nodes, on the other hand, is *synchronous*, or *slotted*, since the behavior of packets in an unslotted node is less regulated and more unpredictable, resulting in a larger contention probability.

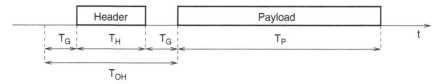

Fig. 3.32 Optical packet format

An ES receives packets from different electronic networks and performs *optical packet* generation. The optical packet is composed of a simple optical header, which carriers the *m*-bit destination address, and an optical payload containing, for example, an IP packet. In principle multiple packets could be packed in the same optical packet payload if they are all addressed to the same ES. The optical packets are buffered and routed through the optical transport network to reach their destination ES, which delivers the traffic it receives to its destination electronic networks. At each intermediate node in the transport network, optical packet headers are received and electronically processed, in order to provide routing information to the control electronics, which will properly configure the node resources to switch packet payloads directly in the optical domain.

Header and payload of an optical packet are transmitted serially, as shown in Fig. 3.32, where header duration is equal to T_H and payload duration to T_P. At each switching node the optical header is read, dropped and regenerated at the node output; therefore, guard times (T_G) are needed in order to avoid payload/header superposition, due to clock jitter in the transmission phase. A guard time $T_G = 1$ ns is felt to be reasonable, assuming that optical transmission is carried out at 10 Gbps. The optical packet header carries not only the *m*-bit destination address but also other information needed to correctly receive and manage the optical packet, such as preamble data, packet length information, etc. It is assumed that 60 bits are enough for carrying all information, thus leading to $T_H = 6$ ns. Hence, the total overhead time is equal to $T_{OH} = T_H + 2T_G = 8$ ns.

The slot duration (T) can be chosen to be equal to the time needed to transmit an optical packet whose payload consists of the smallest TCP/IP packet (i.e., 320 bits, the size of an IP packet carrying a TCP acknowledgment). Time slot duration is therefore equal to $T = T_{OH} + 32$ ns $= 40$ ns. IP packets longer than the minimum size are transmitted, as many consecutive slots as needed are engaged, considering that the optical header is present just in the first slot of the optical packet. The reader interested in a deeper analysis of the motivations of these choices is referred to [221].

3.6.1   Optical Switching Node Architecture

The general architecture of a node of the optical transport network just described is shown in Fig. 3.33. It consists of N incoming fibers with W wavelengths per

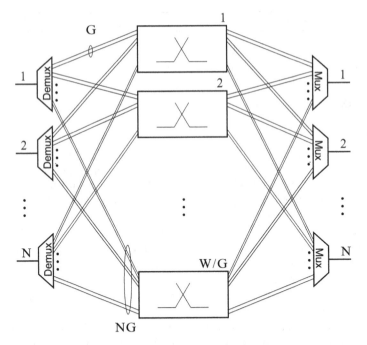

Fig. 3.33 Optical packet-switching node architecture

fiber. The incoming fiber signals are demultiplexed and G wavelengths from each input fiber are then fed into one of the W/G switching planes, which constitute the switching fabric core. Once signals have been switched in one of the second-stage parallel planes, packets can reach every output port on one of the G wavelengths that are directed to each output fiber. This allows the use of wavelength conversion for contention resolution, since G packets can be transmitted at the same time by each second-stage plane on the same output link. Apparently hardware simplicity requirements suggest feeding each plane with the same wavelengths from any input fiber. Nevertheless, in principle there is no restriction in selecting the value of G, even if it can have a significant impact on the node traffic performance.

The optical components envisioned to be used in the switching architecture proposed here are discussed in the following: In some cases the technology involved is really complex and fully commercial products at affordable costs are not yet available. Nevertheless out aim is to show that the proposed architectural solution is feasible, albeit not using off-the-shelf components and systems. Here we do not discuss the issue of optical signal quality. Thus the possible need for optical signal regeneration inside the switch, as well as cost issue, is not investigated, as being closely related to the adopted optical technology, which is likely to improve constantly in the near future.

The structure of one of the W/G parallel switching planes is presented in Fig. 3.34. It interfaces input and output optical links and consists of three main

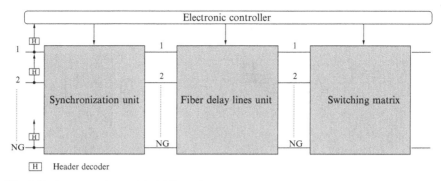

H   Header decoder

Fig. 3.34 Structure of one of the W/G parallel switching planes

blocks: an input *synchronization unit*, as the node is slotted and incoming packets need to be aligned, a *fiber delay lines unit*, used to store packets for contention resolution, and a *switching matrix unit*, to achieve the switching of signals.

These three blocks are all managed by an *electronic control unit*, which carries out the following tasks:

- Optical packet header recovery and processing
- Managing the synchronization unit in order to properly set the correct path through the synchronizer for each incoming packet
- Managing the tunable wavelength converters (TWCs) in order to properly delay and route incoming packets in the second and third unit of the system, respectively

3.6.2 Synchronization Unit

The synchronization unit is shown in Fig. 3.35 and consists of a series of 2×2 optical switches interconnected by fiber delay lines of different lengths. These are arranged in a way that, depending on the particular path set through the switches, the packet can be delayed by a variable amount of time, ranging between $\Delta t_{\min} = 0$ and $\Delta t_{\max} = 2(1 - (1/2)^{n+1}) \times T$, with a resolution of $T/2^n$, where T is the time slot duration and n the number of delay line stages.

The synchronization is achieved as follows: once the packet header has been recognized and packet delineation has been carried out, the packet start time is identified and the control electronics can calculate the necessary delay and configure the correct path of the packet through the synchronizer.

Due to the fast reconfiguration speed needed, fast 2×2 switching devices, such as 2×2 semiconductor optical amplifier (SOAs) switches [51] having a switching time in the nanosecond range, must be used. SOAs are all-optical amplification devices that are already used in a wide range of applications; they can be arranged in a particular structure in order to achieve switching of optical signals. An interesting

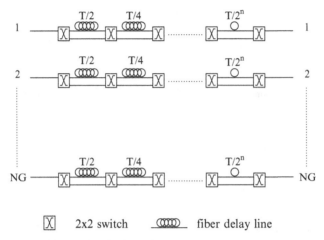

Fig. 3.35 Structure of the synchronization unit

characteristic of SOA switches is that these devices allow the amplification of the traveling signals, making it possible to, besides route functionalities, restore a required given signal level.

3.6.3 Fiber Delay Lines Unit

After packet alignment has been carried out, the routing information carried by the packet header allows the control electronics to properly configure a set of TWCs in order to deliver each packet to the correct delay line to resolve contentions (see Fig. 3.36). On each of the NG inputs of the plane a delay can be applied that is multiple of the basic slot duration T and ranges up to D_{max} slots. An optical packet can be stored for a time slot, with a 40-ns duration, in about 8 m of fiber at 10 Gbps. To achieve wavelength conversion several devices are available [134, 147, 255, 267].

Depending on the managing algorithm used by control electronics, the fiber delay lines stage can be used as an *optical scheduler* or as an *optical first-in-first-out* (FIFO) *buffer*.

- *Optical scheduling*: This policy uses the delay lines in order to schedule the transmission of the maximum number of packets onto the correct output link. This implies that an optical packet P_1 entering the node at time αT from the i th WDM input channel can be transmitted after an optical packet P_2 entering the node on the same input channel at time βT, $\beta > \alpha$. For example, suppose that packet P_1 of duration $l_1 T$ must be delayed d_1 time slots, in order to be transmitted onto the correct output port. This packet will then leave the optical scheduler at time $(\alpha + d_1)T$. So, if packet P_2 of duration $l_2 T$ has to be delayed for d_2 slots,

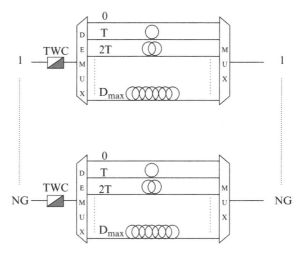

Fig. 3.36 Structure of the fiber delay unit

it can be transmitted before P_1 if $\beta + d_2 + l_2 < \alpha + d_1$, since no collision will occur at the scheduler output.

- *Optical FIFO buffering*: In the optical FIFO buffer the order of the packets entering the fiber delay lines stage must be maintained. This leads to a simpler managing algorithm than the one used for the optical scheduling policy, yielding, however, a suboptimal output channel utilization. In fact, suppose that optical packet P_1 entering the FIFO buffer at time αT must be delayed for d_1 time slots. This implies that packet P_2, behind packet P_1, must be delayed at least d_1 time slots in order to maintain the order of incoming packets. Due to this rule, if packet P_2 could be delayed for $d_2 < d_1$ slots to avoid conflict, its destination output port would be idle for $d_1 - d_2$ time slots, while there would be a packet to transmit.

3.6.4 Switching Matrix Unit

Once packets have crossed the fiber delay lines unit, they enter the switching matrix stage in order to be routed to the desired output port. This is achieved using a set of tunable wavelength converters combined with an arrayed waveguide grating (AWG) wavelength router [190]. This device consists of two slab star couplers, interconnected by an array of waveguides. Each grating waveguide has a precise path difference with respect to its neighbors, ΔX, and is characterized by a refractive index of value n_w.

Once a signal enters the AWG from an incoming fiber, the input star coupler divides the power among all waveguides in the grating array. As a consequence of the difference of the guides lengths, light traveling through each couple of adjacent waveguides emerges with a phase delay difference given by

$$\Delta\phi = 2\pi n_w \times \frac{\Delta X}{\lambda},$$

where λ is the incoming signal central wavelength. As all the beams emerge from the grating array they interfere constructively onto the focal point in the output star coupler, in a way that allows couple an interference maximum with a particular output fiber, depending only on the input signal central wavelength.

Figure 3.37 shows the mechanism described above. Two signals of wavelength λ_0 and λ_3 entering an 8×8 AWG, from input fibers number 6 and number 1, respectively, are correctly switched onto the output fibers number 0 and number 3, respectively the wavelength and the input port of the signals being the only parameters determining the switch permutation. Figure 3.38 shows how a comb of four wavelengths are routed in an AWG of size 4×4.

The most general type of switching operation requires each incoming signal to be routed (switched) to an arbitrary (idle) output port. Achieving such dynamic routing in an AWG requires that an incoming signal could be given a wavelength consistent with the desired routing. This can be obtained by equipping a tunable wavelength converter at each input port. We remark that the AWG is used as it gives better performance than a normal space switch interconnection network, as far as insertion losses are concerned. This is due to the high insertion losses of all the highspeed

Grating array
Input star coupler
Output star coupler
λ_3
λ_0
Input fibers
λ_0
λ_3
Output fibers

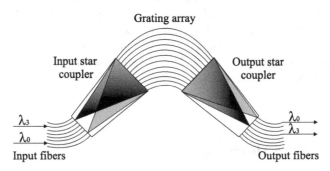

Fig. 3.37 Arrayed waveguide grating (AWG)

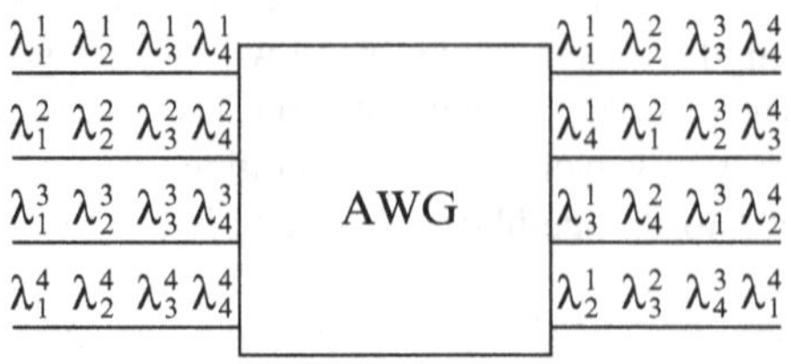

λ_1^1 λ_2^1 λ_3^1 λ_4^1
λ_1^2 λ_2^2 λ_3^2 λ_4^2
λ_1^3 λ_2^3 λ_3^3 λ_4^3
λ_1^4 λ_2^4 λ_3^4 λ_4^4
AWG
λ_1^1 λ_2^2 λ_3^3 λ_4^4
λ_4^1 λ_1^2 λ_2^3 λ_3^4
λ_3^1 λ_4^2 λ_1^3 λ_2^4
λ_2^1 λ_3^2 λ_4^3 λ_1^4

Fig. 3.38 Routing configuration in a 4×4 AWG

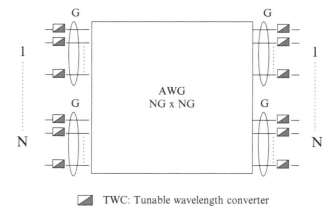

TWC: Tunable wavelength converter

Fig. 3.39 Basic structure of the switching matrix

all-optical switching fabrics available at the moment that could be used to build a space switch interconnection network. Commercially available devices support 40–64 channels with 50–100 GHz spacing and have an insertion loss of less than 6 dB. Other optical switch architectures adopting AWGs as router devices can be found in [36, 167, 238].

The simplest switching matrix structure, referred to as "Basic," is shown in Fig. 3.39. It consists of $2NG$ tunable wavelength converters and an AWG with size $NG \times NG$. Only one packet is routed to each AWG outlet and this packet must finally be converted to one of the wavelengths used in the WDM channel, with attention paid to avoiding contention with other packets of the same channel. This is accomplished by the control electronics through the proper setting of the fiber delay line unit.

In order to improve the system performance and to eventually support different priority classes, some of the AWG ports can be reserved to allow packet recirculation, as shown in Fig. 3.40; this structure is referred to as "Basic-R." To this purpose R AWG output ports are connected via fiber delay lines to R input ports. These lines act as shared queues for all the packets crossing the switch, independently from their respective input line. Recirculation ports allow the switch to support different priority classes, with service preemption. In fact, an optical packet, traveling through a recirculation port delay line, can always be preempted by a higher priority packet and be redirected to a recirculation port, instead of being transmitted. After, recirculation packets cross a TWC in order to select the new AWG output port.

In principle we can adopt either a fixed delay D_{rec} (multiple of the timeslot duration T) for all the R lines, or a delay variable from line to line. In this latter case the selection of the specific recirculation line to be used must be carried out by the control electronics taking into account the specific additional delay being incurred in packet recirculation.

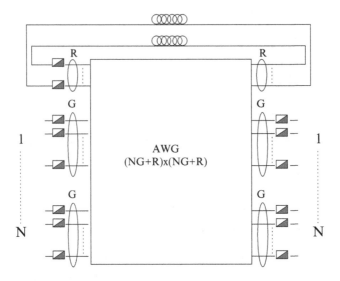

☑ TWC: Tunable wavelength converter   ⬭⬭⬭⬭⬭ FDL: Fiber delay line

Fig. 3.40 Basic structure of the switching matrix with recirculation lines

After crossing the three stages previously described, packets undergo a final wavelength conversion, to deter collisions at the output multiplexers, where W WDM channels are multiplexed onto each output link.

3.6.5 Multiwavelength Switching Matrix

The capability of AWG to route several wavelengths to the same output port makes it possible to reduce the AWG size, given a total number of channels to be handled with the switching matrix. For this purpose we consider now only single-plane implementation of the switching node (i.e., $W = G$) by using a single AWG with size $W \times W$.

The basic structure of the "Multi-λ" switching matrix is shown in Fig. 3.41. The wavelength of the signals entering the switching matrix is converted to an appropriate wavelength, in order to route the signal to the desired output fiber. Unlike the switching matrix considered in [221], the key feature of this switching unit is its ability to route more than one packet from a single AWG inlet to different outlets. In fact, the AWG working principle is such that signals with different wavelengths entering the same inlet will emerge on different outlets, and different wavelengths are needed to route signals from different inlets to the same outlet. So, no superposition can happen at the AWG outlets between signals coming from the same inlet if the TWCs convert them to different wavelengths.

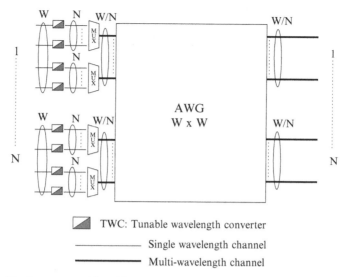

TWC: Tunable wavelength converter

———————— Single wavelength channel

———————— Multi-wavelength channel

Fig. 3.41 Matrix structure with multi-wavelength switching capability

Since NW different channels enter the switching matrix, if N wavelengths are multiplexed on the same AWG inlet, this structure requires a $W \times W$ AWG. So, if the AWG works on the same wavelengths used in the outgoing fibers, no wavelength conversion is needed at the switching matrix output, since packets exit the AWG using one of the transmission wavelengths. Finally, W/N AWG outlets will be multiplexed onto the same output fiber. Therefore, a packet entering an AWG outlet can be routed to the desired output fiber using one of the W/N wavelengths which will route it to an outlet connected to the fiber. Particular attention must be paid by the electronic controller in order to deter wavelength superposition in the output fibers. Two signals coming from different inlets using the same wavelengths will be routed to different outlets, but if these outlets are multiplexed onto the same fiber, wavelength superposition can happen.

As with the previous switching matrix, we can adopt recirculation lines also in the multiwavelength structure by reserving for this purpose R AWG ports to accomplish packet-shared queueing. These recirculation lines can make easier than pure input buffers do the provision of different switching service classes by their dynamically adjusting the priorities of packets being recirculated. The switching matrix structure with R recirculation lines is shown in Fig. 3.42; this structure is referred to as "Multi-λ-R."

It is clear that, since the key property of this structure is to have a $W \times W$ AWG, if R AWG ports are reserved to recirculation lines, a different number k of wavelengths are to be multiplexed now on each AWG inlet. The number of required AWG ports A can be expressed as $A = R + NW/k$. Therefore, since the relationship $A = W$ must be satisfied,

$$W = R + \frac{NW}{k}. \qquad (3.16)$$

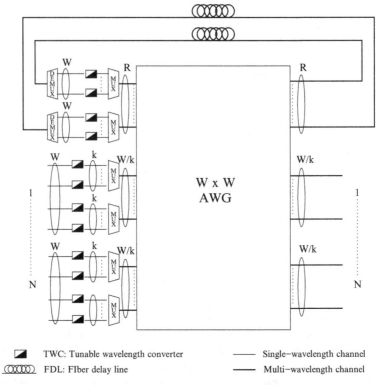

| | TWC: Tunable wavelength converter | —— Single–wavelength channel |
| | FDL: FIber delay line | —— Multi–wavelength channel |

Fig. 3.42 Multi-wavelength switching matrix with recirculation lines

Given the number of wavelengths per channel W and the number of recirculation ports R, the number of wavelengths fed to each AWG inlet k is expressed as

$$k = \frac{NW}{W - R},\qquad(3.17)$$

or alternatively, given W and k, R is obtained by

$$R = \frac{W(k - N)}{k},\qquad(3.18)$$

where obviously N, W, k, and R must be integer values.

Up to W packets on different wavelengths can be concurrently routed to each recirculation line. While allowing us to better exploit the buffering capacity of each delay line, this solution implies that before re-entering the AWG, the different wavelengths traveling through the recirculation lines must be split and sent to different TWCs; therefore a number W of TWCs will be needed to implement a single recirculation line.

Table 3.2 Components of the switching matrices, assuming $W = G$

	AWG size	TWC count	MUX size	MUX count
Basic	$NW \times NW$	$2NW$	–	–
Basic-R	$(NW + R) \times (NW + R)$	$2NW + R$	–	–
Multi-λ	$W \times W$	NW	$N \times 1$	W
Multi-λ-R	$W \times W$	$(N + R)W$	$k \times 1$	NW/k
			$W \times 1$	R

3.6.6 Complexity

The components needed to build a switching matrix with size $NW \times NW$ are listed in Table 3.2, where for simplicity $W = G$ is assumed, so that the architecture includes just one switching plane. Basic solutions where each AWG input and output fiber carries just one channel clearly require a larger size of the AWG, which grows further if recirculation lines must be supported. More advanced solutions for the switching matrix where several channels can share the same input or output AWG port enable the AWG size to be reduced to the number of supported wavelengths (W). The price to pay is apparently the cost of the multiplexers needed to arrange the multiwavelength signals to be fed into the AWG. Notable enough in this last solution is the significantly lower number of TWCs needed, which do not need to be connected to the AWG output ports.

As far as the traffic performance issues are concerned, extensive studies of the basic switching matrices and of multiwavelength solutions can be found in [194, 195].

Chapter 4
Optical Burst Switching

José Alberto Hernández, Víctor López, José Luis García Dorado,
Reza Nejabati, Harald Overby, Ahmad Rostami, Kyriakos Vlachos,
and Georgios Zervas

An all-OPS network architecture displays a very attractive prospect for the future highly flexible optical transport networks. However, due to a variety of technical challenges, there is still a long way to go to accomplish a mature realization of an OPS network that is ready for practical deployments. Optoelectronic packet switching alleviates the implementation difficult to some degree, but a series of technical innovations is still needed in optical signal processing concerning timing and synchronization. In general, OPS is regarded as the long-term solution for high speed optical networks but, in the meanwhile, more feasible network architectures are desired for the efficient transport of highly dynamic and bursty data traffic. This is the case of optical burst switching (OBS).

In OBS networks, a special data unit called *burst* is defined for the transmission of user data. The data burst is generated by aggregating client traffic at the ingress nodes and it may have a variable size. In the network core, such data bursts are switched and transported asynchronously over the optical domain without any O/E/O conversion. The burst switching/routing decision is performed by the electronic processing of an out-of-band signaling message that arrives prior to its associated data burst. Similar to the optoelectronic packet switching, OBS ensures a transparent switching of the optical data traffic and keeps the signal processing and switching control in the electronic domain. In addition, data bursts are transmitted asynchronously in OBS, thus removing synchronization complexity. Also, design that adopts an offset time between the transmission of the signaling message and its associated data burst makes optical buffering not mandatory in the core nodes, thus improving the feasibility of OBS.

This chapter summarizes the fundamentals of optical burst-switched networks and further covers a wide range of the latest research and development issues in the field. Section 4.1 reviews the network and node architecture of OBS networks.

J.A. Hernández (✉)
Department of Computer Science, Universidad Autónoma de Madrid, Spain
e-mail: jose.hernandez@uam.es

J. Aracil and F. Callegati (eds.), *Enabling Optical Internet with Advanced Network Technologies*, Computer Communications and Networks,
DOI 10.1007/978-1-84882-278-8_4, © Springer-Verlag London Limited 2009

Section 4.2 outlines algorithms for burst assembly at the edge node, which have a significant impact on network performance. Signaling and channel reservation protocols in the core network are discussed through Section 4.3. Section 4.4 explores different solutions for resolving contention between data bursts. Section 4.5 investigates the issues of QoS provisioning in OBS networks. Section 4.6 studies the impact of an OBS underlying architecture in the upper layer protocol: TCP. Finally, Section 4.7 summarizes the Erlang Fixed Point (EFP) iterative algorithm that is widely used for the performance evaluation of OBS networks.

4.1 Network and Node Architecture

4.1.1 Network Architecture

OBS is a promising technology for the next-generation networks, wherein bandwidth needs to be accessible to users with different traffic profiles. OBS combines the advantages of circuit and packet switching technologies [201]. An optical burst is usually defined as a number of continuous packets destined to a common egress point. The burst size can vary from a single IP packet to a large data set at milliseconds time scale. This allows fine-grain multiplexing of data over a single wavelength and therefore an efficient use of the optical bandwidth among a number of users through resource sharing (i.e., lightpaths).

The fundamental premise of OBS is the separation of the control and data planes, and the segregation of functionality within the appropriate domain (either electronic or optical). In contrast to OPS which uses on-the-fly routing, OBS follows an in-advance reservation mechanism, which makes it more practical and easier for implementation. In an OBS network, prior to data burst transmission a burst control packet (BCP) is created and sent towards the destination by an OBS ingress node (edge router). The BCP is typically sent out of band over a separate signaling wavelength and processed at intermediate OBS switches. This BCP is sent an offset time in advance of the data burst and informs each node of the impending data burst arrival and sets up an optical path for its corresponding data burst. Data bursts are not typically buffered as they transit the network core all-optically. The content, protocol, bit rate, modulation format, and encoding of data bursts are completely transparent to the intermediate routers. Figure 4.1 shows a generic model of an OBS core router and its functionality.

The main advantages of OBS in comparison to other optical networking schemes are [201]:

- Unlike optical wavelength switched networks, in OBS the optical bandwidth is reserved only for the duration of the data burst.
- There is a clear separation between signaling messages and data as well as the embedded offset time in the OBS protocol.
- OBS can be bufferless, unlike optical packet switched networks.

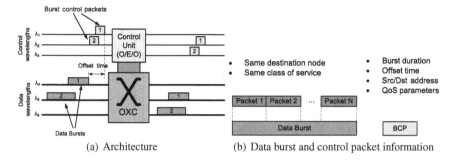

(a) Architecture   (b) Data burst and control packet information

Fig. 4.1 Example of the operation of an OBS switch

4.1.2 Core Node Architecture

As future optical technology moves to 40 Gbps and beyond, networking solutions must be designed to be compatible with such bit rates, in order to reduce the cost per bit [165]. OBS technology is relatively relaxed in terms of switching requirements, as the typical optical switch set-up time (on the order of milliseconds) is small compared to the data burst duration and therefore throughput is almost unaffected. However, the introduction of new bandwidth on-demand services [20] (e.g., grid services: high resolution home video editing, real-time rendering, high definition interactive TV, and e-health) over OBS brings new constrains for the switching speed and technology requirements, which become particularly important when high speed transmission is considered. Such applications usually involve a large number of users that need transmission of relatively small data bursts and possibly with short offset time values. A flexible OBS network must be able to support such small data bursts generated by the aforementioned applications and services.

For example, a MEMS-based switch with switching time of around 20 ms provides a utilization factor of 93.7% on a 10-Gbps system where the burst duration is 300 ms. If the same burst was transmitted at 160 Gbps, then the burst duration would be 18.75 ms and routing through the same switch would decrease the system's throughput to less than 50%. This utilization reduction becomes more severe for smaller bursts with short offset time. For this reason, the deployment of fast-switching technology is essential for future high speed OBS networks with support to such evolving bandwidth on-demand services.

It should be noted, though, that the burst control/header packet (burst control packet (BCP)) requires intensive and intelligent processing (i.e., QoS, routing, and contention resolution algorithms) which can only be performed by especially designed fast electronic circuits. Recent advances in the technology of integrated electronic circuits allow complicated processing of bursty data directly at speeds of up to 10 Gbps [69], which sets the upper limit in the transmission speed of BCPs. On the other hand, the optical data bursts do not have such limitation since they do not require electronic processing and could be transmitted at ultrahigh bit rates

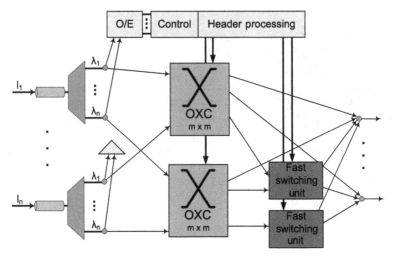

Fig. 4.2 Architecture that combines both slow and fast switching elements

(40 or 160 Gbps), provided the existence of switching elements at such bit rates. Faster burst transmission brings a higher capacity utilization degree of the existing fiber infrastructure, therefore significantly improved network economics.

The deployment of fast switching equipment is an efficient solution in terms of bandwidth utilization, but becomes too expensive when it scales to many input/output ports. Therefore, a trade-off solution may consider a hybrid or combined switch architecture that combines both fast (e.g., based on semiconductor optical amplifiers (SOA)) and slow (e.g., MEMS-based) switching elements. Such switch architecture is shown in Fig. 4.2.

The general idea is based on the use of a MEMS-based optical cross-connect (OXC) that has a number of its output ports connected to fast optical switches. When a BCP arrives, the control mechanism must first recognize whether the BCP belongs to a burst with slow switching requirements (typically long bursts) or a burst with fast switching requirements (usually short bursts). In the first case, the OXC is configured to switch data bursts to the appropriate output port. This architecture requires all switching paths inside the OXC to be initially connected to the fast switching ports, as shown in the Fig. 4.2. It is worth noticing that special design constrains must be considered to avoid collision at the output ports.

In conclusion, such a hybrid architecture reduces the requirements of fast switching devices, which translates to smaller, cost-efficient matrices. Fast switching can be achieved making use of fast active components, such as SOA, whereas slower switching only requires converting and routing the incoming wavelength to an output port with a passive routing device such as an AWG [164]. This solution is scalable but its switching speed depends on which conversion technique is used. In this light, almost transparent bit rate wavelength conversion schemes have been proposed in the literature and fast switching of asynchronous data bursts at 40 Gbps has been demonstrated, with technology scalable to more than 160 Gbps [164].

This solution provides switching in the range of nanoseconds and therefore can almost eliminate the offset time for short data bursts, offering a substantial throughput increase.

4.1.3   Edge Node Architecture

In an OBS network, the edge routers are responsible for mapping IP traffic into the optical domain in the form of variable-length optical bursts and generating their associated BCPs. The main functionalities required of edge routers are [163]:

1. For the transmitter side:

   - Wavelength agility
   - Traffic aggregation based on class of service (CoS)
   - Variable-length optical burst construction
   - Data burst and BCP transmission

2. For the receiver side:

   - Burst-mode clock and data recovery for both BCPs and data bursts
   - Data burst deconstruction and traffic segregation

Figure 4.3 shows a generic architectural block diagram of an optical burst transmitter [280]. Essentially, an edge OBS router is typically a standard (commercial) gigabit electronic packet switch edge router, which employs one optical burst transmitter per output port. Its architecture comprises the following units:

- Input interfaces to accept incoming IP traffic through the gigabit ethernet links
- IP traffic detectors that classify incoming IP packets based on their class of service and destination address
- Data burst (burst payload) assembly units whereby incoming traffic is aggregated into optical data burst

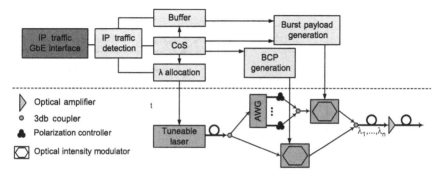

Fig. 4.3 Functional architecture of a tunable optical burst switching interface in an edge router

- BCP allocation mechanisms that generate and transmit a BCP for each optical burst
- Tunable laser source and its controller (λ allocation) to facilitate wavelength assignment for BCPs and data bursts

In this architecture incoming IP traffic enters the edge router in a standard framing format (e.g., gigabit ethernet) through the input interface. Incoming packets are aggregated based on their class of service and destination address with the help of a network processor. Before transmission of each data burst, a BCP is generated and transmitted. Also, the tunable laser is set to emit data at the suitable wavelengths for each BCP as well as data burst.

4.2 Burst Generation and Burst Assembly

4.2.1 Assembly Algorithms

The burst generation and assembly process define how packets are assembled into optical bursts. The burst assembly process starts with the arrival of an IP packet and continues until a predefined criterion is met. The data burst consists of an integer number of variable-size packets, regardless of their protocol or (access) bit rate. In general, each edge router maintains a separate (virtual) queue for each destination node or forwarding equivalence class (FEC), whereby data packets are temporally allocated.

Figure 4.4 shows a block diagram of a typical burst assembler. Each queue is handled by a separate burst assembler, while a single link scheduler is commissioned

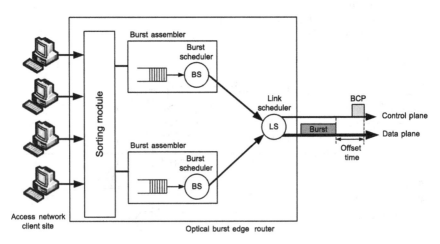

Fig. 4.4 Optical burst switching edge router architecture

to assign wavelengths and schedule bursts for transmission. The burst assembly criterion defines when the actual process of gathering packets stops and a new optical burst is thus generated. This criterion is of paramount importance for the network, since it affects traffic characteristics such as burst size, burst interdeparture times, as well as the assembly delay suffered by each individual packet inside the burst. The assembly delay of packets is defined as the time that the packets must wait before burst transmission [90, 213].

In the literature there are two main burst assembly algorithms: The *timer-based* and the *threshold-based* algorithms. In the timer-based scheme, a time threshold T_{MAX} is defined [75]. A time counter starts any time a packet arrives at the empty assembly buffer and, when the timer reaches the threshold T_{MAX}, a burst is created; the timer is then reset to zero and it remains so until the next packet arrives at the queue. Hence, the ingress router generates bursts of variable sizes depending on how many packets arrived during the time threshold. In the second assembly scheme [261], a *burst-size threshold* is used to determine the end of the process. In most cases the threshold used is the burst length denoted in the literature as B_{MAX}. In that case bursts are thought as containers of a fixed size B_{MAX}, such that a new burst is generated when the container is full of data. Such an assembly scheme results in the generation of equally sized bursts, thus facilitating resource scheduling and provisioning.

The problem with burst assembly is selection of a proper timer or threshold criterion in order that would minimize burst dropping probability at the network core and also minimize the assembly delays at the network edge. For example, the timer-based method limits the delay of packets to a maximum value T_{MAX} but may generate undesirable burst lengths difficult to be handled at core nodes. Similarly, the burst-length-based method generates bursts of equal size, but may result in long delays, especially at low traffic loads. Furthermore, if the B_{MAX} threshold value is too small, the burst assembler tends to generate a large number of small data bursts, which increases control overhead and possibly contention at the network core. In contrast, if the B_{MAX} threshold value is set too high, large size data bursts are generated that alleviate the processing overhead; however, at the cost of the large assembly delays and a large number of packets discarded per burst loss at the network core.

To address these drawbacks, hybrid (mixed time/length-based) assembly algorithms were proposed [278], where bursts are assembled when either the time limit or the burst size limit is reached, whichever happens first. In this light, the min-burst length-max assembly period (MBMAP) algorithm [32] sends out a data burst when its size exceeds a minimum burst length or when the assembly period times out. Performance evaluation and comparison of these schemes in terms of burst length and interdeparture time distribution as well as traffic autocorrelation studies (self-similarity and long range dependence of OBS networks) for various traffic profiles have been carried out in [110, 278]. Additionally, in [52], the burst loss probability of the timer-based assembly algorithm with limited buffer at the ingress node is also studied. Finally [90, 213] study the burst assembly delay experienced by packets for the above mentioned assembly techniques.

The above burst assembly criteria does not take into account the traffic load level so as to adapt the burst assembly process accordingly. This is a very important issue for higher layer protocols such as TCP, since it may limit its effective throughput. To this end, adaptive burst assembly schemes have also been proposed; see for example the adaptive assembly period (AAP) algorithm proposed in [32]. The AAP algorithm dynamically changes the assembly timer at the ingress node according to the length of a sample of recently sent data bursts. Accordingly, the AAP algorithm adjusts the burst transmission characteristics to traffic changes i.e., TCP window increases or decreases. More specifically, after a long burst is sent out, it is very likely that TCP sends more (sometimes twice as many) packets, thus it is better to increase the assembly period. On the other hand, if TCP has just entered in the slow-start stage (e.g., a short burst is sent out), it is desirable to reduce the assembly period significantly. Thus, the appropriate selection of the timer or threshold parameter of burst assembly algorithms is an important and still open issue in the research area. Finally, it is worth mentioning that bounded burst assembly delays allow transport protocols to predict future round trip time (RTT) and thus minimize time out on attempts to improve network performance.

4.2.2 Impact of Burst Assembly on Traffic Characteristics

There is a great discussion concerning the so-called *burstification effect* of burst assembly algorithms. This effect refers to the statistical properties of OBS traffic. It is believed that traffic from access networks is self-similar since the packet arrival process is bursty at all time scales. It was reported that the burst assembly process could reduce the degree of self-similarity (or long-range dependence) of the input packetized traffic; but more recent studies have shown that burst assembly has a smoothing effect on traffic characteristics at small time scales, but cannot remove the long-range dependence property present in network traffic.

In most OBS performance studies, it is assumed that burst arrivals follow a Poisson process and that the burst length distribution is negative exponential, or Pareto (see [276]). In [110], the authors show that, in spite of the long-range dependence nature of incoming traffic, the burst arrival process can be assumed to be Poisson at small time scales. As a consequence, there is almost no influence from self-similarity on the blocking probability experienced by data bursts in bufferless OBS networks.

The impact of burst assembly algorithms on the traffic process can be considered at two different levels: packet level and burst level. The *packet level* approach is usually concerned with the delay that individual packets experience during the assembly and disassembly process at the borders of the OBS network. However, at the *burst level* approach, it is important to understand the statistical characteristics of burst length and burst interarrival times, since they influence the overall performance of the OBS network. The state-of-the-art in this area can be found in [90, 219].

For instance, in [90], the delay distribution of individual packets during the burstification process has been investigated under the assumption that packets of fixed size arrive at the assembly buffer according to the Poisson process with rate λ. Given that S packets are assembled into a single burst, the probability density function (pdf) of the burstification delay d experienced by the ith packet ($i = 1, \ldots, S$) in the burst for the burst threshold assembly algorithm follows a gamma distribution with parameter λ and $N - i$ degrees of freedom. For the timer-based assembly algorithm with parameter T this pdf is given by the truncated gamma distribution evaluated at $T - d$ with parameter λ and $i - 1$ degrees of freedom. Furthermore, the distribution of the assembly delay for the hybrid timer- and threshold-based assembler is a combination of the above gamma and truncated gamma distributions.

Also, in [219] the assembly process has been analyzed at the burst level and exact analytical expressions are derived for length and interdeparture time of bursts that are generated by the three assembly algorithms mentioned above. The analysis is performed under the assumption that the packet arrival process is Poissonian and input packet size is exponentially distributed. For the most interesting case, the hybrid time–size assembly algorithm, the key parameter influencing the burst traffic characteristics is the probability that the assembly timer expires before the length threshold is reached, P_{Tout}. In order to illustrate *this, the cumulative distribution functions (CDFs)* of burst length and burst interdeparture times for a sample scenario are shown in Figs. 4.5 and 4.6, respectively. It is assumed that the input traffic rate is 50 Mb/s with the average packet size equal to 500 Bytes. The length threshold is fixed at 25 KB and the time threshold is varied so that different values of P_{Tout} are achieved, as depicted in Fig. 4.5. The probability distributions in

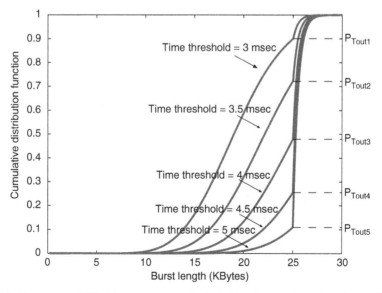

Fig. 4.5 Burst length CDF of bursts generated by the hybrid timer- and size-based assembler at different values of time threshold

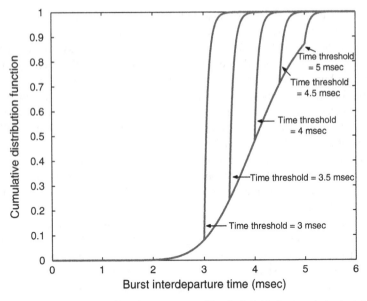

Fig. 4.6 Interdeparture time CDF for bursts generated by the hybrid timer- and size-based assembler at different values of time threshold

Fig. 4.5 can be divided into two regions with the size threshold acting as the boundary between them. The first region (burst length smaller than the length threshold) is associated with those bursts that are generated when the timer expires. The second region, however, refers to bursts that are generated because the length threshold is exceeded. The ratio between the number of bursts in the two regions is determined by P_{Tout}. Therefore, P_{Tout} is the key parameter in characterizing the burst length distribution. Note that P_{Tout} itself is a function of the input traffic rate and the selected time and length thresholds of the assembler. Similar to the burst length case, the probability distribution of the burst interdeparture time can also be divided into two regions (see Fig. 4.6) separated by the time equal to the timer threshold of the burst assembly timer plus the mean packet interarrival time. It is shown that, for small timer thresholds, the range of variations of the burst interdeparture time reduces while that of the burst length increases, and vice versa.

4.3 Signaling Protocols

4.3.1 Classifications of Signaling Protocols

A signaling scheme is required for configuring switches and reserving resources for data bursts in OBS networks. The signaling scheme in an optical burst-switched network is typically implemented using out-of-band burst header or control packets. In such an out-of-band signaling scheme, the header associated with a burst is transmitted on a different wavelength from the burst itself. The out-of-band header packet travels along the route that the burst will later traverse, informing each node on attempts to configure its optical cross-connect to accommodate the forthcoming arriving data burst at the appropriate time. Different signaling schemes for OBS networks have been categorized based on the following characteristics:

1. One-way, also called tell-and-go (TAG), or two-way, also called tell-and-wait (TAW) depending on whether the source awaits an acknowledgement of the reservation or immediately transmits the burst after the control packet.
2. Immediate or Delayed (also called timed) reservation depending if reservation of resources starts immediately after the reception of the control packet or later on upon the actual arrival of the burst.
3. Explicit or implicit release, depending whether the resource release occurs with or without an external resource tear-down message. In the second case, the release of resources is estimated based on the burst size that is encoded in the control packet.

Apart from the aforementioned metrics, there are other classification categories (i.e., centralized or distributed signaling schemes), that however are not widely used. OBS networks have been initially designed based on the one-way reservation concept.

4.3.1.1   One-Way Versus Two-Way Reservation Schemes

An OBS signaling protocol is said to be one-way if upon the creation and transmission of a BCP, the source does not wait for the reservation of resources but rather proceeds with the transmission of the burst after a suitable offset time. Since a reservation is not certain to be accepted, burst transmission is not guaranteed and burst loss may occur at any intermediate OBS node.

The BCP is processed by the nodes across the network path. Based on the information carried by the BCP, the nodes reconfigure their switch fabric to forward the burst to the correct outgoing link. In the case of contention, i.e., the outgoing port is already reserved/occupied by some other burst in the required time duration, the burst is dropped. The advantage of one-way signaling schemes is that the round-trip time delay of the reservation process is avoided and thus data are sent out sooner. This is a significant improvement gain bearing in mind that the round-trip time delay can be comparable to the burst transmission time in high-speed multi-gigabit optical networks.

In contrast, in two-way reservation schemes optical lightpaths have to be fully established before burst transmission. To this end, in two-way schemes the source sends out a control packet and awaits an acknowledgement or reject message to arrive either from the destination node or from an intermediate node respectively.

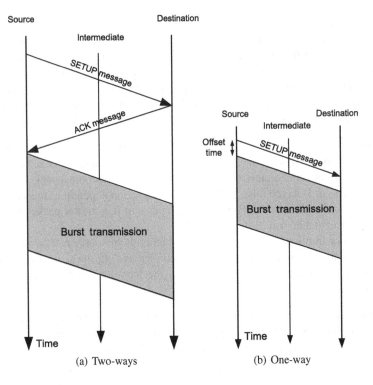

Fig. 4.7 Timing considerations of OBS reservation schemes

The two-way schemes suffer from the round trip time delay, but burst transmission is guaranteed. Figure 4.7 illustrates the timing considerations of these two schemes.

Typical one-way schemes proposed to date include the just-enough-time (JET) [275], horizon [254], just-in-time (JIT) [266] and ready-to-go virtual circuit protocols [259]. The differences among these variants lie mainly in the determination of the time instances at which the channel reservation duration begins (either immediate or delayed reservation) and ends (implicit or explicit release). This is considered in the next section.

4.3.1.2 Explicit/Implicit Release and Immediate/Delayed Reservation Schemes

Explicit or implicit release refers to the way that resources are freed after data transmission. In the first case a control packet notifies every core node of the forthcoming burst arrival, causing the switch control unit to configure its switch fabric to reserve the requested output port. After the burst has traversed it, the switch fabric is not

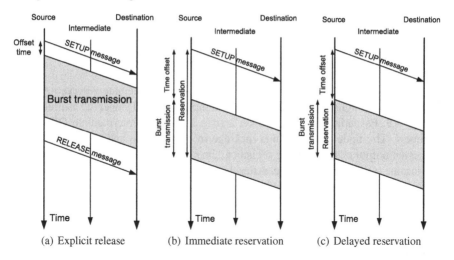

Fig. 4.8 OBS reservation schemes

reconfigured back. Thus, the reservation is not terminated and awaits a new control (release) message that is sent (right after the burst) from the source to the destination node (see Fig. 4.8a). This approach is typically used when the burst size is not known at the time of transmission. The release message basically notifies every intermediate node to free resources at the specific output port. On the other hand, in implicit release resources are freed immediately after the burst departure. In this case the control (reservation) packet announces both the burst arrival time and its duration. Based on this the switch fabric reconfigures its state to free resources in a timely fashion, as soon as the data burst has been forwarded to the destination output port.

Immediate or delayed reservation refers to the reservation duration and, in particular, when such reservation actually starts. There are two options possible upon the arrival of a setup packet at a node: Either to hard-reserve resources immediately, albeit the data burst will arrive later after some offset time (see Fig. 4.8b); or hard reserve resources later only for the burst duration only, thus upon the arrival of the actual data burst (Fig. 4.8c). In the latter case of so-called delayed or timed reservation, the burst size and the offset-time information is encoded within the setup message and is thus known to all intermediate nodes.

Clearly, immediate reservation schemes are simpler but yield a lower resource utilization. This is because the channel is reserved before the actual data arrival and thus wasted. Delayed reservation schemes yield a more efficient utilization but are more complex since the node must keep timing and switch-fabric state information.

4.3.2 Signaling Protocols

4.3.2.1 Just-In Time (JIT) Protocol

The just-in-time (JIT) signaling protocol [266] is an immediate reservation with implicit release signaling mechanism. An example of how JIT operates is illustrated in Fig. 4.9. Essentially, a setup packet arrives at the first intermediate OBS node at time t. The node processes this message in T_{process} time and hard-reserves the requested output channel. In the sequence, the node reconfigures the optical switch fabric state (OXC) in T_{config} time. After these steps, at time $t + T_{\text{process}} + T_{\text{config}}$, the node is ready to (transparently) forward the burst.

It must be noted here that the actual data will arrive at $t + T_{\text{offset}}$ time later. Consequently, the reserved capacity remains idle (and thus wasted) for a time equal to $T_{\text{offset}} - T_{\text{process}} - T_{\text{config}}$. Furthermore, since processing of the setup message and reconfiguration takes place at all nodes, then time-offset decreases along the path from source to destination. To this end, the selection of the appropriate offset time is bounded by the number of hops in the path and the switch's reconfiguration and processing delays. In general, the minimum required offset time is set to $h \cdot T_{\text{process}} + T_{\text{config}}$, where h refers to the number of hops in the path.

In any case, during the offset time, the output port's capacity remains reserved but idle, thus any new setup message that arrives between t and $t + T_{\text{offset}} + T_{\text{burst}}$

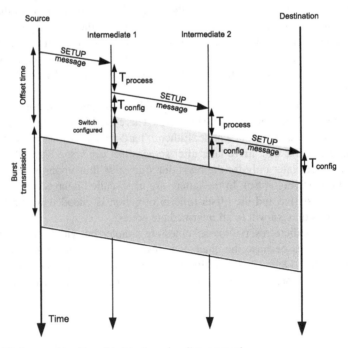

Fig. 4.9 Timing consideration of just-in-time signaling protocol

is rejected (here T_{burst} denotes the burst holding time). Accordingly, data bursts are served following a first come, first served policy, based on the relative arrival time of the setup messages.

4.3.2.2   Just-Enough-Time (JET) Protocol

The just-enough-time (JET) protocol is a delayed reservation protocol with implicit release scheme [275] and is, at present, the most popular signaling protocol in OBS networks. A given output wavelength is reserved only for the duration of the burst and the switch fabric is reconfigured just before the actual arrival of the burst. Figure 4.10 illustrates an example of the timing considerations of JET. A setup message arrives at an OBS node at time t and it carries the actual arrival time of the burst. It is expected that the first bit of the burst will arrive at time $t + T_{offset}$. Assuming that the requested channel is free at that time, the node hard-reserves the outgoing wavelength starting from $t + T_{offset} - T_{config}$ time, and such reservation is held for a duration equal to the burst holding time. At relative time $t_i + T_{offset} - T_{config}$ the node reconfigures its switch fabric so as to transparently forward the data burst to the requested output port upon the arrival of its first bit. To this end, JET allows the reservation of the same outgoing channel for more than one burst, unlike immediate reservation protocols, as long as the actual burst transmission durations do not overlap. Such delayed reservation mechanism results

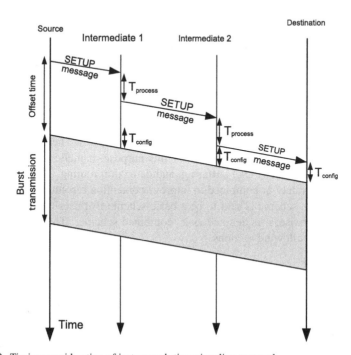

Fig. 4.10 Timing consideration of just-enough-time signaling protocol

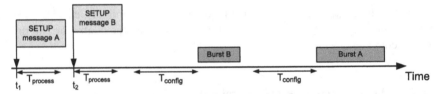

Fig. 4.11 Void filling process; burst B is transmitted before burst A during the void

in the creation of reservation voids and thus JET can benefit from the statistical multiplexing of the arriving bursts on the outgoing wavelengths. This makes JET outperform over the other signaling protocols; however the switching unit must keep track of all the starting and finishing times of all voids on the different wavelengths, resulting in a more complex control plane.

Figure 4.11 illustrates the void filling process of the JET with two data bursts A and B. Upon the arrival of the control packet of burst A at time t_1, the switch control accepts the reservation for burst A but does not reconfigure the switch fabric state immediately. At time t_2, the control packet of burst B arrives and the channel scheduler notes that burst B can be scheduled on the same channel as burst A, inside the void left by burst A. Thus, burst B is also accepted and scheduled for transmission before the arrival of burst A.

4.4 Contention Resolution

In an OBS network that uses a one-way signaling protocol, burst contention occurs frequently among data bursts at core nodes. "Burst contention" here refers to the situation whereby two or more data bursts request the same output channel of a node for periods of time that fully or partially overlap each other. In that case, all contending bursts except the one that has arrived first have to be dropped. This can result in a poor performance operation of the OBS network, therefore lots of efforts are put into devising efficient contention resolution mechanisms. There are three main techniques that are usually considered for this purpose, namely: wavelength conversion, fiber delay line (FDL) buffering, and deflection routing. These techniques can be used separately or combined to improve contention resolution. Thus, a contention resolution scheme is said to be a basic scheme if it uses only one of these techniques; otherwise, it is denoted as a "combined scheme." These strategies are discussed in the following sections.

4.4.1 Wavelength Conversion

Wavelength conversion is a potential way to resolve contention in optical burst switching networks with WDM. Essentially, WDM enables each optical fiber to provide more than one wavelength (therefore) channel over which data transmission is possible, thus increasing the link capacity drastically. Routing with wavelength continuity constrains network performance, since it is not always possible to reserve the same wavelength across a network. Wavelength converters are optical active components that convert an incoming signal's wavelength to a different outgoing wavelength. Thus the same wavelength may be reused to carry different data of different connections in different links. Wavelength converters offer 10–40% increase in reuse values when wavelength availability is small [209].

In OBS networks wavelength conversion can additionally be used to resolve contention. In this case all inputs of the OBS node are equipped with wavelength converters capable of accessing all outgoing wavelengths. In the case that two bursts are competing for the same output port, then one burst is switched to any of the free wavelengths on such outgoing links. To this end both bursts can exit at the same times, but on different channels over the same output port, but again on different channels.

Various scheduling schemes can be applied if nodes are equipped with full or limited wavelength conversion capabilities. In the first case, the contending burst can be switched to any free outgoing wavelength, while in the second case this is restricted to a certain subset. Contention resolution via wavelength conversion is the most preferred scheme in terms of system performance since it does not cause extra latency, jitter, or packet resequencing problems. Furthermore, the current status of technology allows the fabrication of fast wavelength converters with adequate tuning range. High speed operation is not as critical as in optical packet switching, since the typical burst duration exceeds burst conversion speed.

Figure 4.12a displays a typical example of a wavelength conversion-enabled OBS node, whereby the signal on each wavelength from the input link is first demultiplexed and then sent into the switch fabric. The electronic control unit is capable of detecting contention at an output port and selecting a suitable wavelength at the desired output fiber over which conversion is performed. Following this, the next

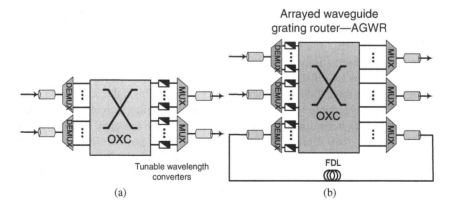

Fig. 4.12 OBS node with wavelength conversion capability for contention resolution

section describes a number of scheduling algorithms to decide over which wavelength data bursts need to be allocated to reduce the probability of burst contention.

The design shown in Fig. 4.12a is the simplest possible, with wavelength converters placed after the switch fabric. The multiplexers at the output ports are simple passive devices that combine all signals. In other schemes, wavelength converters are placed at the switch fabric's input. In that case wavelength converters comprise the arrayed waveguide grating (AWG). Figure 4.12b shows such a scheme, where wavelength converters are placed at the input and might additionally be deployed at the output to form an optical recirculating buffer.

Finally, wavelength converters might be combined with optical buffering units, whereby contending bursts are temporal allocated when no free wavelength channel exists. The next section introduces FDL as the most typical buffering unit available for optical networks.

4.4.1.1 Scheduling Algorithms with Wavelength Converters

Data channel scheduling (DCS) algorithms are in charge of scheduling data bursts on the outgoing wavelengths of core OBS routers. When BCPs arrive at a core OBS router, the switch control unit examines the expected arrival time of its associated data burst and decides the outgoing fiber over which this burst is to be scheduled. On that outgoing fiber a large number of wavelengths are typically available if the switch's architecture provides wavelength converters at the output port. Therefore, the scheduling algorithm must decide which wavelength is most suitable among the available ones. This task entails: (1) to keep the information of all the reserved time intervals on every wavelength; and (2) deciding a suitable gap in one of the available wavelengths upon receiving a reservation request (a burst control packet). Consequently, the goal of such data scheduling algorithms is to maximize the use available network capacity in order to minimize or even avoid (if possible) contention between bursts.

It is worth noticing that, because of the offset time variability, data bursts do not arrive in the order as their associated BCP. This means, that a data burst B_A may arrive at an OBS switch before data burst B_B even though its associated BCP might arrive later than the BCP of burst B_B. Additionally, given the asynchronous nature of burst reservations, outgoing wavelengths show void periods, i.e., periods in which no bursts are allocated. Such effect is known as *channel fragmentation* and has an important impact on the system performance. In this light, scheduling algorithms can be divided into two groups depending on whether such algorithms allow allocation on data bursts in between two other bursts (in the gaps or voids) or do not. The former group is referred to as *non-void filling algorithms*, whereas the latter group is denoted by *void filling algorithms*. Furthermore, different algorithms in each group can be defined depending on the wavelength selection policy. Obviously, void filling algorithms prove to outperform with regard to channel utilization and burst loss ratio; however, this is at the expense of a substantial increase in the algorithms' complexity.

The following section? sections? refs? summarizes a number of burst scheduling algorithms appearing in the literature (see [138, 139, 143, 197, 247, 271, 272] for further details). Additionally, the reader is referred to [73, 99] for a further computation cost and performance trade-off comparison.

4.4.1.2   Algorithms Without Void Filling

The horizon algorithm, also known as latest available unscheduled channel (LAUC), is probably the most widely spread algorithm that does not employ void filling. This algorithm reserves an outgoing channel from the control packet arrival until the last byte of the data burst following the JIT signaling approach, as shown in Fig. 4.13. This approach leads to a low channel utilization, since the channel is reserved for more time than necessary (only the burst duration would suffice). LAUC selects the outgoing wavelength or channel that minimizes the distance between the burst under consideration and the previous scheduled burst. Figure 4.13 shows an example of LAUC's operation. The scheduler choses the first channel because the time difference between the new burst arrival and the already allocated bursts is smaller than if it were scheduled on the second wavelength. Note that the third and fourth wavelengths are not considered, since the new burst arrival overlaps previous reservations.

4.4.1.3   Algorithms with Void Filling

An alternate approach to horizon is to consider the voids between two consecutive allocated bursts whereby an incoming reservation fits. It becomes apparent that the latter reduces fragmentation, albeit this is at the expense of a higher computational cost. The algorithms that allow void filling have been traditionally divided into two other groups depending on whether the scheduler checks all wavelength tables to take a scheduling decision or not. Basically, a scheduler can analyze all the available channels before choosing one of them or, on the other side, it can choose a channel as soon as it finds one available. The former strategies are often referred

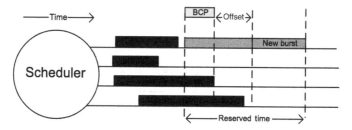

Fig. 4.13 Example of a non-void filling algorithm: horizon

to as *algorithms with full-wavelength evaluation*, whereas the latter are typically named as *first fit unscheduled channel* (FFUC) algorithm.

FFUC algorithms just select the first wavelength in which the incoming burst fits. The distinguishing features of between first fit unscheduled channel (FFUC) algorithms lie in how such algorithms define the order to perform the search of available channels. In this light, the "pure" first fit algorithm numbers the channels in increasing order and these are probed sequentially. This policy increases the load on the former wavelength and leaves unused the latter ones, thus reducing channel fragmentation. However, the number of comparisons needed to find an available void increases since it always tries the former one first and it is more difficult to find an available void on this wavelength. To solve this, it is possible to define a first fit algorithm that uses a round robin order to check the tables. That is, for the first data burst the table search starts on wavelength number one and goes sequentially to wavelength number two and three if the preceding searches were not successful. The search for the second burst would then start on wavelength number two, and so on. This search policy reduces the number of comparisons to find an available void, but increases channel fragmentation. A third first fit policy uses a random number to check the tables. If the randomly selected wavelength cannot allocate the burst, another wavelength is selected randomly. In this case, the number of comparisons and the channel fragmentation that reason is between the pure first fit and the first fit with round robin algorithms. A variant of this algorithm can be implemented to first select a channel randomly, and then proceed sequentially if this channel is not available. Figure 4.14 shows an example of scheduling four data bursts following the "pure" first fit, round robin and random policies.

Algorithms with full wavelength evaluation, contrary to first fit algorithms, analyze all wavelengths in the search table in order to find the "best" void (according to certain policies) on which to allocate the data burst. The *latest available unscheduled channel with void filling* (LAUC-VF) algorithm is probably the most referenced scheduling algorithm in OBS networks. This algorithm searches for the wavelength in which the remaining space between a previous transmitted burst and the starting time of the incoming burst under consideration is minimum. The literature offers some variants of latest available unscheduled channel with void filling LAUC-VF but with small differences and implementation improvements. For instance, in [99] the authors propose an algorithm that gives preference to filling a void between already scheduled bursts with respect to allocating burst at the reservation horizon,

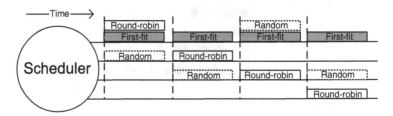

Fig. 4.14 Example of FFUC algorithms: first fit, round robin, and random

i.e., with no bursts scheduled for transmission after the incoming burst. Another full wavelength evaluation algorithm is the *best fit unscheduled channel* (BFUC) algorithm defined in [143]. Such an algorithm considers both the void size at the beginning of the data burst and at the end, in contrast to latest available unscheduled channel with void filling (LAUC-VF), which only considers the former. Consequently, the best fit unscheduled channel (BFUC) algorithm checks the remaining space both before and after the burst if this has been allocated on a given wavelength, to find the void that minimize the sum of both quantities. Figure 4.15 graphically shows the difference behaviors of such full wavelength evaluation algorithms with void filling.

4.4.2 FDL Buffering

A practical way of buffering a burst without converting it to the electronic domain is to send it through a piece of optical fiber, whose length is large enough so that, when the burst leaves the fiber from the other end, the contention period is over. This is the main concept of building FDL buffers that usually comprise a specific number of parallel delay lines. Depending on the type of the basic delay lines applied, an FDL buffer can be classified into two major categories, namely *fixed-delay* and *variable-delay* buffers. In a fixed-delay buffer each basic delay line provides only a fixed delay (see Fig. 4.16a). On the other hand, in a variable-delay buffer each basic delay line is a multistage structure (Fig. 4.16b), where each stage consists of a 2×2 switch and a fixed-delay line. In every stage a burst passes either through the associated delay line or through the line of zero delay. This makes it possible to

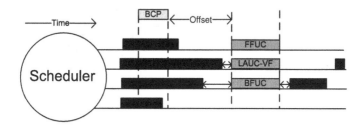

Fig. 4.15 Void filling algorithms: FFUC, BFUC, and LAUC-VF

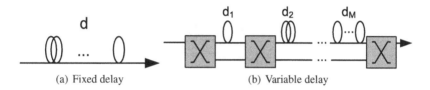

Fig. 4.16 Basic element of an FDL buffer of type (**a**) fixed delay and (**b**) variable delay

obtain different delay values by appropriately changing states of the FDL switches. Obviously, variable-delay FDL buffers are more complicated, and therefore more costly than fixed-delay buffers.

4.4.2.1 Architecture of OBS Nodes with FDL Buffers

Depending on how FDL buffers are employed, two types of OBS nodes can be designed:

- *Feed-forward vs. feedback:* In a feed-forward architecture, burst buffering is performed while the burst traverses the switch from input to output. On the contrary, in a feedback architecture, FDL buffers feed the blocked bursts back to the input of the switch (see Fig. 4.17a). In this way a burst may be circulating between the input and output ports of the switch several times.
- *Dedicated vs. shared:* In a dedicated architecture, separate buffering units exist on every output port of the switch. Alternatively, a single buffering unit can be shared among some or all output ports, as shown in Figs. 4.17b and c.

4.4.2.2 Scheduling Algorithms with FDLs

There are two general types of algorithms for scheduling data bursts over the output channels of a switch with FDL buffers, namely first in, first out (FIFO) and

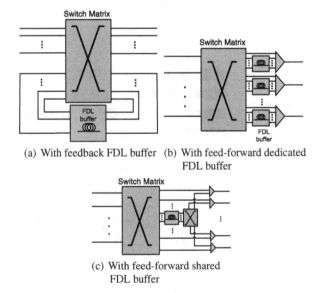

(a) With feedback FDL buffer   (b) With feed-forward dedicated FDL buffer

(c) With feed-forward shared FDL buffer

Fig. 4.17 FDL switch architectures

non-FIFO algorithms. In the former one, the order of bursts remains unchanged, whereas in the latter one burst reordering might frequently happen during buffering. To illustrate the difference between the operation of the two algorithms, we consider a fixed-delay buffer that is employed in the feed-forward architecture and discuss how bursts are delayed in case of contention.

Under the FIFO algorithm, when a new burst arrives at the system and there is at least one burst waiting in the buffer or being served over the channel, the scheduler calculates the earliest time t after which there would be no bursts in the system. Then, the smallest idle delay line that provides a delay larger than t is assigned to the burst and the channel is accordingly reserved in advance. If there is no idle delay line that can provide such required delay, the burst has to be dropped or other contention resolution techniques have to be used. Following this policy, the most recently buffered burst experiences the largest delay among all bursts in the buffer, thus ensuring that bursts are served in the same order as they arrived at the system.

With the FIFO scheduling algorithm, bursts usually experience a larger delay than necessary to resolve a contention. As a result, some gaps are created between the time at which the last bit of a burst left the channel and the time at which the next scheduled burst becomes ready for transmission. These gaps may reduce the system's throughput and global performance. To solve this, a non-FIFO scheduling algorithm can be defined to use these gaps for transmission. That is, a new burst can be served in the gap between two already scheduled bursts. Although such non-FIFO policy increases network throughput, it tends to change the order of bursts, which, in turn, can have a negative impact on the performance of higher layer protocols such as TCP. Moreover, it is shown in [218] that the smoothing effects of burst assembly algorithms on the length of bursts may reduce the performance gain that comes from using a non-FIFO scheduling algorithm, and it further makes the system design more complicated.

4.4.2.3 Performance of FDL Buffering

The effectiveness of FDL buffering in resolving burst contention depends on different factors such as the buffering type, i.e., whether it is of fixed or variable delay, the architecture into which it is incorporated, and the scheduling algorithm used. Additionally, the performance of FDL buffering in OBS networks is greatly influenced by the traffic shaping effect of burst assembly algorithms, as shown in [218]. More specifically, the burst assembly process tends to smooth out traffic at short-time scales, which results in the improvement of burst-loss ratio on switches with small optical buffers.

As a numerical example, let us assume we need to achieve acceptable performance levels in a high load scenario, say for instance a burst drop rate in the range of 10^{-6} at network load 80%. To achieve this a switch with dedicated feed-forward architecture and FIFO scheduling algorithm requires a few hundred delay lines at every output channel if we use fixed-delay buffering [23]. However, if the same

FDL buffering is used in the shared architecture, the number of delay lines needed is reduced very significantly, as shown in [282].

4.4.3 Deflection Routing

Deflection routing, also referred to as "hot-potato routing," utilizes the space domain to resolve contentions. When two bursts contend for the same output wavelength channel, with deflection routing, one burst is transmitted on the contended wavelength channel, while the other burst is deflected to another output fiber link with an available wavelength. If such an alternative output link is not available, the contended bursts are dropped at the current node.

With the application of the deflection routing, the burst takes an alternative route to its destination, which may lead to additional delay and increased network load, since (generally) deflected packets follow a nonoptimal route. The performance gain from utilizing the space domain to resolve contentions has been investigated in several OBS studies showing that deflection routing generally improves network performance only if the normalized traffic load is low and always depending on the specific network topology and traffic matrix.

4.4.4 Combined Schemes

Both FDL buffering and wavelength conversion are effective techniques that can resolve contentions locally. However, relying merely on the former necessitates the use of a huge amount of bulky fibers, something the might not be feasible. On the other hand, equipping a switch with only wavelength converters might not suffice to overcome the contention problem if the number of wavelength channels is small or it might be too costly if the number of channels is large. Alternatively, one can use these two techniques in a combined approach, in which contentions are resolved either through wavelength conversion and/or FDL buffering. Several simulation investigations have shown that such a combined scheme has a very good potential for resolving burst contention [229].

Different combined approaches can be devised by combining different types of FDL buffers and wavelength converters. One can design a scheme incorporating a fixed-delay FDL buffer in the dedicated feed-forward architecture and a shared wavelength converter pool. It is also possible to use multiple stages of FDL buffers and wavelength converters. For example, in a combined scheme with two stages of conversion and one stage of buffering, a burst arriving on wavelength w_a might undergo conversion in order to use FDL buffering on wavelength w_b, and then be transmitted over the outgoing link on wavelength w_c after being converted at the second stage.

In a combined scheme with one stage of buffering and conversion the question reduces to whether one should apply wavelength conversion before or after FDL buffering. In either case, when the contention is resolved in the first step, the second one is no longer considered. This notion can be utilized to optimize the operation of the system from different perspectives. For example, by applying FDL buffering after wavelength conversion, one can design a contention resolution scheme that minimizes the delay experienced by bursts. Additionally, by appropriately selecting the number and the order of the stages one can design a combined scheme that minimizes the use of FDL buffers or wavelength converters for a given target drop rate.

Finally, a combination of deflection routing with wavelength conversion and FDL buffering has been shown to improve the performance of OBS networks very significantly at low- and medium-load levels. However, it is not efficient at high-load levels since the additional load caused by the deflection routing strategy may overload the network, thus producing even more burst contentions in an already loaded network. Also, the order in which these schemes are applied is important. A performance study of these techniques in the Pan-European reference network shows that the order of converter–FDL–deflection has a good overall performance in comparison to other schemes [74]. More specifically, the order converter–deflection–FDL improves network performance with respect to the converter–FDL–deflection scheme but only in the low load case, showing very poor performance results at medium and high loads.

4.5 Quality of Service in OBS

4.5.1 Brief Introduction to QoS Concepts

Quality of Service (QoS) is a broad term which has many interpretations. In the following discussion, the considered service is the delivery of data bursts to their correct destination, and the quality of this service is described by its performance, dependability, and security. Further on, we focus on performance-related QoS metrics, mainly on parameters such as the packet loss rate (PLR), throughput, delay, and delay-jitter, which can be quantified. Furthermore, the concept of traffic differentiation refers to the fact that traffic is handled differently, on attempts to achieve different values on one or more of the QoS parameters defined above among a set of service classes or traffic flows [184].

QoS differentiation can be provided based on a per-flow or on a per-class classification of the traffic, which is an analogue to the IETF IntServ and DiffServ architectures, respectively. In a per-flow classification, admitted traffic flows are differentiated and given appropriate network resources based on the application requirements. In the core network where thousands of flows are aggregated, per-flow classification results in an enormous overhead and state information. In order to avoid this, a per-class classification may be utilized. Here, admitted traffic is grouped into a finite set of service classes, which are managed according to their service class only. That is, we focus on a per-class classification of the traffic [184].

Furthermore, in the per-class approach, QoS parameters can be expressed as relative or absolute guarantees. Relative guarantees can be further divided into qualitative guarantees and proportional guarantees. With relative qualitative guarantees, the QoS parameters of the various classes are qualitatively ordered, e.g., PLR for class 0 traffic <PLR for class 1 traffic. With relative proportional guarantees, QoS parameters of a certain class are given quantitatively, relative to another class, e.g., PLR for class 1 traffic / PLR for class 0 traffic $= 10^2$. With absolute guarantees, QoS parameters of a certain class are given absolute upper bounds, e.g., PLR for class 0 traffic $<10^{-4}$. Absolute guarantees are crucial for the successful operation of interactive, multimedia, and mission-critical applications.

Existing QoS differentiation schemes for traditional store-and-forward networks mandate the use of buffers to isolate different traffic classes, i.e., by the use of active queue management (AQM) algorithms. Here, all packet arrivals to a switch are stored in an electronic buffer and managed according to an AQM algorithm. However, such schemes are not suitable for OBS networks for the following reasons: First, electronic buffering necessitates the use of O/E and E/O converters, which results in a significant increase in the switch's cost and loss of data transparency. Second, although optical buffering can be realized by utilizing fiber delay line (FDL), this approach can only give limited buffering capabilities compared to electronic buffering. Hence, we must utilize the WDM layer in order to isolate the different service classes in future OBS networks.

4.5.2   Packet/Burst Loss Rate Service Differentiation

PLR-based QoS differentiation can be achieved in OBS by using one or many of the following strategies: offset-based QoS differentiation, preemption, and resource restriction, as shown in [185].

4.5.2.1   Offset-Based QoS Differentiation

In the case of using the offset values to provide PLR differentiation, incoming traffic to an OBS network is divided into a set of service classes, and given different offset values according to their priority level. That is, by giving large offset values to high priority traffic and small offset values to low priority traffic, the control packets associated with high priority traffic will arrive before control packets associated with low priority traffic. Therefore, the former control packets have a higher probability of finding available resources over the latter in the OBS network. Thus, the PLR between the service classes may be controlled by adjusting the offset values in the different traffic classes as stated in [276]. The reader is referred to [10, 11, 91] for a further study on the mathematical modeling of offset-based QoS differentiation. Nevertheless, such offset-based QoS differentiation introduces extra delay to the packets of such high priority traffic, which might not be tolerated by some applications.

4.5.2.2   Preemption-Based QoS Differentiation

In OBS all resources are typically available to all traffic classes. However, when resources become scarce, preemption-based QoS differentiation permits high-priority bursts to take over (preempt) the resources currently occupied by low priority bursts, which are then (at least partially) lost. On the other hand, low priority bursts can never preempt any other burst. Hence, on average less resources are available to low priority data bursts than to high priority bursts, resulting in a lower PLR for high priority traffic. In the preemptive drop policy (PDP) [186], a class 0 burst may preempt a class 1 burst that is occupying a wavelength when all N wavelengths at the tagged output port are occupied. This means that a class 1 burst is lost instead of a class 0 burst, which intuitively results in a lower PLR for class 0 traffic relative to class 1 traffic. If there are only high priority bursts occupying the wavelengths, preemption is not possible, and the arriving class 0 burst is lost. In the preemptive drop policy (PDP) [186] the design parameter p denotes the probability of preemption, and can be used to adjust the isolation/differentiation level of QoS classes. That is, when all wavelengths at the tagged output port are occupied, and a class 0 burst arrives, there is a probability p that preemption take place given that there are class 1 bursts currently in transmission. Hence, with $p = 0$ one expects the PLR for class 0 and class 1 traffic to be equal, while the maximum class isolation is obtained for $p = 1$. In the latter case, class 0 traffic is lost only when a class 0 arrival finds all output wavelengths occupied transmitting class 0 bursts.

Figure 4.18 shows the resulting PLR for class 0 and class 1 traffic (class 0 traffic has priority over class 1 traffic) as a function of the preemption probability parameter p in a switch with $N = 16$ wavelengths, full wavelength conversion, 50% traffic load, Poisson traffic arrivals, uniform traffic pattern and 20% class 0 traffic. As shown, the PLR for both class 0 and class 1 traffic is equal for $p = 0$, but when p increases the PLR for class 0 traffic decreases until full class isolation is achieved at $p = 1$. The PLR for class 1 traffic increases slightly as p increases.

4.5.2.3   Resource Restriction-Based QoS Differentiation

In resource restriction-based QoS differentiation, a subset of the available resources (wavelengths, wavelength converters, buffering space, etc.) is exclusively reserved for high priority traffic only. This means that low priority traffic has fewer resources available than high priority traffic, which results in a lower PLR for high priority traffic compared to low priority traffic.

An example of a QoS differentiation scheme based on resource restriction is the wavelength allocation (WA) algorithm. Here, $n < N$ wavelengths at a tagged

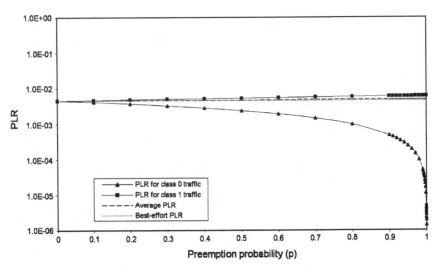

Fig. 4.18 The PLR as a function of the preemption probability parameter p

output port are exclusively reserved for class 0 traffic. That is, as long as less than $N - n$ wavelengths at the tagged output port are occupied, both new class 0 and class 1 arrivals are accepted. In the opposite case, only class 0 arrivals are accepted, while class 1 arrivals are dropped, resulting in a lower PLR for service class 0 than for service class 1. The class isolation may be controlled by adjusting the number of wavelengths (n) reserved for service class 0. Figure 4.19 shows the PLR as a function of the number of wavelengths (n) reserved to class 0 traffic. The PLR for class 0 traffic decreases as the n value increases, while the PLR for class 1 traffic increases since fewer wavelength resources are available for class 1 traffic.

4.5.3 Comparison of QoS Differentiation Strategies

A crucial issue when introducing QoS differentiation in OBS networks is the associated reduction in the average throughput as the isolation between service classes increases. This throughput penalty is due to the nonoptimal resource utilization when the WDM layer is used to isolate service classes. We consider the case where the network migrates from the typical best-effort scenario to a service-differentiated scenario with two service classes, which translates into a throughput change from G_{be} to G_{sd}. Denote S as the relative decrease in throughput when introducing QoS differentiation:

$$S = \frac{G_{sd}}{G_{be}} = \frac{1 - (S_0 P_0 + S_1 P_1)}{1 - P_{be}} \tag{4.1}$$

Here, S_i denotes the relative share of class i traffic, while P_i denotes the resulting burst loss rate for class i traffic. A value of $S = 0.80$ refers to a total throughput

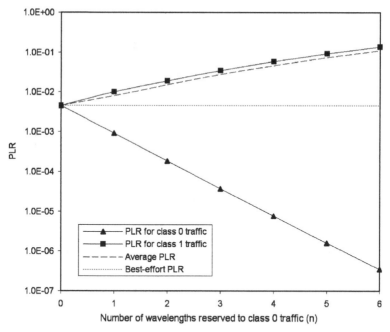

Fig. 4.19 The PLR as a function of the number of wavelengths (n) reserved for class 0 traffic

experienced of 80% of its original throughput before introduction the QoS strategy introduction. Hence, the ideal situation is to have $S = 1.0$, which means that employing QoS differentiation does not influence the total network throughput. In this case, there is a one-to-one mapping between lost class 0 and class 1 bursts, i.e., each class 1 burst that is lost due to QoS differentiation actually prevents a class 0 burst from being lost. However, in practice we often find situations where $S < 1.0$, which means that there is a nonoptimal utilization of the network resources in a service differentiated scenario. Figure 4.20 shows the PLR penalty as a function of class isolation for the WA and the PDP, as well as for the intentional packet dropping (IPD) scheme. We observe that the PDP has a $S \approx 1.0$, while for the WA, $S < 1.0$. The reason for the observed differences between the schemes is that in WA bursts are dropped although wavelengths are idle, while in the PDP all wavelengths are shared among all arrivals.

Another issue related to QoS differentiation is the associated hardware complexity of QoS differentiation algorithms. Increased performance may not always be justified, due to an increase of system complexity, resulting in an unacceptable increase in the total cost only for supporting QoS differentiation. We make a clear difference between hardware complexity and scheduling complexity. Increased hardware complexity stems from additional hardware resources needed to manipulate optical bursts in order to accomplish the QoS differentiation scheme, while increased scheduling complexity results from additional electronic processing associated with implementing the QoS differentiation scheme. Regarding WA,

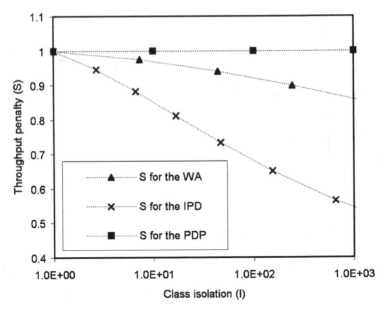

Fig. 4.20 Throughput penalty as a function of the class isolation for three different QoS differentiation schemes

no additional hardware is required. However, when it comes to scheduling, the switch must compare the number of occupied wavelengths at each output port with n, so it drops class 1 bursts when there are $N - n$ or more wavelengths occupied. For the PDP the output wavelength state information must also include the service class of the burst, so it preempts only class 1 data bursts. An improvement of PDP is achieved by preempting the latest class 1 arrival to minimize the "wasted bandwidth." This requires including information about when the currently switched bursts arrive. Regarding hardware complexity, additional hardware is required to erase the portion of the preempted burst that has already been transmitted to minimize the bandwidth utilization in downstream nodes.

A final challenge related to QoS differentiation in OBS is how one provides absolute QoS for a given service class, or more specifically, how to ensure a PLR below a certain fixed value for a given service class, measured over any time interval. The adaptive PDP (APDP) algorithm measures the PLR for class 0 traffic over a certain time window (w). By adjusting the parameter p of PDP, it is possible to ensure a given PLR value for class 0 traffic within a fixed bound, regardless of changes in class 0 traffic patterns. Figure 4.21 illus this statement by showing how class 0 and class 1 traffic change as a result of increased overall system load. Each observation in Fig. 4.21 is a measurement of the PLR over a fixed time window, together with its 95% confidence interval. We observe that class 0 PLR is kept within a bound of 10^{-4} by estimating the burst loss rate for every time window and adjusting the parameter p accordingly. As a result of a constant level for class 0 traffic, the PLR for class 1 traffic increases.

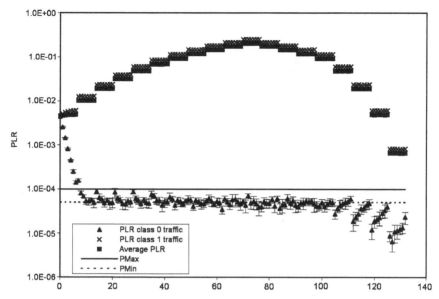

Fig. 4.21 The PLR as a function of the window number (w) in a changing system load scenario

4.5.4 Delay-Based Service Differentiation

The delay experienced by packets traversing an OBS network can be further exploited to differentiate between several classes of service. Essentially, packets traversing an OBS network suffer two main types of delay: burst assembly delay and offset delay, given that propagation delay is almost negligible compared to the other two. The former comprises the time spent by packets at the burst assembler until the data burst is completed, and this value is governed by the burst assembly algorithm. On the contrary, the offset delay is generally fixed by the network topology and rarely modified, unless it is used to provide PLR-based QoS differentiation as stated above.

In this light, the variability of packet delay in OBS networks is mainly due to the burst assembly algorithm employed at the ingress nodes, since all the other sources of delay are constant. As stated in Section 4.2, the delay of each packet is determined by its relative position within the burst, that is, if a packet arrives when a burst is almost completed, it generally suffers less delay than if it arrives when the burst is still empty. This feature of OBS networks can be exploited to provide delay-based service differentiation, as noted in [90, 213].

In [90] the authors propose a mechanism to bound the maximum burst assembly delay experienced by packets that belong to different classes of service. Essentially, the burst assembly algorithm follows a timer-based policy, but with two different timers: T_h for high priority traffic and T_l for low priority traffic, such that $T_h < T_l$, and it proceeds as follows: When the first packet arrives at the burst assembler, the assembly algorithm resets the timer to either T_h if the packet was of high priority

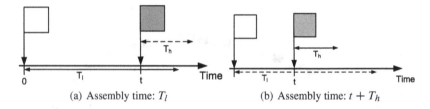

(a) Assembly time: T_l (b) Assembly time: $t + T_h$

Fig. 4.22 $[T_l, T_h]$ QoS differentiation burst assembly algorithm

or T_l if it was of low priority. In the first case the burst is completed and further released when the timer expires, thus no packet in it suffers more assembly delay than T_h. However, if the first packet was of low priority, subsequent packet arrivals may change the timer to T_h only if they are of high priority. Essentially, every low-priority packet arrival after the first packet suffers less than T_l assembly delay, but if a high priority arrives t seconds after, it updates the timer to the minimum value of $[T_h, T_l - t]$. The result is that no high priority packet suffers more than T_h delay and no low priority packet suffers more than T_l delay.

Figure 4.22a shows a case where a low priority packet (white) starts a burst formation process. A second high priority packet (grey) arrives t units of time later, such that $t + T_h > T_l$. In that case, the high priority packet suffers an assembly delay of $T_l - t$ units of time which is smaller than T_h, thus the assembly timer remains unchanged. However, if such high priority packet arrives at time t such that $t + T_h < T_l$ (Fig. 4.22b), then the timer needs to be reset to T_h units of time after the arrival time of the high priority packet t. Otherwise, the high priority packet would suffer an assembly delay value of $t - T_l < T_h$.

Although the maximum assembly delay is a good metric to define delay differentiation between different classes of traffic, it poses one main problem: This metric says nothing about the actual delay experienced by packets in each class. In this light, it may well happen that low priority packets experience less delay, on average, than high priority packets, although the latter satisfy a more restrictive maximum delay bound. Thus, in practice it might be a better choice for one to define service differentiation mechanisms based on "average delays," rather than on "maximum delays" experienced by packets, since this gives a more realistic view of the actual delay experienced by the packets of the same class.

To this end the authors in [213] define an average burst assembly delay metric that measures the delay, on average, that a packet of given service class would experience if it randomly arrived at a burst assembler. Such a metric averages the cases whereby the packet arrival occurs when the assembly process has just started as well as when the burst is almost finished and ready for transmission. Let $(x_1, x_2, \ldots, x_n)$ denote the packet interarrival times of $n + 1$ packet arrivals at a burst assembler. Then, the average assembly delay, namely z_{n+1}, is defined as a mean value of the assembly delay experienced by each packet of the burst:

$$z_{n+1} = \frac{1}{n+1}[(x_1 + \cdots + x_n) + (x_2 + \cdots + x_n) + (x_3 + \cdots + x_n) +$$

$$+ \cdots + (x_{n-1} + x_n) + x_n] = \frac{1}{n+1}\sum_{j=1}^{n} jx_j, \tag{4.2}$$

whose average value is

$$E[z_{n+1}] = \frac{1}{n+1}\sum_{j=1}^{n} jE[x_j] = \frac{n}{2}E[x_1] \tag{4.3}$$

if all packet interarrival times have the same mean $E[x_1]$.

In this light, the authors in [213] define a two-class, size-based burst assembly policy with two thresholds: N_l and N_h. The former controls the maximum number of packets in the burst assembled after a low priority packet has arrived, whereas the latter regulates the maximum number of packets in the burst after a high priority packet arrival. The average delay defined in Eq. (4.3) can then be computed separately for the high and low priority packets giving an average delay of $D_{(N_l,N_h)}^{lp}$ and $D_{(N_l,N_h)}^{hp}$, which determines the average delay experienced by low and high priority packets during such two-class (N_l, N_h) size-based burst assembly processes, respectively.

A case example with $N_l = 24$ and variable N_h is shown in Fig. 4.23. In this case, parameter p_h refers to the probability of a high priority packet, that is, the probability for a given packet arrival to be of high priority. As shown, delay-based

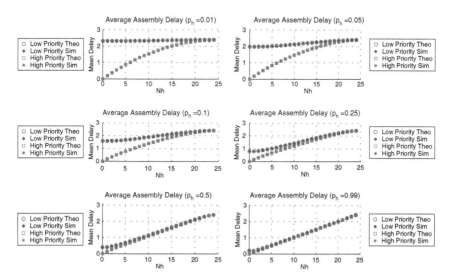

Fig. 4.23 Mean average delay experienced by high priority and low priority for different N_h values ($N_l = 24$ fixed) in several p_h scenarios

service differentiation is achieved when $N_h \ll N_l$, but almost no service distinction can be achieved when N_h approaches $N_l = 24$. Finally, Fig. 4.23 bottom shows that, when most of the packets are of high priority (high values of p_h), the burst assembly policy is most often regulated by size threshold N_h, thus yielding almost no distinction between the two classes.

4.6 TCP over OBS

OBS is capable of providing a huge amount of bandwidth capacity and flexibility for data transmission. However, the final end-to-end user perception depends crucially on the optimal cooperation and coordination of all communication layers in the protocol stack, that is, the application layers as well as the transport and network layers. Thus, it is crucial to understand such interaction between the transport layer and the underlying OBS network.

TCP is the dominating transport protocol in the internet today (more than 80% of the IP traffic today uses TCP) and it is generally assumed that TCP will continue to dominate in the forseeable future. The following briefly reviews the fundamentals of TCP (the reader is referred to [240] for further details) and the implications of the burstification process on the transport protocol.

4.6.1 Brief Review of TCP

Transmission Control Protocol (TCP) has been evolving since its original design in a time where very low bandwidth was available; both its implementation and default configuration have evolved. Both the implementation and default configuration have been adapted to the existing networks. For example, in the implementation of TCP in "old" operating systems, the parameters of TCP are often set in a conservative way, optimized for few Mbps bandwidths, while the newest operating systems have the TCP stack improved and tuned for higher bandwidth values. For a good performance over OBS networks, it is recommended one use the latest TCP implementations which automatically selects a high transmission window value and uses the selective acknowledgements by default.

TCP sends chunks of data, called *segments*, which are acknowledged by the receiver after a correct reception. Each segment is numbered with the aim of facilitating both reordering in the destination node and detecting lost segments. Additionally, TCP uses a sliding window mechanism for flow control purposes. The transmission window determines the maximum number of TCP segments that can be simultaneously in transit, that is, the number of segments transmitted without acknowledgement. Each time an acknowledgement is received, the transmission window is updated, and TCP is allowed to send new segments.

The *Round trip time* (RTT) plays a very important role in TCP. The RTT is defined as the time elapsed between the transmission of the segment and its acknowledgement (ACK) arrival. In a normal situation, all TCP segments in a window are transmitted within an RTT. Thus, an estimate of the TCP transmission rate, $X(t)$ in segments per second, is (assuming there is no bandwidth bottleneck) $X(t) = W(t)/RTT$, where $W(t)$ denotes the transmission window size.

In TCP the transmission window size is computed as the minimum of two quantities: the receiver's advertised window (imposed by the receiver), which indicates the amount of data that it is able to buffer at reception; and the sender's congestion window (imposed by the sender), which limits number of TCP segments in transit in order to not overload the network.

Finally, it is worth remarking that TCP has several phases/states of operation, whereby each state defines the dynamics of the sender's congestion window. Initially, TCP has a low congestion window, typically of one segment, and its size is increased by one segment every time an acknowledgement (ACK) is received. This phase is called *slow-start*, and results in an exponential increase of the congestion window. This behavior ends when the congestion window reaches a certain threshold, namely "ssthresh" (slow-start threshold), after which the congestion window increases linearly with the arrivals of ACKs, not exponentially. This phase is known as "congestion avoidance" and its use is a measure toward avoiding network overload. The congestion window is finally decreased if segment loss occurs.

In this light TCP defines two different ways for detecting segment losses, either by the timeout of the retransmission timer, and by means of the reception of (usually) three duplicated ACKs. The former considers that segment loss occurs when the acknowledgement of a TCP segment is not received before the retransmission timer expires. In this case TCP enters the slow-start phase with drastic throughput decrease. The latter case refers to the situation whereby a sequence of packets arrive at the receiver, but one is missing. In that case, the receiver requests the missing packet several times after the reception of successive packets, thus generating duplicated ACKs. When three duplicated ACKs arrive at the TCP sender, this reduces its congestion window by one half, entering the fast-recovery and fast-retransmit phases.

4.6.2 Impact of Burst-Assembly Algorithms on TCP

We remark that in OBS networks packets are aggregated into data bursts before being transmitted, hence the behavior of TCP differs with respect to ordinary packet-switched networks. First of all, packets suffer an additional delay in the transmitter due to the burstification process and the offset values. Secondly, burst losses have a different impact on TCP depending on whether or not such data burst contains more than one segment from the same TCP connection. Thus, OBS networks are more prone to suffer consecutive segment losses than they do in packet-switched networks.

4.6.2.1 Impact of Delay Penalty

In OBS the assembly process of datagrams introduces an additional delay due to the waiting time until the burst is completed, which increases the RTT experienced by TCP connections. This clearly implies a throughput decrease. Let T_b denote the maximum burst assembly delay suffered by packets at the ingress nodes. The round trip time of a given TCP connection may thus be increased $2 \cdot T_b$ units of time given the fact that both packet and its ACK may suffer such maximum delay, as noted in [47].

4.6.2.2 Impact of Burst Losses

The most influential aspect on TCP performance is the loss of data bursts due to contention at intermediate nodes. The loss of a burst generally implies the loss of several consecutive TCP segments belonging to the same flow. TCP detects segment losses either by means of the reception of duplicated ACKs, or by means of the expiration of a retransmission timeout. Thus, concerning the former mechanism, depending on the number of TCP segments from the same flow in a lost burst, TCP reacts differently, namely: (1) If a lost burst contains a complete transmission window, the retransmission timer will therefore expire and the TCP sender will enter the slow-start phase; but, (2) if the lost burst does not contain a complete window, the receiver will experience out-of-order arrivals, thus transmitting duplicated ACKs back to the source which will immediately enter the fast-recovery and fast-retransmit phases.

In conclusion, burst losses in OBS networks have a different impact on the performance of TCP depending on the number of TCP segments from the same flow contained in a lost burst.

4.6.2.3 Impact of a Burst Carrying Only One Segment of a TCP Flow

Let us now consider a data burst traversing an OBS network. This data burst only carries one TCP segment from a given flow and is lost at some point inside the OBS network.

In this light, Fig. 4.24 shows the dynamics of the congestion window of the TCP sender (version TCP Reno) in this scenario. Figure 4.24a shows such evolution during the complete transmission period, while Fig. 4.24b only shows a zoom around the instant when the burst loss takes place. In addition, a few noteworthy points have been numbered: At point 1, the burst loss occurs. In such a case if the transmission window is large enough, additional segments will have been sent in other bursts after that lost segment. Hence, if at least three segments reach the destination node after the loss, the TCP receiver will detect such packets have arrived out of order, thus sending duplicated ACKs (one for each out-of-order segment). When the third duplicated ACK reaches the TCP sender, the TCP source triggers the fast-retransmit and fast-recovery mechanisms, which has the following consequences: First of all,

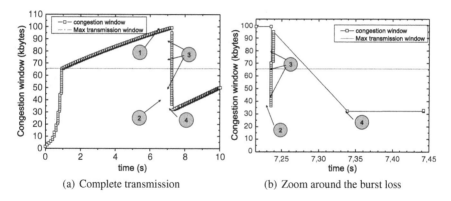

(a) Complete transmission   (b) Zoom around the burst loss

Fig. 4.24 Evolution of the congestion window for TCP Reno when a burst containing one segment of the flow is lost

the congestion window is reduced to flightsize/2 + 3 (point 2). Flightsize is the number of segments that have been sent but have yet to be acknowledged, that is, the number of segments in transit, and its value usually matches that of the transmission window. Then, the lost TCP segment is retransmitted, and the congestion window is increased every time a new duplicated ACK arrives (point 3). Finally, when the ACK that acknowledges the retransmitted segment arrives, the congestion window is reduced by one half of flightsize (point 4). In this scenario the duplicated ACKs arrive at the TCP source before the expiration of the retransmission timer. Thus, the reduction of the transmission rate is not as significant as if the timer had expired (slow-start phase).

The behavior of the SACK version of TCP is shown in Fig. 4.25. After the burst loss (at point 1), when three duplicated ACKs have arrived, the congestion window is reduced to half of flightsize (point 2), and the lost segment is retransmitted. Then, new duplicated ACKs arrive (points 3 and 4). One RTT after the lost segment was retransmitted, its ACK arrives confirming the reception at destination. Then, the size of the congestion window starts growing according to the congestion avoidance phase (point 5). Therefore, both TCP Reno and SACK recover from the segment loss in a short time, one RTT after receiving the three duplicated ACKs. After the recovery, the congestion window is reduced by one half of flightsize. Hence, in this scenario, the behavior of both versions is very similar.

4.6.2.4   Impact of a Burst Carrying Two Segments of a TCP Flow

Now, Figs. 4.26 and 4.27 show the behavior of TCP Reno and TCP SACK, respectively, when a data burst carrying two segments of a TCP flow is lost.

In the case of TCP Reno (Fig. 4.26), after the detection of the burst loss by means of duplicated ACKs (point 1), the TCP sender retransmits the first segment lost and reduces the congestion window to flight size/2 + 3 segments (point 2). Then, as

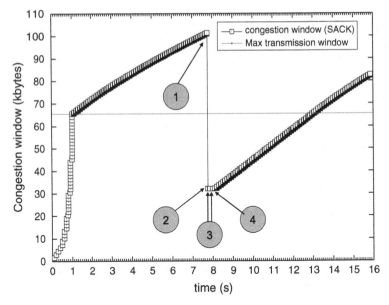

Fig. 4.25 Evolution of the congestion window for TCP SACK when a burst containing one segment of the flow is lost

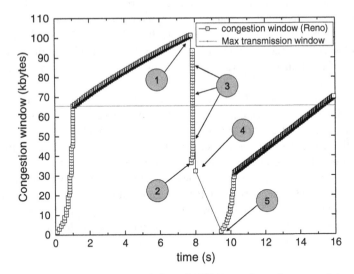

Fig. 4.26 Evolution of the congestion window of TCP Reno when a burst containing two TCP segments of a flow is lost

new duplicated ACKs arrive, the congestion window is increased by one segment (point 3). In the example shown in Fig. 4.26, the sender has in transit as many segments as the receiver's advertised window. Hence, no matter the value of the congestion window, the TCP sender cannot send any new data. If the receiver's

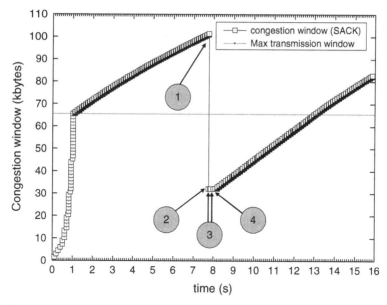

Fig. 4.27 Evolution of the congestion window of TCP SACK when a burst containing two TCP segments of a flow is lost.

advertised window had been higher than the congestion window when fast recovery started, the sender could have been allowed to send any new segment in some of these window updates (but this is not the case considered in the example). Then, the ACK of the first lost segment (which was generated after the reception of the retransmitted segment) arrives, and the congestion window is reduced (point 4). At this point in the example, the number of segments in transit is reduced by just one (thanks to the segment that has arrived correctly, but not more, because the second segment is lost and the remaining segments are still unacknowledged). Hence, the sender's congestion window does not allow new segments to be sent, so the receiver cannot send three duplicated ACKs. Therefore, the sender remains inactive until the retransmission timer associated to the second lost segment expires (point 5). Then, the segment is retransmitted and the sender enters the slow-start phase again. In general, TCP Reno usually has to wait for the retransmission timeout to recover from a two-segment loss, and almost always in case of three or more segment losses.

In the case of TCP SACK, after burst loss detection by means of duplicated ACKs (point 1), the congestion window is reduced to flightsize/2 (point 2). As new duplicated ACKs arrive, the congestion window remains constant (point 3). These acknowledgements contain selective ACK information, which can be used to retransmit all consecutive lost segments. When the ACKs confirming the reception of these segments arrive, the transmission window starts growing as stated by the congestion avoidance phase (point 4).

In summary, this experiment describes the behavior of a burst loss with two segments belonging to the same TCP flow. In general, the same behavior is expected if more than two TCP segments are lost within such burst loss, as long as three duplicated ACKs arrive at the TCP sender after the burst loss.

Finally, as shown, TCP Reno almost always recovers with a timer expiration, thus entering the slow-start phase, which implies a drastic throughput decrease. On the other hand, TCP SACK recovers in approximately one RTT and continues the transmission just with its congestion window halved instead of reducing it to one segment, like in the Reno case. Therefore, SACK offers an important performance improvement in this scenario. Since this is an expected scenario in OBS networks, the use of the SACK version of TCP is highly advisable.

4.6.2.5 Loss of a Data Burst Carrying a Complete Window of a TCP Flow

When a data burst contains all the segments sent in a TCP transmission window, its loss immediately implies a retransmission time-out. This is because the TCP sender (in both Reno and SACK cases) does not receive any duplicated ACK (Fig. 4.28).

In conclusion, the behavior of TCP over OBS networks highly depends on the number of TCP segments transmitted in a lost burst, and the TCP version employed by the sender and receiver. In this light, TCP SACK presents benefits over TCP Reno in the case of multiple segment losses.

4.6.2.6 Amplification and Synchronization Effect of TCP over OBS

One of the benefits of OBS is the so-called *amplification effect* or *correlation benefit* of TCP. Let us illustrate this effect with an example. Consider the transmission of 1,000 TCP segments over an OBS network with burst loss probability of 10^{-2}, and

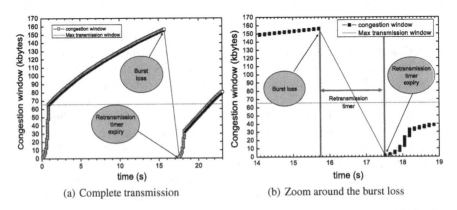

(a) Complete transmission   (b) Zoom around the burst loss

Fig. 4.28 Evolution of the congestion window when a burst containing a complete transmission window of the flow is lost

the following two segment-per-burst ratios: (1) five segments/burst, and (2) ten segments/burst. The first scenario requires the transmission of 200 bursts for that TCP connection which, on average, brings the loss of two data bursts. If, for instance, TCP Reno is employed the presence of, such two burst losses implies entering the slow-start phase twice. In the second case, only 100 bursts are needed, leading to a single burst loss on average. Hence, the TCP sender enters the slow-start phase only once. Since the behavior of TCP is basically the same when either five or ten consecutive segments are lost, the second scenario gives a better throughput performance than the first case. This effect is known as the correlation benefit of TCP.

Finally, it is worth remarking that a burst loss triggers the congestion control mechanisms of all TCP sources, which loses a segment simultaneously. This is often referred to as the *synchronization effect* of OBS on TCP. Essentially, synchronized TCP sources lead to a nonsmooth use of the available bandwidth.

For example, let us consider a case scenario whereby N different TCP flows with the same RTT arrive at a burst assembler in an OBS network. Figure 4.29a and b show $W(t)$ the average transmission window of the TCP flows over a 600 ms simulation experiment. If no synchronization between the sources occurs, the used bandwidth exhibits the nearly flat appearance of Fig. 4.29a, whereby when TCP sources are synchronized, the effect is the sawtooth use-of-bandwidth appearance of Fig. 4.29b. The reader is referred to [81, 82] for further details on this issue.

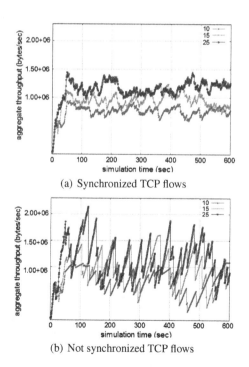

(a) Synchronized TCP flows

(b) Not synchronized TCP flows

Fig. 4.29 Aggregated throughput of TCP flows over a 600 ms simulation

4.6.3   Techniques to Increase Performance of TCP over OBS

Once the behavior of TCP over OBS has been analyzed, the following strategies have been proposed in the literature to improve its behavior over OBS networks.

4.6.3.1   Modifying the Implementation of TCP

Since TCP is not specifically designed for a particular access or network technology, modifying the standard TCP, can lead to a performance optimization in specific environments, see for instance the new TCP versions proposed for wireless networks [252]. However, in high speed networks such as OBS, TCP is questioned as to whether it can achieve the ultra high performance that would be expected in a next-generation high speed network. A great amount of novel TCP versions have been proposed in the literature (see for instance [45, 88]). At the moment, there is no consensus on whether a completely new TCP version is needed, and which new TCP version should be standardized among all of them.

To give an idea of the number and type of modifications which are currently being proposed, the list below summarizes a set of TCP modifications that may be suitable for high speed optical burst-switched networks:

- *TCP-Peach:* Employs sudden start (sends dummy packets to increase the transmission window faster) and rapid recovery (uses dummy packets during recovery). This version needs modification at routers.
- *TCP Westwood:* Estimates the available bandwidth by means of the ACK received rate.
- *Byte counting:* The TCP window grows according to the number of bytes that are acknowledged instead of the number of ACKs received.
- *High speed TCP:* Alters the way that the window is opened on each round trip time and closed upon congestion events as a function of the absolute size of the window. When the transmission window is small, HS-TCP behaves exactly like ordinary TCP, but when it is large, it increases the window by a larger amount and decreases it by a smaller amount than ordinary. Such increase and decrease ratios are chosen based on the precise value of the window in operation. This is good for long distance high speed links.
- *Fast TCP:* The congestion indication is given by queuing delay instead of packet loss. Good for long distance high speed links.
- *TCP-NCR:* Includes a set of TCP sender modifications to provide noncongestion robustness (NCR) to TCP. In particular, these changes are built on top of TCP with selective acknowledgments (SACKs) and the SACK-based loss recovery scheme given in RFC 3517. This is good for networks with reordering.
- *TCP-PR:* Packet loss is detected by the use of timers instead of duplicated acknowledgments. This is good for networks with reordering.
- *TCP-Aix:* Initiates loss recovery before congestion control. While system awaits more information on which to base the congestion control decision, packet

conservation is used to keep the acknowledgment clock running while not stressing the network unfairly. This is good for networks with reordering.

Apart from modifying TCP, network designers can adjust several aspects of OBS networks to improve the performance of TCP. The next section shows how to modify the burst assembly algorithms to make them more TCP-aware.

4.6.3.2   Window-Based Burst Assembly

Conventional burst assembly techniques are not TCP-aware, and can only be tuned for optimal performance for individual flows with similar characteristics (i.e., file size, size of window, blocking, etc.). In order to enhance TCP performance, it has been proposed that we consider the instant TCP window as a metric for determining the optimum assembly time. Moreover, instead of using a single fixed timer for burst assembly, a dynamic process is preferred whereby either the TCP sources control the time instant at which the burst is completed, or it forwards packets to different assembly queues with different assembly timers. For example, the authors in [208] propose a multi-queue burstification system with different assembly timers for TCP sources with small, medium, and large congestion windows. This study shows a significant increase on the performance of TCP. In this light, data bursts with packets in the slow-start phase (small window) go to preferred assembly queues, which dispatches data bursts more quickly than other assembly queues for TCP packets with lager window values.

4.7   Performance Analysis of OBS Networks

The EFP iterative procedure was first introduced by F. P. Kelly in the late 1980s to evaluate the performance behavior of conventional circuit-switched network topologies at low loads [121]. The authors in [216] extended the conventional circuit-switched formulation of the original EFP procedure to the analysis of optical burst-switched networks using either JET or JIT signaling, and whose OBS switches are equipped with full wavelength conversion capabilities (see Section 4.4).

Essentially, the Erlang fixed point (EFP) algorithm is an iterative procedure that operates as follows: Let $G(N, L)$ denote a given network topology characterized by N border OBS nodes, and a total number of links L. Let l_i denote the ith link in the network, where $i = 1, 2, \ldots, L$, and let f_j, $j = 1, \ldots, J$, $J \leq N^2$, denote the jth end-to-end flow or connection between any two pairs of border nodes in the OBS network. Also, let B_{l_i} denote the blocking probability experienced at link l_i and B_{f_j} denote the end-to-end blocking probability observed by end-to-end flow f_j. Finally, let the input traffic at border OBS nodes be assumed to follow a Poisson process.

For mathematical tractability, the assumption is generally accepted that blocking events occur independently from link to link along any end-to-end route j

(reduced load approximation). If this is the case, the EFP algorithm provides an iterative methodology to derive the blocking probability and traffic carried by each link l_i, $i = 1, \ldots, L$, in the network and, consequently, by every end-to-end flow f_j, $j = 1, \ldots, J$. The following summarizes the steps of EFP:

1. Start the algorithm with a random set of link-blocking probabilities $B_{l_i} \in (0, 1]$, $i = 1, \ldots, L$.
2. With values B_{l_i}, obtain the end-to-end blocking probability experienced by flow f_j, that is, B_{f_j}:

$$1 - B_{f_j} = \prod_{i \in f_j} (1 - B_{l_i}), \quad j = 1, \ldots, J, \qquad (4.4)$$

   which arises as the product of individual blocking probabilities of the links traversed by end-to-end flow or connection f_j, given the assumption of independent link blocking.
3. The flow blocking probability set B_{f_j}, with $j = 1, \ldots, J$, determines the amount of traffic carried by each individual link I_{l_i}, given by:

$$I_{l_i} = \sum_j I_{f_j} \prod_k (1 - B_{l_k}), \qquad (4.5)$$

   which takes into account the total number of end-to-end flows traversing link l_i, multiplied by the path blocking probability up to each flow's previous link in the source destination path j.
4. Finally, the blocking probability experienced by each link B_{l_i} in the network is given by the Erlang-B equation applied to the total offered traffic on that link I_{l_i}, say:

$$B_{l_i} = E_B(I_{l_i}, M_i), \qquad (4.6)$$

   where M_i denotes the total number of wavelengths available in link l_i.
5. Return to step 2 making use of the new set of link-blocking probabilities B_{l_i}, $i = 1, \ldots, L$, derived from step 4 and repeat until convergence.

The reader is referred to [121] for a detailed analysis of the EFP iterative loop above, and convergence behavior. It is important to remark that Eq. (4.5) has been modified from the original study by F. P. Kelly to deal with the fact that, when using a one-way reservation algorithm such as JET or JIT, the traffic offered to link l_i depends on the blocking probability of all links l_k which precedes l_i for flow f_j, as described in [216].

The literature also offers a number of studies whereby the EFP methodology is applied to evaluate the performance of OBS networks; see [214, 260, 279].

Chapter 5
Advanced Optical Burst Switched Network Concepts

Reza Nejabati, Javier Aracil, Piero Castoldi, Marc De Leenheer,
Dimitra Simeonidou, Luca Valcarenghi, Georgios Zervas, and Jian Wu

5.1 Role of OBS for Grid Computing, Distributed Applications, and Collaborative Services

In recent years, as the bandwidth and the speed of networks have increased significantly, a new generation of network-based applications using the concept of distributed computing and collaborative services is emerging (e.g., Grid computing applications). The use of the available fiber and DWDM infrastructure for these applications is a logical choice offering huge amounts of cheap bandwidth and ensuring global reach of computing resources [230]. Currently, there is a great deal of interest in deploying optical circuit (wavelength) switched network infrastructure for distributed computing applications that require long-lived wavelength paths and address the specific needs of a small number of well-known users. Typical users are particle physicists who, due to their international collaborations and experiments, generate enormous amounts of data (Petabytes per year). These users require a network infrastructures that can support processing and analysis of large datasets through globally distributed computing resources [230]. However, providing wavelength granularity bandwidth services is not an efficient and scalable solution for applications and services that address a wider base of user communities with different traffic profiles and connectivity requirements. Examples of such applications may be: scientific collaboration in smaller scale (e.g., bioinformatics, environmental research), distributed virtual laboratories (e.g., remote instrumentation), e-health, national security and defense, personalized learning environments and digital libraries, evolving broadband user services (i.e., high resolution home

R. Nejabati (✉)
Department of Computing and Electronic Systems, University of Essex, Colchester,
United Kingdom
e-mail: rnejab@essex.ac.uk

J. Aracil and F. Callegati (eds.), *Enabling Optical Internet with Advanced Network Technologies*, Computer Communications and Networks,
DOI 10.1007/978-1-84882-278-8_5, © Springer-Verlag London Limited 2009

video editing, real-time rendering, high definition interactive TV). As a specific example, in e-health services and in particular mammography applications due to the size and quantity of images produced by remote mammography, stringent network requirements are necessary. Initial calculations have shown that for 100 patients to be screened remotely, the network would have to securely transport 1.2 GB of data every 30 s [230]. According to the above explanation it is clear that these types of applications need a new network infrastructure and transport technology that makes large amounts of bandwidth at subwavelength granularity, storage, computation, and visualization resources potentially available to a wide user base for specified time durations. As these types of collaborative and network-based applications evolve addressing a wide range and large number of users, it is infeasible to build dedicated networks for each application type or category. Consequently, there should be an adaptive network infrastructure able to support all application types, each with their own access, network, and resource usage patterns. This infrastructure should offer flexible and intelligent network elements and control mechanism able to deploy new applications quickly and efficiently.

Optical burst switching technology is a suitable candidate for implementing a scalable network infrastructure to address the needs of emerging collaborative services and distributed applications. Its advantages are as follows:

- Its transport format can be ideally tailored to user's bandwidth requirements and can therefore provide efficient use of network resources.
- Unlike the optical wavelength switched networks, the optical bandwidth can be reserved for a specified time, i.e., only for the duration of the burst.
- Unlike the optical wavelength switched network, its transport format and protocol is scalable and can support a dynamic and large user-based network.
- It offers separation of control and data plane that allows all-optical data transmission with ultrafast user/application-initiated lightpath setup.
- Electronic processing of the burst control packet as well as the advanced reservation mechanism at each node can enable the network infrastructure to offer application layer or middleware functionalities (e.g., intelligent resource (computing and network) discovery, reservation, and allocation).

This chapter discusses how an OBS network can support a ubiquitous distributed platform such as distributed computing, which is able to address requirements of a large number of dynamic users. In Section 5.2, network architectures and requirements in a distributed computing- (i.e., Grid) enabled OBS network are discussed. This section mainly focuses on core OBS and edge OB routers requirements, OBS control protocol issues, and burst aggregation considerations for supporting distributed computing applications. Section 5.3 describes three different OBS network scenarios and their specific implementations with ability to support advanced network services for distributed applications.

5.2 OBS Network Supporting Distributed Computing Applications

5.2.1 Network Architecture

OBS technology, by providing subwavelength bandwidth granularity with advanced and dynamic bandwidth reservation mechanism, is an attractive solution compared to the traditional circuit switching and future optical packet switching technology.

Similar to OBS network scenario, distributed applications and services such as Grid computing deploy an advanced reservation mechanism where, according to the user requirements, network and nonnetwork resources (e.g., computing) are reserved for a specific duration of time. Therefore a natural and efficient way to enable OBS network to support such services is to extend its advanced reservation mechanism for co-allocation and co-reservation of nonnetwork and network resources. This approach will directly affect both physical layer (router architecture and functionality and also burst format) and control layer of the traditional OBS network. Figure 5.1 shows a generic OBS network architecture supporting distributed computing applications such as Grid (in this chapter, the concept of "network-based distributed computing" is referred to as "Grid computing") .

In a Grid-enabled OBS network, the burst format has to be extended to accommodate the application-related information. One approach is to combine computing resource requirements information with physical layer information (e.g., bandwidth requirements) and accommodate them into the same burst control header packet, which will be followed by data burst that carries the data to be processed

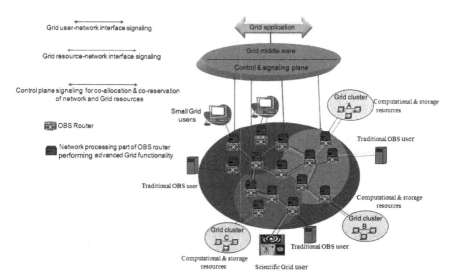

Fig. 5.1 A generic architecture for a Grid enabled OBS network

(i.e., Grid job) in remote computing resources. Another approach is to use the traditional burst format and transport the application-related information in the payload of the two independent bursts such that payload of one burst accommodates computing and network resource requirements information and following that another burst carries the actual data to be processed remotely.

A Grid-enabled OBS network, at the physical layer, is similar to the traditional OBS network and comprises two types of routers, i.e., edge and core OBS routers. At the edge of the network, the ingress router, in addition to traffic aggregation, burst assembly and transmission, provide the interface functionality between Grid users/applications and OBS network. Is a similar way, at the egress of the network the OBS router in addition to burst data recovery and traffic segregation provides the interface functionality between computing resources and OBS network.

A traditional core OBS router performs burst forwarding and advanced reservation through the processing of the information carried by the burst control header. In a Grid-enabled OBS network, the processing power and of the core router need to be extended and deployed for co-reservation and co-allocation of computing and network resources. In addition, at the control layer, the OBS signaling and control protocol functionality, has to be extended for interfacing with application layer to support middle ware functionality, such as enquiring resource requirements related information, resource reservation, and allocation.

5.2.2 Core OBS Router Supporting Distributed Computing Applications

As future optical technology moves to 40 Gbps and beyond, networking solutions must be designed to be compatible with these bit rates in order to reduce the cost per bit [165]. OBS has been introduced as a switching technology relaxed on fast switching requirements, as the relatively slow switch set up times (milliseconds rather than nanoseconds) are small compared to the payload duration (usually hundreds of milliseconds or seconds) and therefore throughput is almost unaffected [201]. However, this is true for an OBS network transmitting large data bursts with low bit rates. Introduction of new network services such as Grid services over OBS implies new constraints for switching speed requirements, which become particularly important when high speed transmission is considered.

A flexible network supporting a large number of users that need access to distributed resources across the network will require the support of users with small data and also transmission of resource request information which implies transmission of small bursts. For example, with a MEMS-based switch with a typical switching speed of 20 ms to achieve throughput better that 90% (considering only switching time) at 10 Gbps the data burst size must be in region of several hundreds of ms. If the same burst is transmitted at 160 Gbps then the throughput of the network will drop significantly as the burst duration becomes extremely small compared to switching time. This becomes more severe when users with small data to be processed remotely are treated in the network or when the network scenario is such that small and frequent resource requests are transported through separate bursts. These small sets of information are implied in the network by the small bursts and maybe with short offset time. These types of bursts with small length and possibly with short offset time require ultrafast switching in nanoseconds regime to achieve high throughput in the network. Additionally, the support of multicasting is particularly essential, in order to support distributed application and enable parallel processing services over remote resources [146] as well as resource discovery in a dynamic network. For these reasons the deployment of fast switching technology with multicasting capability is mandatory for future high speed OBS networks that can support distributed computing applications.

The fast-switching solutions that have been proposed are based on the use of fast active components, like semiconductor optical amplifiers (SOA). Switching is achieved, either by broadcasting the signal (passive splitting) and selecting the appropriate routes using fast gating [237] or by converting the signal's wavelength and routing it to an output port of a passive routing device (AWG) [127]. The deployment of fast switching assists efficient bandwidth utilization, but provides an expensive solution when it scales to many input ports. On the other hand, there is no additional benefit for long bursts of data (e.g., originated from large Grid users) if fast switching is utilized. Figure 5.2 shows a generic architecture for a Grid-enabled OBS core router.

Central to this architecture is the possibility of using network processors (NPs) capable of analyzing data traveling through the network at wire speed. The NP enables the router to efficiently route data based on applications and their resource requirements. The OBS routers utilize high performance NPs capable of executing specific processing functions on data contained within bursts at line rates

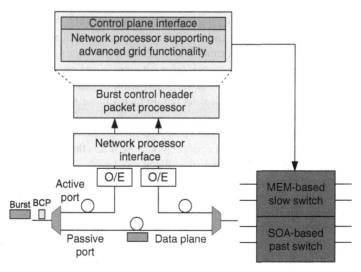

Fig. 5.2 Generic architecture of a Grid-enabled core OBS router

(e.g., computing resource discovery algorithm). This can only be performed by specially designed fast electronic circuits and network processor (NP)s. Recent advances in the technology of integrated circuits allow complicated processing of bursty data directly up to 10 Gbps [69]. This sets the upper limit in the transmission speed of the control information and burst control header (BCH). On the other hand the much longer transparently switched optical bursts (i.e., no conversion to electronic domain) are those that determine the capacity utilization of the network. In summary, core OBS routers equipped with NPs are key enablers for the support of network-based services and distributed applications functionalities: (1) QoS provisioning; (2) reliable multicasting; and (3) resource base routing.

5.2.3 Edge OBS Router Supporting Distributed Computing Applications

An edge OBS supporting distributed computing application such as Grid Node must be able to fulfil distributed computing application requirements and make efficient use of network resources by using OBS technology. The edge router architecture should introduce a mechanism that can process application traffic and maps it onto optical bursts. In such networks a data burst and its burst control header are transmitted separately on different wavelength channels and switched respectively in optical and electronic domains. Thus, in an OBS network an ingress edge router able to initiate a burst control header and also map user traffic into the optical domain in the form of variable length optical bursts is mandatory, and such an edge router must be able to perform the following functionalities: application data classification, traffic aggregation and optical burst assembly, optical burst transmission and user-to-network as well as computing resource-to-network signaling interface.

- *Application data (job) classification:* The job classification at the edge of the network must provide fair and specialized services—differentiated services (DiffServ). Application performance and network utilization can be enhanced by efficiently matching nonnetwork (computational) and network resources to user/application requirements. A flexible and scalable classification mechanism can process jobs based on application requirements in terms of nonnetwork and network resources.
- *Burst aggregation:* The burst aggregation algorithm at the edge router can greatly impact the overall OBS network operation because it sets the burst characteristics and therefore shapes the burst arrival traffic at the core.
- *User and resource network interface functionality:* To facilitate on demand access to network-based services and access to remote resources (e.g., Grid computing services), interoperable procedures between users and optical network for agreement negotiation and service activation have to be developed. These procedures constitute the grid user optical network interface (G-OUNI). The G-OUNI in an OBS network needs to provide the following main functionalities:

- Flexible bandwidth allocation
- Support for claiming existing agreements
- Automatic and timely lightpath setup
- Traffic classification, grooming, shaping, and transmission entity construction

In summary the G-OUNI connects the Grid users from IP domain into optical network and must carry out the following main functionalities:

- Job differentiation and classification scheduler to recognize incoming IP packets type (job request, job submission) and extracts the required information for classification. It enables quality of service (QoS) in Grid-OBS network through a traffic classification method.
- Burst control header (BCH) and data burst construction and transmission: The burst control header must be constructed and transmitted based on differentiation and classification outcome. The IP packets are assembled into bursts and transmitted over different wavelengths after an offset time required for the BCH to set up the path.
- Agile wavelength assignment: to generate the required wavelengths for each data burst.

On the other hand, geographically distributed processing and storage resources across the network constitute fundamental elements of the large scale Grid network. In such a network scenario the resources (i.e., storage and processing) can dynamically enter and leave the OBS network based on pre-established agreements. This fact imposes another important role for the edge OBS router, which is providing a dedicated signaling and control interface between nonnetwork resources and the network. Main functionalities of such an interface can be:

- Support for existing agreements
- Job (application data) submission to local computing resources
- Support for advance resource reservation schemes
- Propagation state of the local resources (available storage/processing resources)
- Propagation of service-related events
- Sending back results to source or multiple alternative destinations

5.2.4 Traffic Aggregation and Burst Assembly Based on Application's Specific Requirements

Photonic infrastructure supporting distributed applications has to rely on application requirements if it is to be useful to the user community. However, each application has its own reasons for communicating and its own types of information to be communicated, which may impose very different requirements on both network and computational sectors. Some applications may run more effectively on one architecture than on another. By executing each application (or phase of application) on the remote computing resource with the most suitable available resource architecture and configuration and appropriate communication infrastructure, the overall application may run in much less time than on a homogeneous system of the same aggregate power. Thus, obtaining peak application performance can depend on careful selection of the type, number, and location of processors, memory and storage, the available network bandwidth, latency, and physical layer constraints to link users with remote resources or even resources with each other. Furthermore, such an infrastructure is dynamic and heterogeneous, and resources are owned by several entities where the availability of resources can change at any time, and new types of resources are continuously added to the network. Therefore, a QoS-aware network supporting distributed application should provide a differentiated services mechanism (DiffServ) based on user/application requirements, available computational and network resources, and fairness on both user and resource level. The starting point of the such a differentiated services mechanism is the classification mechanism that is applied at the edge OBS router. Edge routers deploy this mechanism to classify jobs/packets and determine which flow they belong to and in turn what Grid-DiffServ they should receive. Network-based distributed applications (e.g., Grid computing) have their own distinct requirements, which can be divided into three main categories: network, computational, and timing requirements.

The main *network parameters* are the latency, bandwidth, throughput, jitter, and loss, and can even incorporate physical layer constraints, such as residual dispersion, nonlinear effects, and crosstalk. In the *computational requirements* dimension, CPU, operating system, granularity, storage, and parallelism are the critical parameters. Parallelism determines granularity and frequency of communication between programs of a single application. Dependency between programs of the same application will affect the application data (job) submission distribution approach. *Timing requirements* incorporate RTT, which is determined by the time from the point of job request until the end for the job process. Furthermore, resource discovery time and priority also represent the timing requirements. The classes of services defined based on computational requirements (CR), network requirements (NR) and timing requirements (TR) should support any type of application requiring access to distributed resources interconnected with optical network.

Clearly, a good understanding of the burst generation process, that is, the burst assembly algorithms implemented at edge nodes, is crucial in determining meaningful network performance measures and further designing and engineering an OBS network supporting distributed computing applications[50]. For instance, the size characteristics of optical bursts clearly impact on the probability of finding available time slots at intermediate nodes at which bursts can be scheduled. Also, the design of the burst assembly algorithm determines the level of link utilization. Typically, the process of burst assembly, often referred to as "burstification," follows one of the following policies: size-based [261], time-based [75], and mixed-based [31]. The first strategy consists of generating fixed-size bursts, thus gathering input packets until such targeted burst size is reached. On the other hand, time-based algorithms assemble input packets for a certain amount of time, which is controlled by a given assembly timer and generates the optical burst only when such timer expires. Finally, the mixed-based policy combines the two strategies above and generates the optical burst as soon as the time or the size constraint is met, whichever occurs first.

5.2.5 Control Plane Issues and Transport Protocols in OBS Network Supporting Distributed Computing Applications

Distributed applications such as Grid computing are currently moving from a dedicated local area network (LAN) scenario, where all the network resources are under the customer control, to a wide area network (WAN) scenario, where heterogeneous applications share the same network resources and the QoS connectivity is not guaranteed [223]. In such an environment the Grid middleware needs to be enhanced with network awareness capability to take under control the resources of network infrastructure, in particular QoS-enabled connectivity [12].

Grid middleware currently implements network awareness capability using the informative services provided by IP-based applications probes (e.g., Ping, Traceroute, or Pathchar) or using executive services that allocate network resources by increasing the active application sessions (e.g., GridFTP) [13]. Within the grid high performance networking research group (GHPN-RG) in global grid forum (GGF), the formalization of these operating approaches is ongoing by introduction of a specification of Grid services, named Grid network services (GNSs), which combined with other Grid services allow Grid application to gain network awareness capability. Example of GNSs are the network information and monitoring service (NIMS) that provides up-to-date information on the Grid network status, and the data transport service with network quality of service (DTSNQoS) that establishes QoS-enabled link connections among Grid Nodes [42].

The service oriented automatic switched transport network (SO-ASTN), presented in [151], was introduced in order to enhance the ASTN architecture with a middleware, named SP. By composing the connectivity services offered by the ASTN control plane (CP), the SP provides technology-independent network services with a level of abstraction suitable for being invoked by applications. Accordingly, applications can request network services without going through the details of the metro/core network infrastructure. In case of Grid applications, the GNSs can dynamically invoke network services to designated service nodes unburdening the Grid middleware about any technology details or actual topology of network infrastructure.

A component to be inserted in the currently proposed NIMS is the topology discovery service (TDS) presented in [256]. The TDS is a Grid network service that, similar to the network capability discovery service, provides either the Grid users or the Grid middleware with a snapshot of the current Grid network infrastructure status. The status is defined through different TE parameters, such as node adjacency at different network layers, bandwidth, and latency.

Upon collection of network status information the next key issue to be addressed for providing Grid-based application connectivity services is the choice of the most suitable connection granularity. Applications with diverse network requirements might need the deployment of optical circuit switching (OCS) paths (long-lived wavelength paths) or OBS (short-lived bandwidth reservations). For this purpose a common control plane for the hybrid OPS/OBS network architecture can be implemented through the integration of GMPLS control plane and OBS signaling . In addition, means for evaluating the most suitable connection granularity as a function of the application requirements and of the connection setup latency must be provided. A possible solution is represented by the insertion of a decision box at the network edge nodes to choose the most suitable switching granularity. Only edge nodes are allowed to choose the switching granularity based on the collected network status and application requirements. The edge node architecture is depicted in Fig. 5.3.

The decision box controls the buffer where upper layer packets are stored and assembled, the switching fabric, and the control protocol for resource reservation in the case of OCS and OBS. A more detailed functional description of the decision box is provided in Fig. 5.4.

The decision box is present in any edge node. It collects application requirements and characteristics (e.g., minimum latency) and network status and characteristics (e.g., network load). Based on the collected information it decides the switching

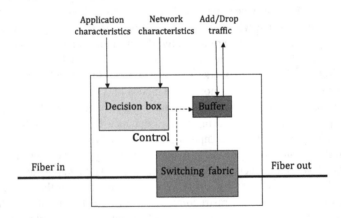

Fig. 5.3 Edge node structure

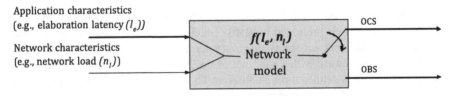

Fig. 5.4 Decision box

granularity to be utilized to transmit packets belonging to a specific application. This allows for dynamically choosing the switching granularity most suitable to a specific application under a particular network status. The choice is based on the computation of function $f(l_e, n_l)$, where l_e is the elaboration latency and n_l is the network load, for instance. The function $f(l_e, n_l)$ is based on OCS and OBS models. Several models are available in the literature to be used in the decision box [52, 122, 200, 215, 270]. The models are utilized to obtain a specific parameter, for example, the delay in delivering a communication from source to destination, given, for example, the network load. The obtained value is compared with the application request and the most suitable switching granularity is then chosen.

Finally, the utilized transport protocol might impact grid-based application performance. In networks in which the bandwidth delay product is large, the file transfer protocol (FTP) protocol, which is based on TCP, shows low efficiency. Novel transport protocols such as GridFTP have been proposed to improve file transfer performance [231]. The joint choice of transport protocol and connection granularity represents an issue yet to be solved and its optimization might potentially improve network performance.

5.3 Advanced OBS Network Scenarios and Their Specific Implementations

This section describes three different OBS network scenarios and their specific implementations with ability to support advanced network services for distributed applications.

5.3.1 Wavelength-Routed OBS Network for Grid Computing Applications

The WR-OBS deploys two-way resource reservation mechanism and a centralized control unit in the core network, which deals with all resource requests from all of the edge nodes [52]. Evidently, centralized control WR-OBS needs a powerful control unit to make a decision as to all the wavelength requests [53]. Also, in order to make accurate response to real-time resource requests, it is necessary to distribute all of the real-time resource information to the centralized control unit. These two factors confine scalability of the WR-OBS network to centralized control.

Distributed control wavelength-routed OBS (DWR-OBS), whose concept comes from the centralized control WR-OBS, however, solves this problem by the distributed control mechanism. Clearly, employing the distributed control mechanism, makes it unnecessary to keep the powerful centralized control node and distribute real-time information to it, which makes up a more feasible and scalable network.

5.3.1.1   Applying Grid Application in WR-OBS

In this section centralized control WR-OBS and distributed control wavelength-routed OBS (DWR-OBS) mechanisms are united and a novel network architecture for Grid application is proposed as shown in Fig. 5.5. In this architecture the functionality of edge router and core router is enhanced and the control plane is extended. An edge Grid-OBS router must be able to fulfill Grid application requirements and make efficient use of network resources, that is, the edge router should act as not only a Grid user network (GUNI) but also Grid resource network interface (GRNI). Furthermore, in the proposed architecture the edge router is a key part of local virtualized organization (VO), where all local Grid resource will be registered there.

Electronic processing of burst control packet at core node enables core node to offer Grid protocol layer functionalities such as resource discovery and security. In the control plane, a hierarchy for Grid resource management is introduced with respect Grid functionality. The Grid resource management hierarchy of the network is shown in Fig. 5.6. The edge routers are layer one node, which manages all Grid resources of local VO. The edge router will report local Grid resource status to the connected core routers in a timely, which form the layer 2 node. Also layer 2 nodes will report information to layer 3 nodes. As a special kind of Grid resource, bandwidth status is also reported from the lower layer to the higher one.

The workflow of how a Grid job is posted to the network and how it is completed is described in detail below.

First of all, the Grid user (or application) has a computing task that cannot be reasonably met within the local VO, and so decides to post it to the core network to accelerate processing. This job is contained in one burst and it is delivered to the edge router and transformed in an optical burst, accompanied by a control packet

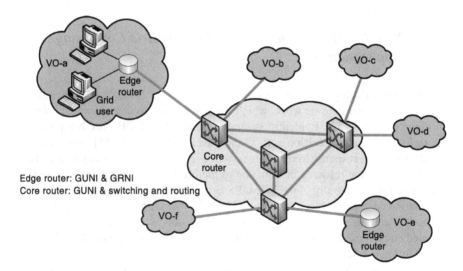

Fig. 5.5 WR-OBS network architecture for Grid application

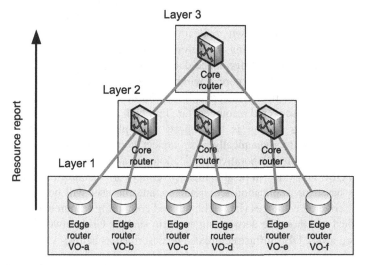

Fig. 5.6 Hierarchy for Grid resource management

indicating various resource requirements parameters. The control packet will be sent to the higher layer node unless the current node finds that this job can be completed using Grid resources that it manages. After resource discovery the corresponding node will assign an end-to-end lightpath for the corresponding data burst using fast dynamic routing and wavelength assignment algorithms. The desired bandwidth is also reserved along the lightpath by this node. After the reservation a backward control packet is generated and sent to the source edge router. Once the source edge router receives this message, the data burst can be released to the network.

After the job is completed, its result may need to be delivered. Clearly there is a distinct return address, and more traditional forwarding solutions have to be used. In that case, "normal" burst switching can be used, that is, once the current layer node finds there is enough bandwidth for the result, a lightpath will be assigned for the result transmission.

5.3.2 Application-Aware OBS Network

As collaborative network services and distributed applications evolve, it becomes unfeasible to build a dedicated network for each application type. Consequently, there should be a dynamic and application-aware network infrastructure that is able to support all application types, each with its own access and resource usage patterns. This infrastructure should offer flexible and intelligent network components able to deploy such new applications quickly and efficiently. Application-aware translates into faster and more flexible service provisioning, while optical networking offers high performance transport mechanism. The development of application-aware optical network allows future network users to construct or choose their own application-specific optical network topology and do their own traffic engineering. Therefore, such a network has the ability to dynamically provision high performance data paths to support future and emerging network applications. Furthermore, it will be able to discover network resources and nonnetwork resources based on application requirements and the user will be able to choose among discovered resources (i.e., lightpath and computing resources).

The aim of this section is to propose an application-aware OBS network infrastructure able to dynamically interconnect computing and nonnetwork resources and perform collaborative applications in a user-controlled manner. The proposed OBS network will be able to discover network resources and nonnetwork resources based on application requirements, and the user will be able to choose among discovered resources (i.e., lightpath and computing resources).

A typical collaborative networking scenario such as Grid networking using the application aware OBS infrastructure can be described as below:

1. The user/application sends the request for a service through user-network interface (edge router) by using dedicated optical bursts (namely, active burst).
2. The request is processed and distributed through the network for the resource discovery (both network and nonnetwork resources) by active core OBS routers using optical multicast or broadcast.
3. After resource discovery, an acknowledgment message determines type and identity of computing resources (processing and storage) as well as associated network resources such as allocated lightpath and the time duration that each lightpath is available.
4. Consequently the user can select among available resources to send the job (application data) by using another optical burst (namely nonactive/normal burst) through the appropriate lightpaths.
5. Once the job has been completed (data have been processed), the results have to be reported back (if there are any results for the user (sender). On the way back, based on the type of results as well as their requirements in terms of the network resources, a new path can be reserved using a new OBS signaling.

One of the advantages of this scenario is that both traditional data traffic and distributed application traffic can be supported by a common infrastructure. Core OBS routers perform burst forwarding when normal traffic transits across the network, while in addition they support transport of traffic related to collaborative services by performing advance Grid networking functionality such as resource discovery.

Central to this network scenario is deployment of active OBS routers for resource discovery and routing of the user data to the appropriate resources across the network, as shown in Fig. 5.7. An active OBS router, in addition to the burst forwarding, can intercept with data carried by some optical bursts (active bursts) and perform dedicated appellation layer functionality. It is capable of executing specific processing functions on data contained within an active burst at very high speed (wire-speed). These functions are: (1) resource requirement classification;

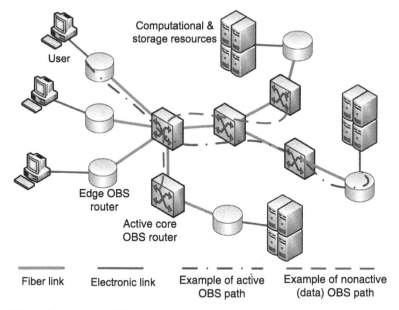

Fiber link   Electronic link   Example of active   Example of nonactive
                                              OBS path   (data) OBS path

Fig. 5.7 Application-aware OBS network architecture

(2) network requirement classification; (3) network and resource constraint policy-based classification; and (4) matchmaking between classified resource requirements and available resources. The proposed networking scheme (active OBS networking scheme) has the potential to offer global reach of computing and storage resources to a large number of anonymous users with different traffic profiles. In such a network, OBS offers efficient network resource utilization while active networking offers intelligent application layer functionality such as computing resource discovery and allocation.

For a realistic and efficient implementation of the aforementioned OBS networking scenario supporting Grid applications, a two-stage OBS networking scheme including an active stage and a nonactive stage is required. In the proposed networking scheme the resource requirement or Grid job specification is transmitted in the form of active burst prior to the actual data or Grid job (user data), which is transmitted in the form of a nonactive burst as shown in Fig. 5.8.

There are several major OBS variants differing in bandwidth reservation schemes. Among all of them, the JET is the most appropriate protocol for implementation of the proposed scenario. The JET protocol employs a delayed reservation scheme that operates as follows: An output wavelength is reserved for a burst just before the arrival of the first bit of the burst; if, upon arrival of the burst header, it is determined that no wavelength can be reserved at the appropriate time, then the burst header is rejected and the corresponding data burst is dropped. The JET is a suitable protocol for implementation of application-aware OBS network scenario in both active and nonactive network operations. The normal traffic is transmitted to

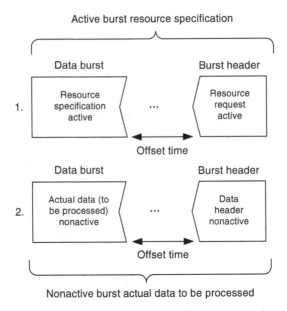

Active burst resource specification

Fig. 5.8 A complete user job/application data comprises the resource requirements burst (active) and the actual data burst (nonactive)

the network in the form of normal (nonactive) OBS packets, and active routers do not intercept with their data burst. In this mode when data are ready for transmission to the network a burst header is sent in advance to the network by the edge router and reserves the required resources across the network for the duration of the data burst. After an offset time the data burst is transmitted through the network. The traffic that needs access to remote computing resources, is transmitted in two stages as discussed above (i.e., active control info/job specification and nonactive user data/actual job). The user/application sends a request to the edge router informing about the specification and requirements for network and nonnetwork resources. The edge router then constructs and transmits the active optical burst (Fig. 5.8), for which the burst header only informs that the incoming optical burst is active. After an offset time the active burst is transmitted carrying information about the resource requirements (network and computing). With this mechanism active routers prior to arrival of the resource specification burst have been informed about the arrival of an active burst. An active router on arrival of a resource specification burst performs a resource discovery algorithm to find out whether there are available local computing resources for the job. In addition each active router multicasts both the burst header and data burst of an active burst toward the other active routers in the network.

In order to accommodate the requirements of the active network scenario, the JET scheme is modified. As mentioned before and illustrated in Fig. 5.9, data transmission is divided into two steps: (1) the active burst header is sent to all active routers through intermediate nodes (active or nonactive). After an offset time the active data burst is sent down to the network path. The result of the resource

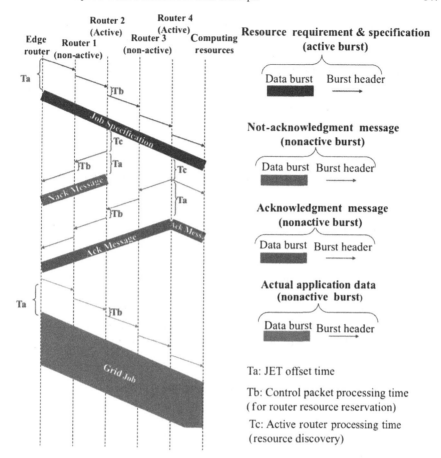

Fig. 5.9 Active OBS resource request and data transmission processes based on JET and delayed bandwidth reservation. It is assumed the network comprises four core OBS routers of which two routers are active

discovery algorithm in each active router produces an acknowledgment (ACK) or a not-acknowledgment message (NACK). These messages are transmitted back to the user after (Tc + Ta) through an optical burst (nonactive burst). In case of acknowledgement, the active OBS router also informs the corresponding resource manager. At that point the resource manager reserves the local resources for a predefined and limited duration of the time. (2) Receiving all ACK and NACK messages, the user can choose one or multiple appropriate destinations among all available resources across the network. The actual data to be processed remotely are now sent within the reservation period to the appropriate destination in normal (nonactive) optical burst format. In summary, the proposed programmable OBS network is a two-mode networking scheme where it is an active network when the resource specification or requirement is routed through the network to discover the suitable resources, and it is nonactive when actual data traffic are routed across the network. This combination provides bandwidth efficiency, especially when a large data set needs to be transferred because the actual data are submitted to the network only when both the computing resources and the network resources have been reserved. In addition it provides a secure and policy-based environment where the users have ability to choose among the available resources in different domains across the network, and, also, active routers in each domain can respond positively only to the requests that are matched with the applied policy in their corresponding domain.

5.3.3 OBS Network for Consumer-Based Grid Applications

Mainly, application requirements drive research and development of consumer Grids. As such, this section will present a use case scenario detailing current and future requirements of consumer applications. This description will be generalized into several characteristics of the job generation process. Consequently, the impact on the underlying Grid system will be discussed, and the desirable properties of the architecture will be deduced. This section will also present practical anycast routing algorithms together with an evaluation in a number of specific usage scenarios. Furthermore, an overview of possible techniques and protocols, and their improvements in the operational behavior of the consumer Grid will be discussed.

5.3.3.1 Application Drivers for Consumer Grids

In what follows, some typical application requirements are presented and their impact on the underlying Grid system are discussed. Consider a multimedia editing application; integrated audio and video manipulation programs are widely adopted and allow users to manipulate video clips, add effects, restore films, etc. Advances in recording, visualization, and effects technology will demand more computational and storage capacity, especially if the editing is to be performed within a reasonable time frame (allowing user feedback). More specifically, 1080p HDTV offers a resolution of up to $1,920 \times 1,080$ pixels, amounting to around 2 Mpixel per frame. Suppose that applying an effect requires ten floating point operations (Flop) per pixel per frame, and the user would like to evaluate the effect for ten different options; then processing a 10 s clip (25 fps) would over 50 GFlop. This will take about 5 s to complete locally, assuming local processing power is 10 GFlops. However, if service providers offer resources having a 100-fold capacity, execution time should only take 50 ms. Transmission time of 10 s of compressed HDTV video (bitrate 20 Mbps or a 25 MB file size) on a 10 Gbps access link is 20 ms. A Grid user can thus create an optical burst containing the multimedia material to be processed and hand over this burst to the network. The network is then responsible for delivering this burst to a resource with sufficient capacity. As such, important improvements in application response times can be achieved, making interactivity possible for applications that are otherwise too resource intensive. Also, observe the rather modest requirements of the Grid job for both the computational resource and the network resources, although a large number of such jobs will be generated at unpredictable times and locations in the network. Several important properties of the job generation process in consumer Grids can be identified:

- A large number of jobs are generated.
- Individual jobs have fairly modest resource requirements.
- Job sizes are quite small, usually in the order of a few megabytes. This means that network holding times are short in comparison to optical switching times. For instance, a 1 MB burst is transmitted in 0.2 ms over a 40 Gbps link, while current photonic switches have setup times in the millisecond range.
- Time and location of job submissions are highly unpredictable. This can lead to frequent mismatches in available versus generated load, indicating remote execution of jobs is a necessity.
- Several application types will be interactive in nature (e.g., immersive learning environments, haptic feedback systems, etc.), indicating a strict deadline must be met for successful completion. Other applications have different degrees of tolerance for various system parameters, which implies the existence of several QoS classes.

5.3.3.2 Resource Discovery and Reservation. Anycast Routing Protocols

Currently, deployed networks employ shortest-path routing for transferring data from source to destination. In a Grid scenario, however, a user's interest typically lies in successful job execution subject to certain predetermined requirements. Since multiple processing and/or storage locations likely exist in the network, the exact location and network route used is of less importance to the user. Anycast routing specifically enables users to transmit data for processing and delivery, without assigning an explicit destination. This approach is especially useful for delivering consumer-oriented services over an optical network to a large number of users, as centralized job scheduling and Grid status monitoring can be avoided. To enable efficient job delivery in optical grids, several routing algorithms are proposed: SAMCRA*, which is an update of the SAMCRA algorithm; maximum flow pseudo-optimal bound; and best server and best delay heuristics.

Self-adaptive multiple constraint routing algorithm (SAMCRA) is an online algorithm to determine the shortest path subject to multiple constraints [257]. Unfortunately, its traditional method of ordering subpaths (based on a nonlinear length function) can cause suboptimal results, eventually leading to routing loops. A novel path ordering, which guarantees optimality, is therefore introduced and the resulting algorithm is named *SAMCRA** [239]. Application of SAMCRA* is only possible for a unicast routing problem. Anycast routing requires the introduction of a virtual topology, consisting of a virtual resource linked to all physical resources. Each client will then route towards that virtual destination. SAMCRA* is available as a source-based, centralized algorithm, making routing decisions for the whole network on the edge routers, or as a suboptimal, distributed hop-by-hop version, executed on each participating network router. *Maximum flow* is an optimal, offline technique to determine the maximum amount of flows between a given source and destination. It essentially locates paths between source and destination with free capacity (referred to as "augmenting paths"), and routes as many flows as possible over these paths. Similar to SAMCRA, support of the anycast scenario also requires the incorporation of a virtual resource, whereby the capacity of the virtual links is proportional to the processing rate of the attached resource. In case job characteristics of individual clients (e.g., required processing capacity and average runtime) remain identical, a virtual source can be introduced in the network, together with links connecting the virtual node to the physical clients. Virtual link capacities are proportional to the job arrival rate of the attached client, and the classical, single-commodity, maximum flow algorithm can be employed. However, in case job characteristics differ between clients, a virtual client cannot be introduced and a multi-commodity, maximum flow algorithm would need to be used between all clients and the single, virtual destination. The remainder of this section only considers the single-commodity, maximum flow algorithm.

Finally, the incorporation of a deadline as job constraint causes the pseudo-optimal behaviour of the maximum flow technique. Indeed, paths violating the deadline constraint are not considered as a possible augmenting flow path, and thus the true maximum flow is not attainable. Heuristic techniques, which implement straightforward strategies for resource and path selection, are introduced for comparison purposes. First, in *best server*, the client selects the server with the highest available capacity, and uses fixed shortest-path routing to reach that server. In contrast, the client selects the server that can be reached within the smallest network delay in the *best delay* approach.

As show in Fig. 5.10, the acceptance rate of the intuitive heuristics best server and best delay is much lower than both SAMCRA* variants. When wavelengths are sparse, best delay can approach the acceptance probability of SAMCRA*s. Unfortunately, as network capacity increases, job requests are frequently scheduled

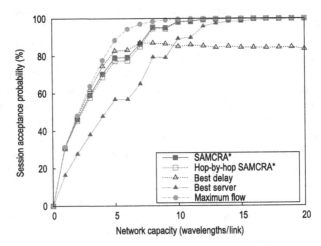

Fig. 5.10 Session acceptance probability versus network capacity for different anycast algorithms

on overloaded resources. The best server heuristic consumes too many network resources (lambdas), and therefore converges only slowly to a maximum acceptance rate for an overdimensioned network. The close match between the SAMCRA* scheduling results and the maximum flow, pseudo-optimal bound emphasizes the effectiveness of this algorithm.

5.3.3.3 Specific Requirements of Network and Control Plane: General Versus Grids over OBS

An important problem of global communication networks is the difficulty of efficiently managing such networks. Indeed, large-scale networks are generally composed of smaller subnetworks, usually referred to as *domains*. The control and management of a single domain is performed locally, and information concerning state and availability is in general not shared with other domains. Special agreements called *service level agreements* (SLAs) are usually required between different domains to create peering connections and allow transit data transfers. Problems arise for the control and management of interconnections of domains, i.e., a multi-domain network, since this domain's size and heterogeneity make it difficult to collect all information needed to make optimal management decisions. The scale of the network directly influences the number of events related to network state and availability; transferring these data to the controlling entities, and in turn processing it, can generate a considerable overhead, leading to inefficient network operation. Controlling the timing of sending the state information, together with aggregation of this information (e.g., sending average values, aggregating information of multiple network links into a single value, and so on), can significantly reduce control plane overhead. In essence, two different approaches are possible for the control of such networks, each having specific advantages and disadvantages:

- *Centralized:* A single control entity is aware of the full network and resource state of the multi-domain network. It receives all communication requests and is responsible for all scheduling decisions (i.e., when data transfer can start, which network route must be used, what level of reliability is available). The main strengths of this approach are its straightforward deployment and reconfiguration possibilities. However, this approach is not scalable for larger networks and suffers from a single point of failure.
- *Distributed:* In this case resources send updates to all clients directly, and clients individually perform the network control. An important assumption is that this approach requires total transparency between domains (which in reality is difficult to achieve). This means the number of status updates sent will increase dramatically compared to the centralized setup. An advantage of this setup is the removal of the single point of failure.

In the following an alternative to these approaches is proposed, one which tries to combine the advantages of both techniques while minimizing their respective problems.

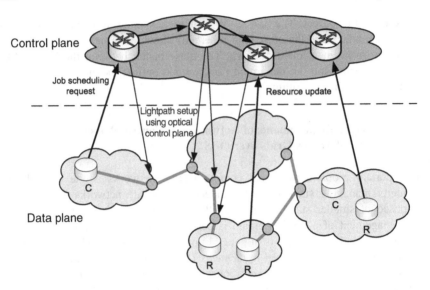

Fig. 5.11 Overview of the proxy-based anycast architecture (R = resource, C = client)

Figure 5.11 presents an overview of a proxy-based control plane. Using this approach, a resource only forwards state information to its closest proxy using anycast communications. Typically, this proxy belongs to the same domain as the resource node, and from the resource perspective it also behaves like a local scheduler. Likewise, a client who wants to submit a job to the multi-domain Grid forwards its request to the nearest proxy, also using anycast communications. Upon reception of the job request, the proxy selects the most suitable target proxy to forward the request to, such selection being based on aggregated state information of the resources connected to this proxy. We assume the proxy in the client domain will take the necessary control plane actions to set up the lightpaths for actual job transmission in the data plane. Once the job request is processed by the Grid and optical control plane, the client is notified about this and the actual job can be submitted. This approach has the following benefits:

- Increased cooperation between independent optical Grid sites due to the network and resource state distribution in aggregated form.
- Grid sites maintain their autonomy, and configuration details are not revealed.
- Control plane scalability: The intelligent state aggregation results in reduced control plane traffic.
- Flexibility in migration and deployment: Whenever a domain deploys a proxy, it can participate immediately in the multi-domain Grid network.
- Adoption of novel data transport and control plane technologies is straightforward, by adding new interfaces to the anycast proxy servers that can understand and control these new protocols.
- System-wide optimization of the Grid network is possible, e.g., minimal job blocking, global load-balanced resource utilization, etc.

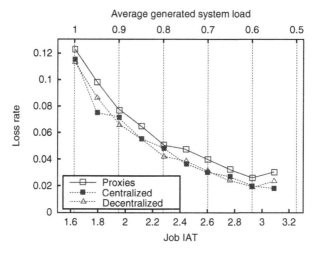

Fig. 5.12 Job loss rate for varying interarrival times (load)

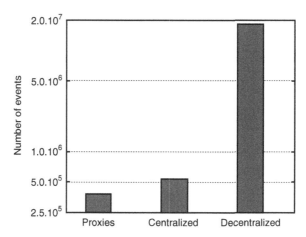

Fig. 5.13 Number of control plane events for different multi-domain routing approaches

- Support of any subset of parameters available to the routing protocol is possible, i.e., computational resource states, physical parameters of photonic network, etc.

Results for the job loss rate related to the job IAT (and corresponding average generated system load on the second axis) are depicted in Fig. 5.12. We can conclude that there is no significant difference in job acceptance rate between the three alternative approaches; the less frequent distribution of aggregated resource state by the proxy system does not prevent efficient resource allocation.

Observing the corresponding number of events generated in the simulator (Fig. 5.13) we can conclude that a proxy-based interdomain job allocation approach significantly reduces the control plane overhead, while job loss rates are comparable with those associated to the other strategies. As such, it offers a scalable solution for a growing network with an increasing number of clients and computational resources. Indeed, when proxies aggregate state for a larger number of resources, their state will be even more accurate and less volatile. At the same time, proxies prevent frequent resource update messages from propagating through the network.

Chapter 6
Optical Switch Fabrics (OSFs) and Their Application

Kyriakos Vlachos, Lambros Raptis, Antonio Teixeira, Giorgio Maria Tosi Beleffi, and Kostas Yiannopoulos

6.1 Applications of Optical Switches

6.1.1 Introduction

The core component of the different optical network elements are the optical switches, which are combined for the construction of complex switching systems, such as OXCs and OADMs. Optical switches have attracted significant attention due to these feature:

- The transparency to higher layer protocol formats they allow. Since, there is no opto-electronic (OE) conversion, thus no electronic processing of the incoming signal, there is no need to know the timing of the incoming data/bits. However, as the need for more bandwidths continues to increase, it becomes clear that current optical networks will become increasingly constrained by the need to convert optical signals into electronic form to allow the signal to be switched. For speeds beyond 10 Gbps per wavelength, optical regeneration is needed.
- Cost reduction due to the absence of OE conversion or, if this is not completely feasible, to the minimization of OE conversion.
- Lower power consumption and footprint compare to their electronic counterparts.

Generally, the term "optical switches" is not ubiquitously used, which leads to various kinds of misunderstanding when the functionality of complex optical network elements lik e OXC and optical add/drop multiplexers (OADMs) should be studied. Roughly, the following classification can be introduced [58]:

- *O/E/O network elements:* The majority of deployed network element belong to this category. Optical signals are first converted to electrical, they are then

K. Vlachos (✉)
Computer Engineering and Informatics Department, University of Patras, Greece
e-mail: kvlachos@ceid.upatras.gr

J. Aracil and F. Callegati (eds.), *Enabling Optical Internet with Advanced Network Technologies*, Computer Communications and Networks,
DOI 10.1007/978-1-84882-278-8_6, © Springer-Verlag London Limited 2009

processed and switched in the electrical domain and finally are converted to optical signals in order to be transmitted to the optical fibers.

- *Opaque network elements:* This is an evolution of the O/E/O network elements. The main difference between these elements and the O/E/O network elements is the fact that switching is performed optically, not electronically. However, electronics still exist to support auxiliary functions like performance monitoring, signal regeneration, etc.
- *All-optical network elements:* All-optical network elements process signals in the optical domain and have no electronics. The main challenges that manufacturers and researchers are facing in the construction of all-optical network elements are the lack of memory and bit processing, two major limitations of the optical technology. Size is also a significant parameter, since the large size of different prototypes does not permit the construction of compact switches. All-optical switching ensures higher throughput and less power consumption. Depending on the switching granularity, we can further differentiate an all-optical packet switch from an OXC. The former is able to perform packet-level switching whereas the latter is able to switch at coarser granularity such as wavelengths, fiber, and so on.

The structure of this chapter is the following: First we present some key performance indicators of optical switch components, which allows us to understand and compare the different optical switch technologies that are presented in the next chapter. Then, different applications of optical switches are described focusing on the two main network elements that are used in optical networks, namely optical cross connects (OXC) and optical add/drop multiplexers (OADM). Special attention is also given to the protection switching, an attribute that is the most important factor for the provided quality of service. Based on the provided material the reader should be able to understand simple and well as complex optical network topologies based on OXC and OADM nodes.

6.1.2 Key Performance Indicators and Requirements of Optical Switches

Different technologies like optical MEMS-based switch, thermal optical switch, electro-optical switch, opto-optical switch, and holographic grating switch [236] can be used for the realization of an optical switch. Each technology has its own advantages and disadvantages and not all technologies can be used for the same network applications. [144] provides an in-depth comparison of the different optical switching technologies. An overview of the different technologies is presented in Section 6.2.

Key performance indicators for evaluating different optical switches, independent from the technology are:

- *Switching time/speed:* Refers to the time needed to change the state of the switch, and therefore it is associated with the maximum supported throughput as well as the reconfiguration rate of the devices.
- *Signal quality:* In general, optical switches are deployed to work in a specific band and for a specific bit rate. Outside of this band and/or for higher values of the bit rate, the quality of the switching with respect to crosstalk, loss, dispersion, and polarization mode dispersion (PMD) may be significantly reduced. This is called *performance variation due to parameter sensitivity.* The most significant parameters are:
  - *Insertion loss.* This refers to the signal power that is lost due to the switch. Ideally, the insertion loss should be the same for all the sets of input-output connections.
  - *Crosstalk.* Crosstalk is generated when signals following one path through the switch leak power to another path through the switch.
  - *Polarization-dependent loss (PDL).* If the loss of the switch is not equal for both states of polarization of the optical signal, the switch is said to have polarization-dependent loss. It is desirable that optical switches have low PDL.

- *Reliability:* Due to the vast amount of traffic every link carries, any fault in the network can disrupt the service of millions of end users. Existing telecommunication networks offer high reliability (99.999% uptime) and thus redundancy of switch paths inside a fabric, redundancy of switch fabrics, and of switches as a whole may be needed to provide sufficient reliability.
- *Size and power:* This refers to their size and power consumption, which should both be comparable to that of their electronic counterparts.
- *Temperature:* This refers to cooling requirements.

For example, an optical switch should be capable of switching an optical signal faster than electronic switches do; the insertion loss and crosstalk should be kept at levels that do not disturb the quality of service (less than $-40\,dB$) and it should be wavelength-independent. All the previous parameters are interdependent and the performance of all the optical switches of every optical network element affects the whole optical network. Therefore, from a network element perspective, designers should take into consideration all these parameters in order to produce an optical network element/node with characteristics like:

- *Nonblocking:* The nonblocking attribute refers to the capability of the switch to reroute any input channel to an output free/unoccupied channel.
- *Switching dimension:* This parameter is associated with the switching capacity of the optical switch, depending on the position of the optical switch in the network. The switching dimension is also related to scalability, which is a significant attribute when large switches must be constructed from smaller ones.
- *Stability/reliability:* Since existing networks carry a vast amount of traffic, the stability of the optical switches is extremely important. Stay should take into account different environmental requirements like temperature variations, humidity, vibrations, etc.

- *Power consumption:* Power consumption should be kept as low as possible in order to minimize the system's cost and the required cooling system.

Optical switches serve optical networking efficiency in many different domains. The main applications of optical switches are [211]:

- *Fast provisioning:* Optical cross connects use optical switches as a means to set up/tear down or reconfigure lightpaths/channels. Such functionality allows the replacement of fiber patch panel with intelligent network elements, which transform optical transport network (OTN) into intelligent automatic switched optical network (ASON) [114].
- *Packet switching:* Although OTN follows the approach of connection-oriented technologies, advances into optical packet switching technology allow the switching of data at 10 Gbps line rate. Such rates require switching times on the order of ns.
- *Protection switching:* In case of a link failure, traffic should be switched from the primary link/fiber to a backup link/fiber in less than 50 ms. Taking into consideration the fact that it takes some time to detect the fault and notify the adjustment nodes, optical switch components should be capable of switching the traffic in less than 50 ms time.

Having defined optical switch applications as well as the parameters used to characterize a switch, the following guidelines can be used for evaluating the switches for a certain application:

- Identification of the application's minimum requirements with regard to the switching time. Not all switches are suitable for all applications.
- The maximum port number of the switch, possibly using the higher order architectures described in Section 6.1.3, determines its scalability in size.
- Comparison of the crosstalk characteristics for any chosen architecture. The influence of optical transmission impairments should be taken into account, as this gives the scalability with respect to number of nodes in the network.
- Comparison of the uniformity of loss characteristics (wavelength dependency).
- Evaluation of power consumption.
- Evaluation of cost. It should be noted that the price of the final optical switch product would depend largely on the fabrication volume since mass–scale production can reduce the cost.

In the following sections we examine in more detail the most important applications of optical switches, namely optical cross-connect (OXC), optical switching, and optical add/drop multiplexers (OADM).

6.1.3 Optical Cross-Connects (OXCs)

OXCs are emerging as the fundamental building block of a seamless optical transport network with distributed intelligence, automated circuit provisioning, and rapid time-to-service being the main characteristics to be addressed. OXC are the descendents of traditional digital cross-connects (DXC) and are used for the implementation of complex mesh topologies with a large number of lambdas/wavelengths carried per fiber.

OXCs are used particularly at hub locations handling a large number of fibers. The importance of OXCs today and in future optical networks is continuously increasing since OXCs are the basic elements for routing, grooming, and optimizing transmission paths.

6.1.3.1   Reference Architecture of Small OXC

Depending on the granularity that OXCs operate, they can be classified into the following categories:

- *Fiber switching OXC:* The OXC simply links fibers according to the network needs. The design of this OXC contains an optical space switch that is capable of interconnecting different fiber pairs.
- *Lambda switching OXC:* Such OXCs are more advanced compared to the fiber switching-capable OXC, allowing the switching of different wavelengths/lambdas from one fiber to the other one. Such OXCs are based on more complex and complicated architectures using tunable/selectable filters and advanced optical space switching mechanisms.
- *Wavelength conversion OXC:* This is the most complicated and most expensive OXC, but it offers however, the greatest degree of flexibility in terms of network design and provisioning. Wavelength conversion OXC permits the switching of different lambdas/wavelengths to the same fiber, even if two of more of the switched lambdas are using the same lambda/wavelength. Such functionality is feasible by converting the same lambdas into different ones. When in an optical transport network there are no wavelength conversion OXCs, wavelength routing is an extremely complicated and costly procedure.

Figure 6.1 depicts a simplified diagram of the three previous categories of OXC. By mixing different components like multiplexers/demultiplexers and optical switches large OXCs can be constructed. The simple case is a fixed nonconfigurable OXC in which each wavelength of every input port/fiber is always cross-connected/routed to the same output port/fiber. Such OXC uses only multiplexers and demultiplexers (Fig. 6.2).

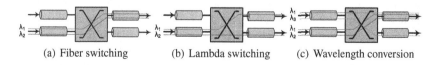

(a) Fiber switching   (b) Lambda switching   (c) Wavelength conversion

Fig. 6.1 Simplified Diagram of a 2 × 2 OXC structures

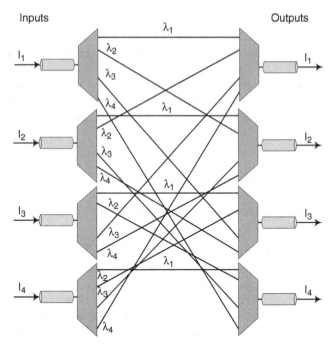

Fig. 6.2 Block diagram of a 4 × 4 nonconfigurable OXC

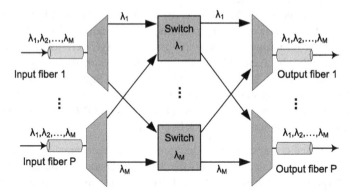

Fig. 6.3 Block diagram of a P × P lambda OXC

Wavelength conversion OXC is an extension of lambda switching OXC, where wavelength conversion functionality is added. There are different flavors of wavelength conversion OXC, depending on the number and the positioning of the wavelength converters (WCs) into the OXC architecture. Figure 6.4 illustrates the simplest case of a dedicated wavelength conversion OXC. The use of both multiplexers/demultiplexers as well as of 2 × 2 optical switches allows the creation of a P × P lambda switching OXC (see Fig. 6.3).

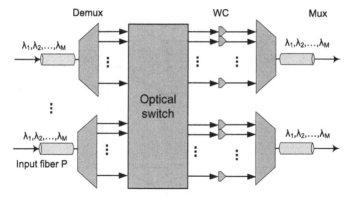

Fig. 6.4 Block diagram of a 2 × 2 wavelength conversion OXC

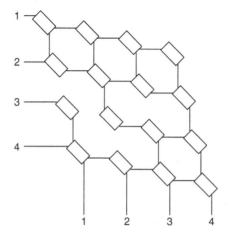

Fig. 6.5 Crossbar architecture

6.1.3.2   Reference Architecture of Large OXCs

Large OXCs are constructed by combining many 2 × 2 optical switches in different architectures [189]:

- *Crossbar architecture:* The crossbar architecture has a 2 × 2 optical switch at each of the N^2 junctions between an input row and an output column, as illustrated in Fig. 6.5. The architecture is wide sense nonblocking, meaning that blocking can be avoided with an intelligent routing strategy in the fabric. The disadvantage of the crossbar architecture is the high component count. It scales with the number of input ports as N^2.

- *Benes architecture:* The Benes architecture (see Fig. 6.6) is an efficient architecture in terms of the 2 × 2 optical switches that are needed. Any N × N Benes

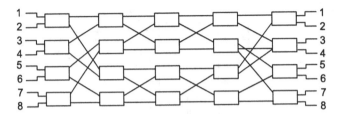

Fig. 6.6 Benes architecture

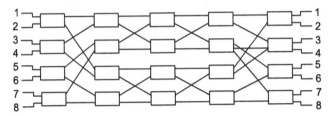

Fig. 6.7 Spanke–benes architecture

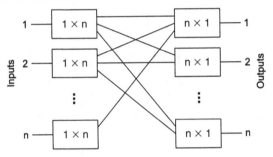

Fig. 6.8 Spanke architecture

switch requires $(N/2)$ $(2\log_2 N - 1)2 \times 2$ optical switches. The main issues with this architecture include that it is not wide-sense nonblocking and that a number of waveguide crossovers are required.

- *Spanke–benes:* This it is a combination of the two previous architectures. The Spanke–Benes architecture (see Fig. 6.7) requires $N(N - 1)/2$ switches. Spanke-Benes architecture alleviates the need for waveguide crossovers, but it is not wide-sense nonblocking.

- *Spanke:* The Spanke architecture allows the reduction of the required optical switches since it uses only free space $1 \times N$ and $N \times 1$ switches. The number of the required optical switches increases linearly with the port count. Additionally, each connection only passes through two switch elements, which allows for low loss. Figure 6.8 depicts an example of the Spanke architecture.

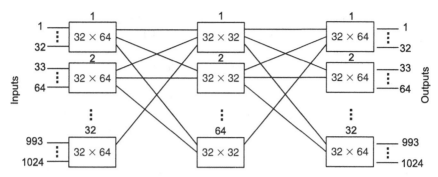

Fig. 6.9 Clos architecture

- *Clos:* Clos architecture is based on the crossbar architecture. The Clos architecture separates the switch into a number of stages, with every stage consisting of a number of crossbar switches. Figure 6.9 depicts an example of the Clos architecture. Clos switches are strict-sense nonblocking.

6.1.4 Protection Switching

Network survivability is nowadays an important characteristic of telecommunication networks. Although the term is quite generic, it is used to describe all the mechanisms that are used in order to recover a network from node and/or link failures. Two main categories of recovery mechanisms can be identified: protection and restoration. *Protection* reserves in advance backup paths, which can be used in the case of a failure. Protection is faster and simpler than restoration. However resources are wasted to protect the working paths. Protection is usually the vanguard of the recovery mechanisms. On the contrary, *restoration* dynamically searches for new paths in order to reroute the working ones. Restoration is slower and more complex compared to protection. Restoration is the second line of the recovery mechanisms.

The establishment of the Synchronons digital hierarchy (SDH) technology as the dominant transport technology has introduced some de facto standards in network recovery schemes. Therefore, it is logical that the proposed recovery mechanisms of the optical layer are based on the same concepts as the SDH recovery [109]. A short description of the available mechanisms for recovery in optical networks, classified according to topology, is the following [181]:

- *Linear topology:* For linear configuration there are the following protection schemes at the optical channel (OCh) and optical multiplex section (OMS) layer: 1 + 1 protection, 1:1 protection, 1:N protection and M:N protection.
- *Ring topology:* There are mainly two basic mechanisms for protection in WDM rings. The main difference between is them granularity. The fine-grained approach (OChDPRing, OChSPRing) is applied on an optical channel basis, while

the coarse-grained approach (OMSDPRing, OMSSPRing) is applied on the optical multiplexing section. The difference between DPRing and SPRing is in the consumed backup resources. In the DPRing approach there is a 1:1 mapping between the working and the backup resources. In the SPRing, N working resources are protected by 1 shared backup resource.

- *Mesh topology:* The recovery mechanisms in mesh topologies are based on the generalization of the SPRing approach. There are many proposals in the literature (protection cycles, optical path protection). The reader is referred to [59, 65] for more information about restoration/protection in mesh OTN networks.

Despite the plethora of recovery mechanisms, in the majority of optical networks 1 + 1 OCh protection and 1 + 1 OMS protection are used [76]. It seems that network operators are reluctant to deploy more sophisticated recovery mechanisms in the optical layer, relying instead on the client networks like SDH or IP/MPLS when more sophisticated mechanisms are needed. When the granularity of the offered optical services becomes finer, all optical protection schemes in mesh topologies will be gradually adopted. In the next paragraph we elaborate more on 1 + 1 OCh and OMS recovery mechanisms.

Dedicated protection schemes rely predominantly on 1×2 and 2×2 optical switching components achieving protection switching on the order to 10 ms [7]. The OChDPRing scheme is based on head end permanent signal bridging to provide a receiver-based protection that protects the signal at the path/channel layer. This scheme requires almost no protection signaling between the two nodes. Similarly, in the OMSDPRing scheme protection is performed at the optical multiplexing layer. OMSDPRing is implemented by performing fiber loopback switching at the node adjacent to the failure. Those two recovery mechanisms are based on the capability to split the optical signal of the input channel between several output channels, controlling at the same time the ration of optical energy splitting. Such a feature is part of optical switches, which can energetically split the input channel to several output channels through an externally controlled dynamic process. This feature, which is feasible in the latest optical switch implementations, makes those recovery schemes applicable to interconnected rings as well as various mesh architectures. Finally, it should be noted that large OXCs, which consist of switch fabric with large port count, are achieving switching between 50 ms and 100 ms, which may exceed the 50 ms of SDH however, this is still acceptable.

6.1.5 Optical Add/Drop Multiplexing

SDH add/drop multiplexers (ADM) have been widely deployed and almost all existing SDH networks use ADMs. Such systems are used especially in metropolitan area networks (MANs) where ring topologies are the most common architecture. They provide the necessary functionality to add/drop N SDH signals, i.e., 4 STM-1, multiplex them and transmit to a single optical fiber. Similarly, optical add drop multiplexers OADMs are providing the necessary functionality to add/drop N lambdas,

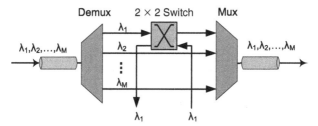

Fig. 6.10 A simplified fix wavelength optical add/drop multiplexer

which are then multiplexed into a single fiber. Figure 6.10 depicts a simplified optical add drop multiplexers (OADM) block diagram. The OADM receives N different lambdas from a single fiber. After de-multiplexing the different lambdas, it selectively drops/removes one lambda (i.e., lambda-1), adds new data within the same lambda, and multiplexs again all lambdas in order to be transmitted into a single fiber. In general, OADM have two types of ports: *tributary ports*, which add/drop new wavelengths, and *aggregation ports*, which receive/transmit the traffic from/into the optical fiber.

With respect to the number of wavelengths that can be added/dropped or translated, OADMs can be classified into the following three categories:

- *Fixed OADMs*: These provide no or low reconfigurable add-drop functionality.
- *Reconfigurable optical add drop Multiplexers (ROADM)*: These offer wavelength routing functionality in the sense that some wavelengths can be dynamically directed to the output.
- *Reconfigurable and wavelength-translating OADM*: These provide fully reconfigurable routing functionalities.

6.1.6 OADM architectures

From an architectural point of view the deployment of OADM can be classified into the following categories:

- *Parallel OADM architecture*: In parallel OADM architecture all lambdas are separated and multiplexed back. This architecture is not very cost-effective when the number of dropping lambdas is small (Fig. 6.11). Parallel OADMs are easy to manage but often have a high insertion (add–delete) loss. A modified version of the parallel architecture is one consisting of many stages, adding and dropping a band of lambdas at each stage. This approach is more scalable when the numbers of channels become large.

- *Cascade OADM architecture*: In cascade OADM architecture, all lambdas are dropped and added one at a time (Fig. 6.12).

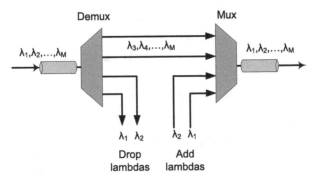

Fig. 6.11 Parallel OADMs

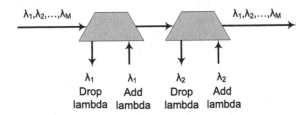

Fig. 6.12 Cascade OADMs

6.1.7 ROADM

A reconfigurable add/drop multiplexer (ROADM) is a remotely reconfigurable version of an OADM allowing fast provisioning. Despite the different variations for implementing an reconfigurable optical add drop multiplexers (ROADM), there are two major architectures: the wavelength blocker (WB) architecture [265], which is the most widely deployed, and the wavelength selective switch (WSS), architecture [49, 265]. In the WB architecture, the incoming multi-lambda signal is split over a drop and a pass-through path. Pass-through signal traverses a wavelength blocker module that is used to block the dropped lambdas and power balance the rest of them before the added lambdas are inserted. In the WSS architecture the incoming multi-lambda signal is directed to the WSS, which is capable of redirecting a lambda to one or more output ports.

6.1.8 Summary/Conclusions

Optical transport networks are gradually evolving from a simple point-to-point transmission system to a unified intelligent optical layer providing features like rapid end-to-end provisioning of optical connections, efficient utilization of network resources, fast recovery mechanism, advance OAM mechanisms, and ease of management. OXC and OADM are playing a key role for the deployment of such networks and therefore the evolution of optical network elements functionality affects the features of optical networks. In that respect, optical switches, which are the building blocks of OXC and OADM, have drawn significant attention both by the research community and the industry. This chapter discusses the main applications of optical switches focusing mainly on OXC and OADM. By reviewing and characterize different system architectures, we provide a better understanding of the complexity of existing commercial and experimental optical network elements.

6.2   Optical Switching Fabrics (OSFs) Technologies for Transparent OXC Matrix

An optical switch may operate by mechanical means, such as physically shifting an optical fiber to drive one or more alternative output fibers or by other effects occurring in some material under some conditions (e.g., acousto-optic, electro-optic, magneto-optic, etc.). From these technologies several types of switches have been developed and studied. Switches are mainly grouped in two classes for considering the base-building technology: *free space* and *guided wave*. The first class, free space, encompasses devices that perform switching by working on optical free space collimated beams. Examples of this technology are: MEMS (micro electrical mechanical systems), liquid crystals, electroholography-based devices or ESBG (electrically switchable bragg gratings). In the other group, guided wave, switching is performed recurring to effects occurring in the waveguides; from these are examples: thermo-optic, electro-optic, acousto-optic, gel/oil-based, semiconductor optical amplifier (SOA) and ferromagnetic devices [189,196]. These two classes are schematically presented in Fig. 6.13.

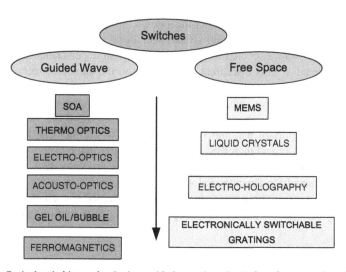

Fig. 6.13 Optical switching technologies: guided wave-based switches; free space-based switches

Usually in free-space to guided wave comparison the latter shows increased losses, but higher switching speeds. Therefore, when chooses a switching technology, a compromise should be reached between these two parameters, loss and speed. Slow optical switches, such as those using moving fibers, may be used for alternate routing of an optical transmission path, such as routing around a fault, which is called restoration and protection. Fast optical switches, such as those using electro-optic or magneto-optic effects, may be used to perform logic operations and bit length switching as optical time division multiplexing /demultiplexing (OTDM). When evaluating the performance of different optical switches, there are several parameters one needs to consider, e.g., switching time, reliability, energy usage, port configurations and scalability, optical insertion loss, crosstalk, extinction ratio, temperature resistance, polarization-dependent loss characteristics, and cost. The requirements on these parameters are different and depend on the final applications.

Optical cross-connect, protection switches, OADM, optical signal monitors (OSM), and network provisioning are some of the applications where switches are the core. In these scenarios, switching time, for example, is one of the crucial parameters to be considered. Switches for inline provisioning—existing inside wavelength cross-connects are used to reconfigure or accommodate new lightpaths, allowing rapid management of connections across a network. For these applications switching time on the order of milliseconds to seconds are needed. Along the same line is protection switching, where the traffic stream must be switched into a secondary fiber if the primary one fails. For SDH/SONET compatibility several tens of ms are required (up to 50 ms). An opposite example is optical packet or burst switching (OPS/OBS) where switching time requirements are set to a few picoseconds in order to be significantly shorter than the packet duration [199]. Insertion loss is another crucial requirement that must be carefully considered. Device losses add to fiber losses and only an efficient scheme and packaging can help lower the total network losses. This reflects directly in network costs related to extra amplification needed, as well as the need (or not) for regeneration. The losses should be kept low especially in the switching fabrics, since in topologies where many will cascade, signal-to-noise ratio (SNR) will decay. Installed equipment has to be reliable, therefore, expected to behave without visible performance degradation for several decades. This has direct implications in the choice of technologies for places of difficult accessibility. One general example is any equipment with moving parts is expected to have some degradation dependent on the usage (e.g., MEMS in very active reconfigurable nodes). Energy consumption of the switching fabric is also a very important parameter, especially due to the fact that the density of devices is increasing and therefore advanced power dissipation schemes need to be used in order not to disrupt the function of the switch or accelerate the aging. Many technologies have been developed along the years. Each has its own limitations and benefits, and based on these, they are more or less adapted to each of the functions. A summary of actual technologies and applications is presented in Table 6.1.

Table 6.1 Summary of the main characteristics of some of the available technologies

Technology	Advantages	Disadvantages	Applications
Moving fiber	Low loss and low crosstalk	Long switching and stabilizing time, poor scalability	Protection, OADMs
MEMS	Small size	Low reliability due to moving parts	Large OXC
Bubble	Easy to integrate	Long switching time (down to 10 ms), limited reliability, high power consumption	Protection/restoration, OADM, medium OXC
Thermo-optic	Easy to integrate	Long switching times, high loss and crosstalk, high power consumption	Protection/restoration, OADM, medium OXC
Liquid crystal	Good reliability	Temperature-dependent slow switching time (ms)	Protection/restoration, small OXC and OADM
Electro-optic	Fast switching	Medium loss and high crosstalk Polarization-dependent and poor scalability	Protection/restoration, OADM, packet/burst
Acousto-optic	Flexible switching	Medium loss and complexity	Protection/restoration, small OXC and OADM
Electro holography	Highly flexible and (possible) built in wavelength demultiplexing	Medium loss and high power	Protection/restoration, Small OXC and OADM
SOA	Fast switching, gain amplification	Noise addition, actually moderately expensive	Protection/restoration, OADM, packet or bust switching

6.2.1   Opto-Mechanical Technology—Moving Fiber

This technology was the first commercially available for optical switching, namely for the basic functions of protection and restoration. In opto-mechanical switches, the switching function is performed by some mechanical means. These means include prisms, mirrors, and directional couplers. Mechanical switches exhibit low insertion losses, low polarization-dependent loss, low crosstalk, and low fabrication cost. Their switching speeds are on the order of milliseconds, which may not be acceptable for some types of applications. Another disadvantage is the lack of scalability. Opto-mechanical switches are mainly used in fiber protection and very-low-port-count wavelength add/drop applications, whose summary is presented in Table 6.2 [196].

Table 6.2 Summary of the characteristics of the opto-mechanical switches

Scalability	Switching speed	Reliability	Losses	Port-to-port repeatability	Cost	Power consumption
2D medium 3D high	Tens of milliseconds	Moderate	Few dB	High for small switches, moderate for big switches	Medium	Medium

6.2.2 Micro-Electro-Mechanical System Devices (MEMS)

Micro-electrical mechanical machines (MEMS) are switching elements principally based on silicon wafer and mirrors. MEMS working principle is simple. The light is switched from one input fiber to another by routing the light with the help of a mirror whose reflectivity can be increased by highly reflective coating deposition. For this reason, the switch itself is wavelength transparent. If a wavelength-switched matrix is needed filtering must be added to the waveguides or accessing fibers. It is possible to distinguish between two MEMS configurations: two-dimensional (2-D) and three-dimensional (3-D) MEMS [92, 166, 189, 196]. 3-D MEMS have reflecting surfaces that pivot on axes to guide the light, while 2-D MEMS have reflective surfaces that "pop up" and "lie down" to redirect the light beam. In 2-D MEMS, the mirror position is bistable (that means ON or OFF), and are commonly referred to as *digital MEMS*. The basic principle is sketched in Fig. 6.14 [189]. The activation of a mirror redirects the light beams, which are propagating parallel to the substrate, to one of the outputs due to the 45° angle. On the other hand, leaving the mirror in an "off" state, the beam will simply propagate in an undistorted. This switch can be used to implement in the same device add/drop functionalities [189]. In 3-D MEMS, there is a dedicated movable mirror for each input and each output port, like that shown in Fig. 6.15. The path inside the switching matrix is setup by tilting two mirrors independently to redirect the light from an input port to a selected output port.

Each mirror must be able to redirect a beam from each input/output port, needing therefore analogue moving capability. Careful placing of the mirrors is important to minimize the distance between ports. This approach is promising for very-large-port-count switches with more than 500 input and output ports. The problems arise from the complexity in the feedback system necessary to maintain the mirror position or to stabilize the insertion losses, due to environmental effects. Also, for high port counts, due to the density and microscopic size of the lightpaths entering and exiting the substrate, the packaging becomes quite complex and expensive. The switching mirror capability can be implemented by adopting electrostatic, electromagnetic, or thermal forces. Electrostatic actuation is the preferred force due to its ease of fabrication and the extremely low-power dissipation, and it is based on the attraction of oppositely charged mechanical elements. If magnetic forces are used, the principle will be the attraction of the moving parts by one or more electromagnets.

Fig. 6.14 2-D MEMS device concept

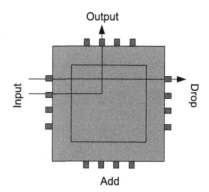

Fig. 6.15 3D MEMS concept

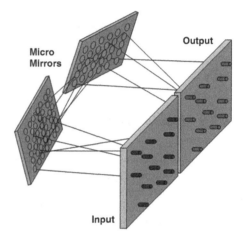

In this case, the fabrication process is more complex and an electromagnetic shield is needed; but the benefit is a large attractive or/and repulsive linear force, [189]. In terms of optical insertion losses and switching speed, performance characteristics of optomechanical switches vary according to architecture. The optical losses in 2-D MEMS increase with the port count. Furthermore, constraints on collimator performance and mirror alignment tolerance, due to the light beam diameter growth, and path dependent time jitter must be taken into account. Therefore, high port count numbers are not suitable for 2-D MEMS. Three-dimensional MEMS are more suitable for high port count switches due to the freedom of the analogue technology of the mirrors, which allow high flexibility. The drawbacks of this technology are related to life cycle limitation of the mechanical actuators and also the sensitivity to the mechanical vibrations. Despite these limitations, many of these switches are already commercially available and are used in real switching matrices. A summary of the main characteristics is presented in Table 6.3 [92, 166, 189, 196].

Table 6.3 Summary of the characteristics of the MEMS switches

Scalability	Switching speed	Reliability	Losses	Port-to-port repeatability	Cost	Power consumption
2D medium 3D high	Tens of milliseconds	moderate	Few decibels	High for small switches, moderate for big switches	Medium	Medium

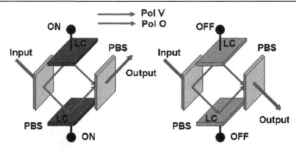

Fig. 6.16 Switching concept based on liquid crystals (LC)

6.2.3 Liquid Crystal Switches

Liquid crystal switches also recur to free space optics to perform switching [92,189]. The most common type of liquid crystal switch has a working principle based on polarization rotation of light by its reflection in a liquid crystal. In these switches the light is split into the two polarizations, which will be then reflected separately in the liquid crystal cells. The liquid crystal cell can be operated by voltage, and can be either bistable or monostable, requiring in both conditions a driving voltage that will cause the cell to behave differently, and rotate or not the polarization of the incident light. In the case where the two previously separated polarization beams are simply reflected in the cells, the output will be combined in a polarization beam combiner and follow the through port. If there is the polarization rotation in the cells, the light will be then deflected in the other direction by the polarization beam combiner. Due to space optics, stability of vibrations can be an issue; however, since there are no moving parts, as long as the temperature issues are handled to allow some stable working conditions, the switch can be considered stable and robust. As mentioned depending on the type of liquid crystal and scheme used, the operation of these switches can be bistable, requiring in this situation only a voltage be switched, or they can be monostable, requiring the voltage be present for all "on" time. Due to the principle behind this technology, liquid crystal switches can also be used as variable attenuators since one can vary in an analogue way the rotation induced in the polarization of light (see Fig. 6.16).

The benefits of liquid crystal technology for optical switch applications include high reliability and lack of moving parts; however, these structures can be affected by temperatures if not properly designed. These characteristic are optimal for low-port-count optical switching in protection, restoration, channel monitoring, and configurable add/drop multiplexing applications. A summary of liquid crystal technology characteristics is presented in Table 6.4 [166].

6.2.4 Bubble Switches

Index-matching gel-and oil-based optical switches can be classified under thermo-optical technology due to the induced heating and cooling needed for the switching process to occur. The presence of a bubble, which is moved by heating or cooling, will create an index matching the existing light guides, resulting in a redirection of the light stream to the desired port [71,92,189]. Two technologies are typically used to achieve bubble switching: a planar lightwave circuit (PLC) with optical waveguides written, and ink jet technology. Instead of using an air bubble to drop an ink tear on a paper sheet, as is done in standard printers, in this case the light is deflected due to the index change caused by the presence or absence of the bubble. The planar waveguides intersect ducts filled with a liquid having the same refractive index as the glass. Microheaters placed on the top of these structures heat the liquid close to the evaporation point, generating a bubble that modifies the refractive index in the duct. The light traveling in the silica waveguides is refracted when it encounters a liquid bubble placed at the intersection of a wave guide and a duct. If in the intersection no bubble present the light waves pass through, see Fig. 6.17. A summary of the main characteristics is presented in Table 6.5.

These bubbles can be moved a hundred of times per second. The temperature of the device must be kept high for proper functioning, and must be carefully controlled in each duct in order to avoid extra heating that could modify the propagation characteristics of the waveguides. There are still questions regarding long-term reliability and optical insertion loss. The limitation of this technology relates to the

Table 6.4 Summary of the characteristics of the liquid crystal switches

Scalability	Switching speed	Reliability	Losses	Port-to-port repeatability	Cost	Power consumption
Medium–high	Slow (ms)	Good	Medium	Moderate	Medium	Medium

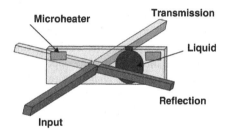

Fig. 6.17 Structure of a refractive-index-matching liquid

Table 6.5 Summary of the characteristics of bubble switches

Scalability	Switching speed	Reliability	Losses	Port-to-port repeatability	Cost	Power consumption
Medium–low	Slow (10 ms)	Good	Low	—	Medium–low	—

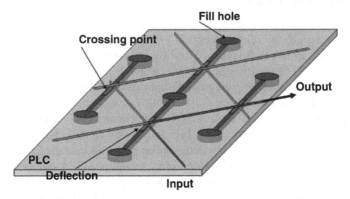

Fig. 6.18 Generic sketch of a bubble switch

optical power losses (deflection losses) and possible inkhead damage. The bubble device combines reasonable switching speeds (around 10 ms) with quite good optical properties and low dimensions. Several results have been attained by many companies, and up to now the most important limit of this technology seems to be the scalability, which is still at 32×32 [166]. There are two main methods based on bubbles. The first one, previously described, is based on air bubbles generated in liquid, using technology originally developed for inkjet printers [67]; the other is based on heat used to move a bubble in a partially fluid-filled groove (Fig. 6.18) [148].

The base element of this switch is made of an upper glass substrate and an intersecting waveguide substrate characterized by several grooves placed at each crossing point. The grooves, sealed, are partially filled with refractive-index-matching liquid. This liquid must possess low viscosity, low volatility, good refractive-index controllability, and high thermal and chemical stability. When the liquid is present at the crossing point of waveguides, the optical signals pass straight through the groove while when the liquid moves away from the crossing point, leaving it filled with air, the optical signals are switched into the crossing waveguide by total internal reflection. A pair of microheaters generate a thermal gradient reducing the interfacial tension of the air–liquid interface. This allows the liquid, present in the groove, to move toward the opposite side of the groove. In this way the switch only consumes power to change state and each state is maintained stably without power. This approach faces quite high losses and high power requirements, limiting the number of available ports to 16×16. The switching time, normally set to around

Table 6.6 Summary of the characteristics of bubble switches

Scalability	Switching speed	Reliability	Losses	Port-to-port repeatability	Cost	Power consumption
Medium–low 3D high	Tens of milliseconds	Moderate	Few decibels	High for small switches, moderate for big switches	Medium	Medium

Table 6.7 Summary of the characteristics of the electro-optic switches

Scalability	Switching speed	Reliability	Losses	Port-to-port repeatability	Cost	Power consumption
Medium–Low	Slow 10 ms	Good	Medium–Low	Poor	Medium	Low

100–50 ms, can be lowered to around 10 ms by properly decreasing the liquid viscosity and making the traveling distances shorter [227]. A summary of the main characteristics is presented in Table 6.6 [67, 148, 166, 189, 227].

6.2.5 Electro-Optical Switches

In certain crystals the refractive index is proportional to the intensity of an electric field applied to it; this is the *linear electro-optic effect* [274]. The effect offers a means to control the intensity or phase of the light propagating through the material. There are several classes of materials where this effect is being explored, e.g., solid state (LiNbO3), polymers, and lead zinconate titane (PZT). Depending on the material used the general conditions differ. For example, LiNbO3 switches are commonly used nowadays as modulators due to their very fast response (ps) and well-established growing and connecting methodologies. As for polymers, a long journey has still to be made before they clearly become an option. The latter have the great advantage of easy growing and cheap processing. PZT is of growing interest due to the low loss and higher electro-optical effect, resulting in higher efficiency devices. Also, due to the material structure, polarization dependence is lower, resulting in a much more suitable device. Electro-optical switches use the index change caused by an electric field to cause switching [189]. Switching can be achieved by the index change, which leads the light through the more index-matched of the available ports, or by interference in a common splitting port, where, depending on the beams' relative phase, the output can be switched to one of the available ports. These types of switches are integrable and cascadable, however, only small port count is nowadays available, due mainly to size and layout difficulties. Nevertheless, these are the most established techniques existing for OBS and OPS techniques. A summary of the main characteristics is presented in Table 6.7 [189].

6.2.6   Thermo-Optical Switches

The thermo-optical effect is similar to the electro-optical. In the latter, the effect is achieved by an electric field, whereas in the thermo-optic the temperature is responsible for the index change. Due to this inherently slow temperature flow and stabilization process, these switches are typically slower than their electro-optical counterparts. Similarly, both configurations, Y-splitter or interferometric, are common for implementing these switches. The heat diffusion in the substrate is one of the major limitations to the implementation of high-port-count thermo-optical switches, since close switches are influenced by the state of their neighbors, due to temperature diffusion. To minimize this effect, usually interferometric switches are used. Always, the switching speed depends on how fast the materials can be heated (e.g., polymers are faster (few milliseconds) than silica (tens of milliseconds)). Also, the power needed to heat the waveguides in order to achieve enough index change is highly dependent on the type of material used (few milliwatts for polymers and hundreds of milliwatts for the silica). There are two basic types of thermo-optic switch: *digital optical switches* (DOSs) and *interferometric switches*. The latter are typically more compact, however, they can be built in several configurations (The Mach–Zehnder interferometer (MZI))—most common (Fig. 6.19), the Michelson interferometer (MI), the Fabry Perot (FP), and the nonlinear optical loop mirror (NOLM). They are also wavelength sensitive, which leads normally to extra temperature control. The DOS, on the other hand, is more robust due to its steplike response. In other words, if more power is applied to the heater, the switch stays in the same state, whether "on" or "off." The simplest device, a 1 × 2 switch, is called a *Y-splitter*. These switches can be scaled, however, power dissipation issues will limit their use in high-port-count matrices. A summary of the main characteristics is presented in Table 6.8 [92, 189].

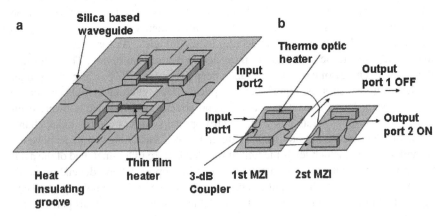

Fig. 6.19 Schematic of two thermo-optic Mach–Zehnder switches: (**a**) simple structure (**b**) double structure

Table 6.8 Summary of the characteristics of the thermo-optic switches

Scalability	Switching speed	Reliability	Losses	Port-to-port repeatability	Cost	Power consumption
Medium–low	Slow (10 ms)	Good	Medium–low	Poor	Medium	Medium–high

Table 6.9 Summary of the characteristics of the electroholography switches

Scalability	Switching speed	Reliability	Losses	Port-to-port repeatability	Cost	Power consumption
High	Low (ns)	Good	Moderate	Moderate	—	High

6.2.7 Electroholography

Electroholography (EH) technology is used to switch wavelengths by the deflection effect of an electrically controlled grating in a specific crystal (e.g., potassium lithium tantalate niobate—KLTN). The applied voltage activates a prewritten hologram that works as a Bragg grating, deflecting the incoming wavelength. In the absence of voltage the light flows directly without distortion. Typically this deflective effect is not very efficient, requiring typically two stages with some absorption parts to lower crosstalk. Due to the characteristics of the phenomenon, the switch can achieve high switching speed (tens of ns). Holographic switches may have high scalability, since thousands of wavelength inputs are independently switchable; many gratings can be written into the same crystal, and the crystals can be operated in series. A summary of the main characteristics is presented in Table 6.9 [92].

6.2.8 Acousto-Optic Switches

The acousto-optic switches are based on the effect of the same name. The effect is based on refractive index change, which travels at sound speed and creates a traveling grating in the material. Depending on the intensity of the sound wave and the angle of the incident beam with respect to the moving grating, the light can be refracted, redirected, and intensity-controlled. The output beam intensity can be controlled by the power of the radio frequency (RF) carrier. More light will be refracted when a stronger grating is formed in the crystal. The direction of the refracted beam can be controlled by the frequency of the RF signal used to write the grating. After the switch, which is usually a crystal, the light can be coupled to fiber by prisms or lenses. The switching time is intimately related to the speed of the sound wave traveling inside the crystal, therefore, actually, the switching time is presently on the orders of few μs, however the port count can be rather high (e.g., 256×256). A summary of the main characteristics is presented in Table 6.10 [92, 189].

Table 6.10 Summary of the characteristics of the Acousto-optic switches

Scalability	Switching speed	Reliability	Losses	Port-to-port repeatability	Cost	Power consumption
High	Few us	Good	Low	—	Medium	—

Table 6.11 Summary of the characteristics of the SOA-based switches

Scalability	Switching speed	Reliability	Losses	Port-to-port repeatability	Cost	Power consumption
Medium	100 ps	Good	Gain	Power-dependent	Medium	High

6.2.9 Semiconductor Optical Amplifiers

Semiconductor optical amplifiers (SOAs) can operate when current is modulated as an optical switch. They are characterized by a high degree of integration. These relatively basic elements can also be integrated with passive functions, such as splitters or wavelength multiplexers, to perform very simple wavelength add/drop functions. Drawbacks of this technology are a high noise factor and interchannel crosstalk; but, with careful design, at the technology and system levels it is possible to overcome these impairments. These devices can be integrated with other technologies and result in very attractive switching functions (e.g., inside arrayed waveguide gratings). Further details will be addressed in Section 6.3. A summary of the main characteristics of the SOA as a basic ON/OFF switch is presented in Table 6.11.

6.2.10 Summary

Several technologies are able to perform switching in the most variable applications. Each switching application has its own requisites, which are or are not critical. Regarding these, the switching properties should be defined and matched to each technology. Up to now there is no clear view as to which will be the prevailing, most accessible, and flexible switching technology, and so many technologies will still occupy their niches depending on application requisites.

6.3 Semiconductor Optical Amplifier Switches

In the current section we discuss semiconductor optical amplifier-based switches. SOA-based switches have been applied to several photonic network systems, including switching matrices, wavelength converters, 2R and 3R regenerators, clock recoveries, burst mode receivers, demultiplexers, header extraction circuits, time slot interchangers, optical gates, and optical sources. In addition to having a wide range of applications, SOA-based switches are of significant importance in optical networks since they combine a plethora of advantageous attributes, as compared to other switching technologies. In particular, SOA-based switches require very low switching energies, which in turn means that the total optical power consumption of the switch fabric remains at low levels. Moreover, it is possible to integrate the SOA-based switches in a monolithic or a hybrid fashion, thus allow, at least in principle, for mass production and subsequent cost minimization. Finally, since the dynamic phenomena that allow for switching in the SOA take place in time scales ranging from femtoseconds to picoseconds, switching is achieved for line rates that reach several tens or thousands of gigahertz.

The dynamic processes that take place in SOA are of key importance for understanding SOA-based switches. We discuss these processes in Section 6.3.1 along with SOA structure. In the next section we detail the deployment of the SOA in optical switches, including electrically controlled optical switches and all-optical switches. The section concludes with the Section 6.3.3, where we summarize the main attributes of the SOA-based switches presented.

6.3.1 *Semiconductor Optical Amplifiers*

6.3.1.1 SOA Structure

The SOA structure is shown in Fig. 6.20. The SOA is essentially a Fabry–Perot laser diode whose input and output mirrors have been replaced by antireflection coatings or tilted facets, so that optical feedback is minimized and the laser diode is transformed into a traveling wave amplifier. The light pulses that are incident on the

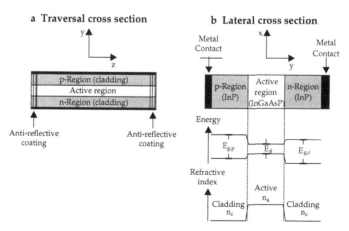

Fig. 6.20 Structure of the semiconductor optical amplifier

SOA chip are amplified inside the active region of the device through the stimulated recombination of carriers, which are electrons in the conduction band and holes in the valence band.

The carriers are supplied by an external driving current and their recombination generates photons whose energy equals the bandgap of the active region material. SOA active regions are typically formed from InGaAsP and the percentage of InGaAsP molecules determines the energy bandgap E_g, thus the operational wavelength of the SOA. In practice, the active region is sandwiched between InP layers with higher energy bandgaps ($E_{g,p}$ and $E_{g,c}$), so that carriers are capable of recombining only, but doing so within the active region (carrier confinement). Moreover, the neighboring InP layers have a lower refractive index (n_c) than the active region (n_a), thus the light is waveguided primarily inside the active region (photon confinement) [1, 43].

6.3.1.2 Physical Description: Intraband and Interband Processes

Pulses that traverse the active region of the SOA cause the depletion of the carrier density due to stimulated recombination. The carrier density is ultimately restored by supplying external current, however the restoration is not instantaneous and this leads to a time-dependent profile of the SOA gain. There are several processes that contribute to the SOA gain profile and they are commonly categorized as being *intra-band* or *interband*, depending on whether the electron transitions take place inside the conduction band or between the conduction and the valence band. Intraband effects do not alter the carrier density and as a result they do not directly contribute to the generation of photons and optical gain. However, they alter the carrier distribution within the valence or conduction band and, consequently, the percentage of carriers that are available for recombination. On the contrary, interband effects generate photons and carriers and, as a result, directly influence the SOA gain.

The intraband transitions commence with the advent of the optical pulse in the active region and the stimulated recombination of electron–hole pairs. The recombination causes a spectral hole (energy hole) in the Fermi–Dirac distribution of the electrons, and the distribution is restored through electron–electron scattering, which takes place in approximately 100 fs. The new Fermi–Dirac distribution corresponds to an electron temperature that is higher than the lattice temperature, and as a result electrons are forced to cool down to a thermal equilibrium with the lattice. This is achieved by means of electron–phonon (lattice vibration) scattering, which takes place in about 0.5–1 ps [96]. The process is summarized in Fig. 6.21.

The above phenomena restore the Fermi–Dirac electron distribution as well as the thermal equilibrium between electrons and lattice; however, the total number of electrons (and holes) is reduced due to the interband carrier recombination that triggered the intraband effects in the first place. Carriers are supplied to the active region of the SOA from the external current source and the carrier-filling

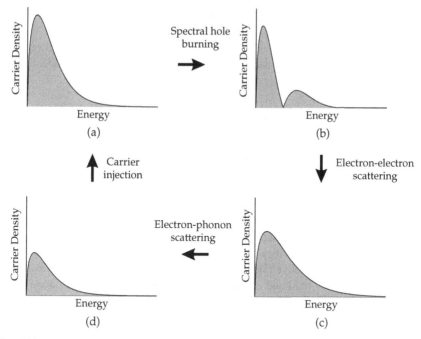

Fig. 6.21 Dynamic processes in the SOA. (**a**) Initial Fermi-Dirac carrier density distribution, (**b**) an energy hole is created in the carrier density distribution due to carrier recombination, (**c**) electron–electron scattering restores the Fermi–Dirac distribution at a higher carrier temperature, and (**d**) electron–phonon scattering equalizes carrier and lattice temperatures

process is complete typically after several hundreds of picoseconds. The aforementioned carrier recovery time is governed by the electron–hole loss rate due to the three recombination processes denoted as *Shockley–Read–Hall, bimolecular*, and *Auger recombination*. During the Shockley–Read–Hall recombination the electron does not directly recombine with a hole, but it falls into an energy trap (within the energy bandgap) that is created by a recombination center (an impurity or lattice defect). The trapped electron finally recombines with a hole in the valence band, but this two-step process does not contribute to photons having energy equal the bandgap; therefore the Shockley–Read–Hall recombination is considered nonradiative. Bimolecular recombination involves the spontaneous radiative recombination of an electron–hole pair and is associated with optical noise. Finally, in Auger recombination an electron–hole pair recombines, however the resulting energy is absorbed by another electron or hole, which transfers to a higher energy level, and as a result the Auger recombination is also a nonradiative process [244].

6.3.1.3 Mathematical Description of the SOA

The physical description of the SOA leads to the following mathematical equation that relates the changes of the carrier density $N(m^{-3})$ to the intraband and interband processes [153, 249]:

$$\frac{\vartheta N(z,t)}{\vartheta t} = \frac{I}{e \cdot V} - (A \cdot N + B \cdot N^2 + C \cdot N^3) - \frac{g \cdot (N(z,t) - N_T) \cdot P(z,t)}{h \cdot v \cdot A_{\text{eff}} \cdot (1 + \epsilon \cdot P(z,t))}. \quad (6.1)$$

The first term of Eq. (6.1) accounts for carrier injection by the external current source. The second term is associated with the carrier recovery time through the Shockley–Read–Hall (coefficient A), bimolecular (coefficient B), and Auger (coefficient C) recombination effects. The last term describes carrier depletion due to stimulated emission of photons. Intraband processes are taken into consideration through the nonlinear gain coefficient ϵ.

A second equation describes the evolution of the power $P(\text{W}/\text{m}^3)$ of the optical field that traverses the active region. Starting from the electromagnetic wave equation for the electrical field and assuming that (a) the reflections at the facets of the SOA are negligible, and (b) the differential gain does not affect the optical mode distribution inside the active region [2], it follows that the optical power obeys

$$\frac{\vartheta P(z,t)}{\vartheta z} = \frac{\Gamma \cdot g \cdot (N(z,t) - N_T) \cdot P(z,t)}{h \cdot v \cdot A_{\text{eff}} \cdot (1 + \epsilon \cdot P(z,t))} - a_D \cdot P(z,t). \quad (6.2)$$

The first term of Eq. (6.1) accounts for optical gain due to stimulated emission (compare with the third term of Eq. (6.2)). However, only the percentage of the optical mode that is located inside the active region experiences gain, thus the total gain is multiplied with the confinement factor Γ. The second term of Eq. (6.2) takes into account power dissipation due to optical waveguide losses.

In a similar fashion, it can be found that the phase of the optical field also changes as the field travels the active region. This is due to the fact the refractive index of the active region material depends on the carrier density. Since the refractive index is a complex quantity, its real part accounts for phase changes on the optical field; the imaginary part has already been taken into account for gain changes as described in Eq. (6.2). Given that conditions (a) and (b) are satisfied, it follows that the phase of the optical field satisfiespower obeys

$$\frac{\vartheta \phi(z,t)}{\vartheta z} = -\frac{1}{2} \cdot \Gamma \cdot g \cdot (N(z,t) - N_T) \cdot \left(a - a_T \cdot \frac{\epsilon \cdot P(z,t))}{1 + \epsilon \cdot P(z,t))} \right). \quad (6.3)$$

Parameters a and a_T are the traditional and temperature linewidth enhancement factors, respectively [89, 249]. Table 6.12 summarizes the parameters used in the previous equations.

Table 6.12   Rate equation parameters

Parameter	Description
I	Injected current
e	Electron charge
h	Planck's constant
V	Active region volume
A_{eff}	Active region cross-section
A, B, C	Shockley–Read–Hall, bimolecular and Auger recombination coefficients
N_T	Transparency carrier density
Γ	Confinement factor
g	Differential gain
v	Photon frequency
ϵ	Nonlinear gain coefficient
a_D	Optical waveguide losses
a	Linewidth enhancement factor
a_T	Temperature linewidth enhancement factor

Fig. 6.22 Output power and phase of a continuous wave probe signal that travels through an SOA when it is saturated by a high power pump pulse

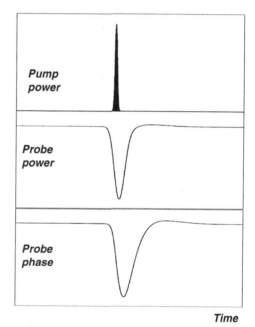

6.3.1.4   Gain Saturation and Recovery by Optical Pulses

Equations (6.1)–(6.3) are numerically solved to calculate the output power and phase that the probe signal acquires while traversing an SOA that is saturated by a high power pump pulse. An indicative solution of Eqs. (6.1)–(6.3) is illustrated in Fig. 6.22 for a continuous wave probe signal. Before the advent of the pump signal, the probe output power is constant. The advent of the pump signal causes carrier density depletion inside the SOA and as a result the probe output power decreases rapidly, within a few picoseconds. The probe output power remains at the minimum level for the whole duration of the pump pulse. After the pump pulse has exited the SOA, the injected current restores the carrier density, thus the probe output power, within several tens of picoseconds. The same remarks hold for the probe phase. The probe phase is constant during the absence of the pump pulse. However, a large phase shift occurs during the pump-induced carrier density depletion. The phase is ultimately restored to its initial value when the carrier density has been restored.

6.3.2 SOA-Based Switches

6.3.2.1 Electrically Controlled SOA-Based Switches

As described earlier in Section 6.3.1, an optical signal that traverses the SOA experiences gain or loss depending on the injected current. The optical signal is boosted when strong external current is present; however, it is heavily attenuated when the SOA is operated at a low or no current. The latter is due to the extreme optical waveguide losses, which typically reach several thousands per meter in InGaAsP.

The gain dependence of the SOA on the injected current has served towards the development of electrically controlled optical ON-OFF switches (EC-SOA switches). The EC-SOA switches have low power consumption, approximately 50 mA per gate, and are therefore suitable for large scale switching matrices. Moreover, the switching time of the EC-SOA switches equals several ns, as determined by the recovery time of the SOA. A recently proposed technique, however, has achieved much shorter switching times of 200 ps [70]. The technique involves injecting a positive/negative electrical pulse to the SOA before turning the bias current on/off, respectively. The positive electrical pulse contributes to an increase of the carrier density when turning the SOA on and consequently to the decrease of the SOA recovery time. Similarly, the negative pulse allows the depletion of carriers and the decrease in the carrier density causes faster switching off of the SOA.

EC-SOA switches may be utilized in broadcast and multicast optical switch fabrics. A bank of EC-SOA switches is located at each output of the switch fabric, while all inputs are driven through a power splitter to all output banks. Multicasting and broadcasting is achieved by adjusting the electrical currents of the EC-SOA switches, i.e., when input i broadcasts a message to all outputs only the ith EC-SOA in each bank is driven by electrical current. The EC-SOA switches have also been deployed in a similar configuration as wavelength selective switches in a broadcast and select packet switching architecture [83].

6.3.2.2   All-Optical Switches Based on Cross-Gain Modulation

All-optical switching based on cross-gain modulation (XGM) involves the saturation of the SOA gain by a high power pump signal. A second probe signal of
significantly lower power traverses the SOA simultaneously or shortly after the
pump signal and samples the saturated gain. Under this scheme, the probe signal
experiences no gain during presence of the pump signal or full gain during the absence of the pump signal. Consequently, the SOA operates as an optically controlled
ON–OFF switch (cross gain modulation (XGM)-SOA switch) with the ON state selected at the absence of the pump signal. XGM-SOA switches require very low
switching energies for the optical signals, ranging from a few nanojoules to several
femtojoule. Their switching time is determined by the SOA recovery time, and may
be as low as a few tens of picoseconds, thus XGMXGM-SOA switches allow packet
switching with ultrashort duration and bit-by-bit signal processing at line rates of a
couple of tens of gigahertz.

6.3.2.3   Cross-Phase Modulation Switches

The saturation of the SOA gain by a strong pump signal causes an analogous change
in the refractive index of the active region, thus a phase shift on the probe signal,
as we have already discussed in Section 6.3.1. This effect is known as cross-phase
modulation (XPM) in SOA and has been taken advantage of in the development of
interferometric optical switches. As elaborated in the following paragraphs, interferometric switches involve splitting the incoming optical signal into two separate
components. The signal components experience differential gains, therefore phases,
while traversing the SOA (or SOAs) of the switch. The two components interfere at
the output of the switch and they either add to or cancel one another, depending on
the relative gains and phases that they have acquired.

   XPM-SOA switches are typically faster than their EC-SOA and XGM-SOA
counterparts, since it is possible to make their response independent of the SOA
recovery time [111, 243, 245]. Moreover, a variety of functionalities has been
demonstrated with XPM-SOA switches, including optical logic, wavelength conversion, demultiplexing of TDM optical signals, signal regeneration, and clock
recovery [241]. We briefly describe the most common XPM-SOA switch architectures in the following sections.

6.3.2.4   Mach–Zehnder switch

The SOA-based MZI-SOA switch is shown in Fig. 6.23. The switch consists of
two identical arms that are spatially separated, and an SOA is located at each arm.
The data signal at the input of the switch is split into two components by means of a
3-dB optical coupler, and each component is directed to a respective SOA. A second

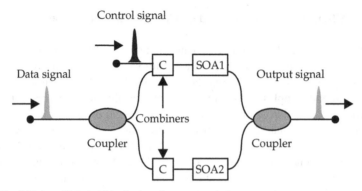

Fig. 6.23 SOA-based Mach–Zehnder interferometer switch

coupler at the output of the switch combines the outputs of the SOAs, while two additional optical combiners introduce the signal that controls the switch in the SOAs.

Switching on and off of the MZI-SOA switch is controlled by the presence or absence of the control signal. The state of the switch may be mathematically described by its switching window, which for the MZI-SOA is given by

$$SW(t) = \frac{1}{4} \cdot \left(G_1(t) + G_2(t) - 2 \cdot \sqrt{G_1(t) \cdot G_2(t)} \cdot \cos\left(\varphi_1(t) - \varphi_2(t)\right) \right). \quad (6.4)$$

$G_{1,2}(t)$ and $\varphi_{1,2}(t)$ are the respective gains and phases that the signal components experience in the SOAs of the respective arm, and are evaluated after solving Eqs. (6.1)–(6.3). It follows from Eq. (6.4) that when the control signal is absent, the data signal components experience identical SOA gains and phases, and as a result cancel out at the output coupler. On the contrary, when the control signal is present in either SOA, but not both, the corresponding data signal component experiences a saturated SOA gain and phase. Therefore, it is possible that the data components add up at the output coupler, provided that the differential gains and phases maximize the switching window.

The mach–zehnder interferometer (MZI)-SOA with 3-dB input and output couplers and identical SOA in the interferometer arms is commonly referred to as a *symmetric* MZI-SOAs switch. Despite the fact that integrated symmetric MZI-SOAs have been extensively deployed in optical experiments, their switching window is sensitive to device fabrication parameters, such as the split ratio of the input and output couplers and the SOA gain and phase characteristics. As such, complete switching off of the symmetric MZI-SOA is not possible if the unsaturated SOA gains are not equal or the splitting ratios of the couplers are not exactly 3 dB, according to Eq. (6.4). The effect of incomplete switching is particularly detrimental in a number of applications; for instance, it introduces channel crosstalk in demultiplexing and a power pedestal in "0" bits in wavelength conversion, and thus must be minimized. Incomplete switching due to minor deviations in the couplers and SOA characteristics are alleviated in symmetric MZI-SOA by imposing different unsaturated SOA gains by means of different external currents. Sensitivity to fabrication imperfections is also alleviated by using asymmetric MZI-SOA switches that incorporate additional phase shifters in the interferometric arms. The phase shifters introduce a constant differential phase between arms and by adjusting them, complete off switching is achieved at the absence of the control signal. The asymmetric MZI-SOAs may also be described mathematically by a switching window function that is similar to Eq. (6.4). However, the asymmetric MZI-SOA switching window is more involved since it accounts for arbitrary splitting ratios in the couplers, different unsaturated SOA gains, and constant differential phase shifts [136].

The main drawback of the above mentioned schemes is that they require a single control signal to set the state of the switch. This in turn means their switching window depends on the SOA recovery time, since one of the SOAs maintains a constant gain, while the gain of the other SOA saturates and recovers under the presence of the control signal. As a result, a differential gain and phase exists for the whole duration of the SOA gain recovery. The practical aspect of the dependence of the switching window on the recovery time is that incomplete switching is achieved for successive bits if the bit period is shorter that the SOA recovery time. This limits the operation speed of the MZI-SOA switch to a couple of tens of gigahertz; therefore switching at higher rates imposes that the duration of the switching window be shortened. The duration of the switching window is minimized by introducing two replicas of the initial control pulse in each interferometer arm [111, 245]. The two replicas are delayed with respect to one another, so that the first replica "opens" the switching window and the second "closes" it. "Opening" the switching window is achieved similar to the single control scheme with only one of the SOAs being saturated. The switch stays open until the second SOA is saturated by the control signal replica and after a short transient, which corresponds to the SOA saturation, the gain recovery of the second SOA forces the switching window to "close". This is feasible since the recovering gains of both SOAs can be made approximately equal by adjusting the relative powers of the control signal replicas and the temporal delay between them. This technique achieves switching windows with duration that equals the temporal delay between the control signal replicas, which is practically a few picoseconds.

MZI-SOA switches have demonstrated a broad range of functionalities. These include optical logic [281], wavelength conversion [161], demultiplexing of TDM optical signals [162], optical sampling, and optical signal processing [120]. A detailed analysis of the SOA-based MZI switch and its applications may be found in [246].

6.3.2.5 Michelson Switch

The SOA-based Michelson switch is illustrated in Fig. 6.24. The Michelson switch consists of two spatially separated arms, quite similar to the MZI switch, and an SOA is located at each arm. Contrary to the MZI, however, the SOA output facets have been removed, and as a result partially reflecting mirrors are formed at the

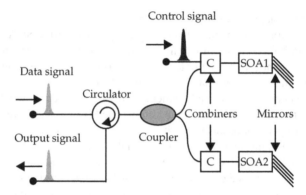

Fig. 6.24 SOA-based Michelson interferometer switch

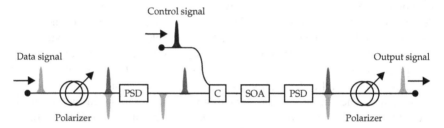

Fig. 6.25 SOA-based ultrafast nonlinear interferometer switch. PSD: polarization sensitive delay

SOA outputs. Therefore, the data signal components traverse the SOAs twice and interfere at the optical coupler at the input of the switch. The output data signal exits the switch through an optical circulator.

The Michelson switch had been proposed as an integration alternative of the MZI switch, since it requires less antireflection coating and fewer SOAs to fiber couplings [156]. The Michelson switch has demonstrated functionalities such as optical logic [66] and wavelength conversion [155].

6.3.2.6 Ultrafast Nonlinear Interferometer Switch

The SOA-based ultrafast nonlinear interferometer (UNI) switch is shown in Fig. 6.25. The data signal that enters the UNI switch is analyzed into two orthogonally polarized components by means of a polarizer whose axes are rotated by 45° with respect to the polarization of the data signal. The two data signal components are temporally separated after propagation through a polarization sensitive delay element (PSD); for instance, polarization maintaining fiber or a birefrigerant crystal. The control signal enters the SOA synchronized with one of the data signal components, and as a result only one of the data components experiences the induced gain saturation and phase shift. The data signal components are temporally merged after propagating through a second PSD element whose optical axes are rotated by 90° with respect to the axes of the input PSD element. The data components, which are still orthogonally polarized, interfere at a 45° polarizer at the output of the switch.

An advantage of the UNI switch is that it is a single arm interferometer, thus requires only one SOA, contrary to the MZI and Michelson switches. However, the SOA gain in the UNI switch should recover in half the time compared to the MZI and Michelson switches. Moreover, the UNI switch has not been integrated, mainly because of the PSD elements. The UNI switch has been demonstrated in numerous applications, including demultiplexing [192], optical logic [16, 86, 191], all-optical signal processing [95, 193], and optical packet switching [17].

6.3.2.7 Sagnac Switch

The SOA based Sagnac switch is illustrated in Fig. 6.26. Instead of placing the SOA in an interferometric arm, as in the previous switch architectures, the SOA is placed inside an optical loop. The data signal is split by means of a 3-dB coupler into two components that travel inside the loop to opposite directions (clockwise and counterclockwise). An offset delay is imposed on one of the data signal components before it enters the SOA and as a result the data components do not coincide inside the amplifier. Similar to the UNI switch, the control signal is synchronized with one of the data signal components, thus it imparts a differential gain and phase. The two countertravelling data signal components finally interfere at the output coupler.

The Sagnac switch maintains the advantage of requiring only a single SOA and has also been integrated [112, 154], but the SOA gain recovery time should be faster than the MZI and Michelson switches. The Sagnac switch has found application in wavelength conversion [154], demultiplexing [56, 112, 234], and optical logic [94]. A more comprehensive analysis of the Sagnac switch, its variations, and its applications may be found in [220].

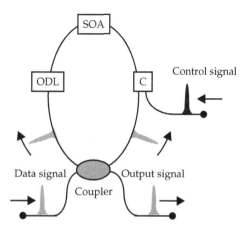

Fig. 6.26 SOA-based Sagnac switch. ODL: optical delay line

6.3.3 Summary

The current section has reviewed a number of SOA-based switches that are capable of operating at ultrahigh speeds. The realizability of such switches owes to the picosecond time scales within which the SOA carrier density depletes and recovers. As such, nanosecond switching is feasible at electrically controlled optical switches, where the signal that controls the switch modulates the injected current. Switching at picosecond scales, however, requires the switch be controlled optically. Optically controlled switches rely upon the phenomena of cross-gain and cross-phase modulation. The former effect is due to the SOA gain saturation by the control pulses and allows for switching within tens of picoseconds. The latter effect is due to the change in the refractive index of the SOA material by the control pulses, and has been taken advantage of to perform picosecond switching in interferometric setups, such as the Mach–Zehnder, Michelson, Sagnac and ultrafast nonlinear interferometers.

References

1. Agrawal, G. and Dutta, N. (1993). Semiconductor Lasers, 2nd ed. Van Nostrand Reinhold. McGraw-Hill, New York.
2. Agrawal, G. and Olsson, N. (1989). Self-phase modulation and spectral broadening of optical pulses in semiconductor laser amplifiers. IEEE Journal of Quantum Electronics **25**(11), 2297–2306.
3. Agrawal, G.P. (1992). Fiber-optic communication systems. Series in Microwave and Optical Engineering. Wiley McGraw-Hill, New York.
4. Al-Zaharani, F.A., Habiballa, A., Fayoumi, A.G., et al. (2005). Performance tradeoffs of shared limited range wavelength conversion schemes in optical WDM networks. In: Proceedings of Second IFIP International Conference on Wireless and Optical Communications Networks. pp. 18–22.
5. Aleksić, S. and Krajinović, V. (2002). Comparison of optical code correlators for all-optical MPLS networks. In: 28th European Conference on Optical Communication (ECOC 2002). Copenhagen, Denmark.
6. Almeida, R., Pelegrini, J., and Waldman, H. (2005). A generic-traffic optical buffer modeling for asynchronous optical switching networks. IEEE Communications Letters **9**(2), 175–177.
7. Appelman, R. and Zalevsky, Z. (2004). All-optical switching technologies for protection applications. IEEE Communications Magazine **42**(11), 35–40.
8. Banejee, D. and Mukherjee, B. (1996). A practical approach for routing and wavelength assignment in large wavelength-routed optical networks. IEEE Journal on Selected Areas in Communications **14**(5), 903–908.
9. Banerjee, A., Drake, J., Lang, J., et al. (2001). Generalized multiprotocol label switching: An overview of signaling enhancements and recovery techniques. IEEE Communications Magazine **39**(3), 144–151.
10. Barakat, N. and Sargent, E.H. (2004). An accurate model for evaluating blocking probabilities in multi-class OBS systems. IEEE Communications Letters **8**(2), 119–121.
11. Barakat, N. and Sargent, E.H. (2005). Analytical modeling of offset-induced priority in multiclass OBS networks. IEEE Transactions Communications **53**(8), 1343–1352.
12. Baroncelli, F., Martini, B., Valcarenghi, L., et al. (2005). A service oriented network architecture suitable for global grid computing. ONDM, 9th IFIP/IEEE Conference on Optical Network Design and Modeling, Milan Italy.
13. Baroncelli, F., Martini, B., Valcarenghi, L., et al. (2005). Agreement signalling and network service provisioning for grids. 2nd International Workshop on Networks for Grid Applications, GridNets 2005, Boston, MA, USA.
14. Bergman, L., Morookian, J., and Yeh, C. (1998). An all-optical long distance multi-Gbytes/s bit-parallel WDM single-fibre link. IEEE Journal of Lightwave Technology **16**(9), 1577–1582.

15. Bergman, L., Morookian, J., and Yeh, C. (2000). Advances in multi-channel optical multi-Gbytes/sec bit-parallel WDM single fiber link. In: IEEE 50th Electronic Components and Technology Conference. Las Vegas, Nevada, USA, pp. 1504–1510.

16. Bintjas, C., Kalyvas, M., Theophilopoulos, G., et al. (2000). 20 Gb/s all-optical XOR with UNI gate. IEEE Photonics Technology Letters 12(7), 834–836.

17. Bintjas, C., Vlachos, K., Pleros, N., et al. (2003). Ultrafast nonlinear interferometer (UNI)-based digital optical circuits and their use in packet switching. Journal of Lightwave Technology 21(11), 2629–2637.

18. Birman, A. and Kershenbaum, A. (1995). Routing and wavelength assignment methods in single-hop all-optical networks with blocking. In: Proceedings of the Fourteenth IEEE Infocom, pp. 431–438.

19. Blumenthal, D., Prucnal, P., and Sauer, J. (1994). Photonic packet switches: Architectures and experimental implementations. In: Proceedings of the IEEE 82, 1650–1667.

20. van Breusegem, E., de Levenheer, M., Cheyns, J., et al. (2004). An OBS architecture for pervasive grid computing. Workshop on Optical Burst Switching.

21. Brungard, D. (2005). Requirements for generalized multi-protocol label switching (GMPLS) routing for the automatically switched optical network (ASON). RFC 4258, Internet Engineering Task Force.

22. Callegati, F. (2000). Optical buffers for variable length packets. IEEE Communications Letters 4(9), 292–294.

23. Callegati, F. (2001). Approximate modeling of optical buffers for variable length packets. Photonic Network Communications 3, 383–390.

24. Callegati, F., Cankaya, H., Xiong, Y., et al. (1999). Design issues of optical IP routers for internet backbone applications. IEEE Communications Magazine 37(12), 124–128.

25. Callegati, F., Careglio, D., Cerroni, W., et al. (2005). Keeping the packet sequence in optical packet-switched networks. Optical Switching and Networking 2, 137–147. DOI 10.1016/j.osn.2005.09.001.

26. Callegati, F., Casoni. M., Raffaelli, C., et al. (1999). Packet optical networks for high speed TCP-IP backbones. IEEE Communications Magazine 37(1), 124–129.

27. Callegati, F. and Cerroni, W. (2002). Time-wavelength exploitation in optical feedback buffer with trains of packets. In: N. Ghani, K.M. Sivalingam (eds.) Optical Networking and Communications (Opticomm 2002), vol. 4874, pp. 274–285. SPIE. DOI 10.1117/12.475304.

28. Callegati, F., Cerroni, W., Bonani, L.H., et al. (2006). Congestion resolution in optical burst/packet switching with limited wavelength conversion. In: IEEE Global Telecommunications Conference (GLOBECOM '00), p. 5. IEEE, San Francisco, CA, USA. DOI 10.1109/GLOCOM.2006.393.

29. Callegati, F., Cerroni, W., Raffaelli, C., et al. (2004). Wavelength and time domains exploitation for QoS management in optical packet switches. Computer Networks 44(4), 569–582. DOI 10.1016/j.comnet.2003.12.010. Special Issue on QoS in Multiservice IP Networks.

30. Callegati, F., Corazza, G., and Raffaelli, C. (2002). Exploitation of DWDM for optical packet switching with quality of service guarantees. IEEE Journal on Selected Areas in Communications 20(1), 190–201.

31. Cao, X., Li, J., Chen, Y., et al. (2002). Assembling TCP/IP packets in optical burst switched networks. In: Proceedings of IEEE GLOBECOM, pp. 2808–2812.

32. Cao, X., Li, J., Chen, Y., et al. (2002). TCP/IP packets assembly over optical burst switching network. In: Proceedings of GLOBECOM 3, 2808–2812.

33. Chan, K.M. and Yum, T.S.P. (1994). Analysis of least congested path routing in WDM lightwave networks. In: Proceedings of the Thirteenth IEEE Infocom, pp. 962–969.

34. Chao, H.J. (2002). Next generation routers. In: Proceedings of the IEEE 90, 1518–1558.

35. Chen, L.R. and Smith, P.W.E. (2000). Demonstration of incoherent wavelength-encoding/time-spreading optical CDMA using Chirped Moire gratings. IEEE Photonics Technology Letters 12(9), 1281–1283.

36. Cheyns, Y., Van Breusegem, E., Develder, C., et al. (2004). Evaluating cost functions for OPS node architectures. In: Proceedings of 8th Working Conference on Optical Network Design and Modeling (ONDM).

37. Chiaroni, D. (2003). Packet switching matrix: A key element for the backbone and the metro. IEEE Journal on Selected Areas in Communications **21**(7), 1018–1025. DOI 10.1109/JSAC.2003.816569.

38. Chlamtac, I., Farago, A., and Zhang, T. (1996). Lightpath (wavelength) routing in large WDM networks. IEEE Journal on Selected Areas in Communications **14**(5), 909–913. DOI 10.1109/49.510914.

39. Cho, H., Kapur, P., and Saraswat, K.C. (2004). Power comparison between high-speed electrical and optical interconnects for interchip communication. Journal of Lightwave Technology **22**(9), 2021–2033. DOI 10.1109/JLT.2004.833531.

40. Chu, X. and Li, B. (2005). Dynamic routing and wavelength assignment in the presence of wavelength conversion for all-optical networks. IEEE/ACM Transaction on Networking **13**(3), 704–715.

41. Cisco Systems, I. (2004). Next-generation networks and the cisco carrier routing systems. URL http://www.cisco.com/warp/public/cc/pd/rt/12000/clc/prodlit/reqng_wp.pdf.

42. Clapp, G., et al. (2005). Grid network services. Grid Forum Draft, GHPN-RG, draft-ggf-ghpn-netserv-2.

43. Coldren, L. and Corzine, S. (1995). Diode Lasers and Photonic Integrated Circuits. McGraw-Hill, Wiley-Interscience, New York.

44. Cotter, D., Lucek, J.K., Shabeer, M., et al. (1995). Self-routing of 100 Gbit/s packets using 6 bit "keyword" address recognition. IEE Electronics Letters **31**(17), 1475–1476.

45. Dalton, L. and Isen, C. (2004). A study on high speed TCP protocols. In: Proceedings of IEEE Globecom, vol. 2, pp. 850–855.

46. Danielsen, S.L., Hansen, P.B., and Stubkjaer, K. (1998). Wavelength conversion in optical packet switching. IEEE/OSA Journal Lightwave Technology **16**(9), 2095–2108.

47. Detti, A. and Listanti, M. (2002). Impact of segments aggregation on TCP reno flows in optical burst switching networks. In: Proceedings of IEEE INFOCOM, vol. 3, pp. 1803–1812.

48. Dittmann, L. et al. (2003). The European IST project DAVID: A viable approach towards optical packet switching. IEEE Journal on Selected Areas in Communications **21**(7), 1026–1040.

49. Dobbelaere, P.D., Falta, K., and Gloeckner, S. (2003). Advances in integrated 2D MEMS-based solutions for optical network applications. IEEE Communications Magazine **41**(5), 16–23.

50. Dolzer, K. and Gauger, C. (2001). On burst assembly in optical burst switching networks—A performance evaluation of just-enough-time. In: Proceedings of the 17th International Telegraffic Congress, pp. 149–160.

51. Dorgeuille, F., Mersali, B., Feuillade M., et al. (1996). InP-switch matrix based on laser-amplifier gates. SPIE Optical Networks Magazine **8**, 1178–1180.

52. Düser, M. and Bayvel, P. (2002) Analysis of a dynamically wavelength-routed optical burst switched network architecture. IEEE/OSA Journal of Lightwave Technology **20**(4), 574–585.

53. Düser, M., Kozlovski, E., Killey, R.I., et al. (2000). Design trade-offs in optical burst switched networks with dynamic wavelength allocation. Proceedings of the European Conference on Optical Communication Munich, Germany **2**.

54. Dutta, R. and Rouskas, G.N. (2000). A Survey of Virtual Topology Design Algorithms for Wavelength Routed Optical Networks. Optical Networks Magazine, **1**(1), 73–89.

55. Eckberg, A.E. and Hou, T.C. (1988). Effects of output buffer sharing on buffer requirements in an ATDM packet switching. In: Proceedings of INFOCOM. Networks: Evolution or Revolution? Seventh Annual Joint Conference of the IEEE Computer and Communcations Societies, pp. 459–466.

56. Eiselt, M., Pieper , W.G., and Weber, H. (1995). SLALOM: Semiconductor laser amplifier in a loop mirror. Journal of Lightwave Technology **13**(10), 2099–2112.

57. El-Bawab, T.S. and Shin, J. (2002). Optical packet switching in core networks: Between vision and reality. IEEE Communications Magazine **40**(9), 60–65.

58. Ellinas, G., Labourdette, J., Chaudhuri, S., et al. (2003). Transparent optical switches: Technology issues and challenges. International Engineering Consortium Annual Communications Review.

59. Ellinas, G.N. (1998). Fault restoration in optical networks: General Methodology and Implementation. Ph.D. thesis, Columbia University.
60. Eramo, V., Listanti, M., and Pacifici, G. (2003). A comparison study on the number of wavelength converters needed in synchronous and asynchronous all-optical switching architectures. IEEE/OSA Journal of Lightwave Technology **21**(2), 340–355.
61. Eramo, V., Listanti, M., and Spaziani, M. (2005). Resource sharing in optical packet switches with limited-range wavelength converters. IEEE/OSA Journal Lightwave Technology **23**(2), 2095–2108.
62. Eramo, V., Raffaelli, A.G.C., and Savi, M. (2008). Performance analysis of multi-fiber all-optical switches employing fixed-input/tunable-output wavelength converters. In: Proceedings of IT-NEWS (QoS-IP), 4th International Telecommunication Network WorkShop on QoS Multiservice IP Networks.
63. Erramilli, A., Narayan, O., and Willinger, W. (1996). Experimental queueing analysis with long-range dependent packet traffic. IEEE/ACM Transactions on Networking **4**(2), 209–223.
64. Fathallah, H., Rusch, L.A., and LaRochelle, S. (1999). Passive optical frequency-hop CDMA communication system. IEEE Journal of Lightwave Technology **17**(3), 397–405.
65. Finn, S.G., Medard, M.M., and Barry, R.A. (1997). A novel approach to automatic protection switching using trees. IEEE International Conference in Communication.
66. Fjelde, T., Kloch, A., Wolfson, D., et al. (2001). Novel scheme for simple label-swapping employing XOR logic in an integrated interferometric wavelength converter. IEEE Photonics Technology Letters **13**(7), 750–752.
67. Fouquet, J.E., Venkatesh, S., Troll, M., et al. (1999). Compact scalable fiber optic cross-connect switches. LEOS Summer Topical Meeting **1**(1), 59–61.
68. Muretto, G. and Raffaelli, C. (2007). Combining contention resolution schemes in WDM optical packet switches with multifiber interfaces. OSA Journal of Optical Networking, **6**(1), 74–89.
69. Gaither, J. (2004). 300-Pin MSA bit-error rate tester for the ML10G board and RocketPHY transceiver. XILINX, Application note: XAPP677 Virtex-II Pro family.
70. Gallep, C. and Conforti, E. (2002). Reduction of semiconductor optical amplifier switching times by preimpulse step-injected current technique. IEEE Photonics Technology Letters **14**(7), 902–904.
71. Gallo, J.T., Booth, B.L., Schuetz, C.A., et al. Polymer waveguide components for switched WDM cross-connects. www.opticalcrosslinks.com
72. Gambini, P., Renaud, M., Guillemot, F. et al. (1998). Transparent optical packet switching: Network architecture and demonstrators in the KEOPS project. IEEE Journal on Selected Areas in Communications **16**(7), 1245–1259. DOI 10.1109/49.725193.
73. García-Dorado, J.L., Lòpez de Vergara, J., and Aracil, J. (2006). Analysis of OBS burst scheduling algorithms with stochastic burst size and offset time. In: Proceedings of the 10th Conference on Optical Networks Design and Modelling (ONDM). Copenhagen, Denmark.
74. Gauger, C.M., Köhn, M., and Scharf, J. (2004). Comparison of contention resolution strategies in OBS network scenarios. In: Proceedings of 6th International Conference on Transparent Optical Networks. Wroclaw.
75. Ge, A., Callegati, F., and Tamil, L.S. (2000). On optical burst switching and self-similar traffic. IEEE Communications Letters **4**(3), 98–100.
76. Gerstel, O. and Ramaswami, R. (2003). Optical layer survivability: A post-bubble perspective. IEEE Communications Magazine **41**(9), 51–53.
77. Glesk, I., Solokoff, J.P., and Prucnal, P.R. (1994). All-Optical address recognition and self-routing in a 250 Gbit/s packet-switched network. IEE Electronics Letters **30**(16), 1322–1323.
78. Gowda, S., Shenai, R.K., Sivalingam, K.M., Cankaya, H.C. (2003). Performance evaluation of TCP over optical burst-switched (OBS) WDM networks. In: Proceedings of IEEE International Conference on Communications. pp. 1433–1437.
79. Granger, C. and Joyeux, R. (1980). An introduction to long-memory time series models and fractional differencing. Journal of Time Series Analysis **1**, 15–29.
80. Gripp, J., Duelk, M., Simsarian, J.E., et al. (2003). Optical switch fabrics for ultra-high-capacity IP routers. Journal of Lightwave Technology **21**(11), 2839–2850. DOI 10.1109/JLT.2003.819150.

81. Guidotti, A., Rafaelli, C., and González de Dios, O. (2007). Burstification effect on the TCP synchronization and congestion window mechanisms. In: Proceedings of the International Workshop on Optical Burst Switching (WOBS), pp. 24–28.

82. Guidotti, A., Rafaelli, C., and González de Dios, O. (2007). Effect of burst assembly on synchronization of TCP flows. In: Proceedings of Broadband Communications, Networks and Systems (Broadnets), pp. 29–36.

83. Guillemot, C., Renaud, M., Gambini, P., et al. (1998). Transparent optical packet switching: The European ACTS KEOPS project approach. IEEE/OSA Journal of Lightwave Technology 16(12), 2117–2134.

84. Hajduczenia, M., Lakic, B., da Sliva, H.J., et al. (2007). Optimized passive optical network deployment. OSA Journal of Optical Networking 6(9), 1079–1104.

85. Halabi, S. (2003). Metro Ethernet. Cisco Press/McGraw-Hill, New York.

86. Hall, K.L. and Rauschenbach, K.A. (1998). 100-Gbit/s bitwise logic. Optics Letters 23(16), 1271–1273.

87. Harai, H., Murata, M., and Miyahara, H. (1997). Performance of alternative routing methods in all-optical switching networks. In: Proceedings of the Sixteenth IEEE Infocom, vol. 2, pp. 516–524.

88. Hassan, M. and Jain, R. (2003). High performance TCP/IP networking: concepts, issues, and solutions. Prentice-Hall/McGraw-Hill, New York.

89. Henry, C. (1982). Theory of the linewidth of semiconductor lasers. IEEE Journal of Quantum Electronics QE-18(2), 259–264.

90. Hernández, J.A., Aracil, J., López, V., et al. (2007). On the analysis of burst-assembly delay in OBS networks and applications in delay-based service differentiation. Photonic Network Communications 14, 49–62.

91. Hernández, J.A., Aracil, J., de Pedro, L., et al. (2008). Analysis of blocking probability of data bursts with continuous-time variable offsets in single wavelength OBS switches. IEEE/OSA Journal of Lightwave Technology 26(12), 1559–1568.

92. Heywood, P., Rigby, P., and Clavenna, S. (2000). Optical switching fabric. Lightreading 10.

93. Hill, A. and Neri, F. (2001). Optical switching networks: From circuits to packets. IEEE Communications Magazine 39(3), 107–108. DOI 10.1109/MCOM.2001.910597.

94. Houbavlis, T., Zoiros, K., Vlachos, K., et al. (1999). All-optical XOR in a semiconductor optical amplifier-assisted fiber sagnac gate. IEEE Photonics Technology Letters 11(3), 334–336.

95. Houbavlis, T., Zoiros, K.E., Kalyvas, M., et al. (2005). All-optical signal processing and applications within the Esprit project DO_ALL. Journal of Lightwave Technology 23(2), 781–801.

96. Hughes, S. (1998). Carrier-carrier interaction and ultra-short pulse propagation in a highly excited semiconductor laser amplifier beyond the rate equation limit. Physical Review A 58(3), 2567–2576.

97. Hunter, D.K. and Andonovic, I. (2000). Approaches to optical internet packet switching. IEEE Communications Magazine 38(9), 116–122.

98. Zang, H., Jue, J. P. and Mukherjee, B. (2000). A review of routing and wavelength assignment approaches for wavelength-routed optical WDM networks. Optical Networks Magazine 1(1) 47–60.

99. Iizuka, M., Sakuta, M., Nshino, Y., et al. (2002). A scheduling algorithm minimizing voids generated by arriving bursts in optical burst switched WDM network. In: Proceedings of GLOBEC OM 2002, vol. 3, pp. 2736–2740.

100. ITU-T Rec. G.7041/Y.1303: Generic framing procedure (GFP) (2005).

101. ITU-T Rec. G.7042/Y.1305: Link capacity adjustment scheme (LCAS) for virtual concatenated signals (2004).

102. ITU-T Rec. G.707/Y.1322: Network node interface for the synchronous digital hierarchy (SDH) (2003).

103. ITU-T Rec. G.7715/Y.1706: Architecture and requirements for routing in the automatically switched optical networks (2002).

104. ITU-T Rec. G.783: Characteristics of synchronous digital hierarchy (SDH) equipment functional blocks (2004).

105. ITU-T Rec. G.806: Characteristics of transport equipment—Description methodology and generic functionality (2004).

106. ITU-T Rec. G.807/Y.1302: Requirements for automatic transport networks (ASTN) (2001).

107. ITU-T Rec. G.8080/Y.1304: Architecture for the automatically switched optical network (ASON) (2001).

108. ITU-T Rec. X.85/Y.1321: IP over SDH using LAPS (2001).

109. ITU-T Recommendation G.841: Types and characteristics of SDH network protection architectures (1998).

110. Izal, M. and Aracil, J. (2002). On the influence of self-similarity on optical burst switching traffic. Proceedings of IEEE GLOBECOM **3**, 2308–2312.

111. Jahn, E., Agrawal, N., Arbert, M., et al. (1995). 40 Gbit/s all-optical demultiplexing using a monolithically integrated Mach–Zehnder interferometer with semiconductor laser amplifiers. Electronics Letters **31**(21), 1857–1858.

112. Jahn, E., Agrawall, N., Pieper, W., et al. (1996). Monolithically integrated nonlinear sagnac interferometer and its application as a 20 Gbit/s all-optical demultiplexer. Electronics Letters **32**(9), 782–784.

113. Jajszczyk, A. (2004). Control plane for optical networks: The ASON approach. China Communications **1**(1), 113–122.

114. Jajszczyk, A. (2005). Automatically switched optical networks: Benefits and requirements. IEEE Optical Communication Supplement, IEEE Communications Magazine **43**(2), S8–S13.

115. Jeong, G. and Ayanoglu, E. (1996). Comparison of wavelength-interchanging and wavelength-selective cross-connects in multiwavelength all-optical networks. In: Proceedings of the Fifteenth IEEE Infocom, pp. 156–163.

116. Jourdan, A., Chiaroni, D., Dotaro, E., et al. (2001). The perspective of optical packet switching in IP-dominant backbone and metropolitan networks. IEEE Communications Magazine **39**(3), 136–141.

117. Kitayama, K.-I. and Murata, M. (2003). Versatile optical code-based MPLS for circuit, burst, and packet switchings. IEEE/OSA Journal of Lightwave Technology **21**(11), 2753–2764.

118. Kamakura, K. and Sasase, I. (2001). A new modulation scheme using asymmetric error-correcting codes embedded in optical orthogonal codes for optical CDMA. IEEE Journal of Lightwave Technology **19**(12), 1839–1850.

119. Karasan, E. and Ayanoglu, E. (1998). Effects of wavelength routing and selection algorithms on wavelength conversion gain in WDM optical networks. IEEE/ACM Transaction on Networking **6**(2), 186–196.

120. Kehayas, E., Vyrsokinos, K., Stampoulidis, L., et al. (2006). ARTEMIS: 40-Gb/s All-optical self-routing node and network architecture employing asynchronous bit and packet-level optical signal processing. IEEE/OSA Journal of Lightwave Technology **24**(8), 2967–2977.

121. Kelly, F.P. (1986). Blocking probabilities in large circuit-switched networks. Advances in Applied Probability **18**, 473–505.

122. Kermani, P. and Kleinrock, L. (1990). A tradeoff study of switching systems in computer communication networks. IEEE Transactions on Computers **29**(12), 1052–1060.

123. Kitayama, K. (1998). Code division multiplexing lightwave networks based upon optical code conversion. IEEE Journal on Selected Areas in Communications **16**(7), 1309–1319. DOI 10.1109/49.725198.

124. Kitayama, K., Kataoka, N., Yoshima, S., et al. (2006). Optical code label switching and its applications. In: Photonics in Switching, 2006. PS '06. International conference on photonics in switching, pp. 1–3. DOI 10.1109/ PS.2006.4350164.

125. Kitayama, K. and Murata, M. (2001). Photonic access node using optical code-based label processing and its applications to optical data networking. IEEE Journal of Lightwave Technology **19**(10), 1401–1415.

126. Kitayama, K.I. and Wada, N. (1999). Photonic IP routing. IEEE Photonics Technology Letters **11**(12), 1689–1691. DOI 10.1109/68.806889.

127. Klonidis, D., Nejabati, R., Politi, C., et al. (2004). Demonstration of a fully functional and controlled optical packet switch at 40 Gb/s. Proceedings of the 30th European Conference on Optical Communication, Stockholm, Sweden.

128. Kompella, K. and Rekhter, Y. (2005). Label switched paths (LSP) hierarchy with generalized multi-protocol label switching (GMPLS) traffic engineering (TE). RFC 4206, Internet Engineering Task Force.

129. Kovacevic, M. and Acampora, A.S. (1996). Benefits of wavelength translation in all-optical clear-channel networks. IEEE Journal on Selected Areas in Communications **14**(5), 868–880.

130. Krajinović, V., Aleksić, S., Remšak, G., et al. (2001). All-optical address recognition based on Mach-Zehnder interferometer. In: European Conference on Networks & Optical Communications (NOC 2001) Ipswich, UK.

131. Kwong, W.C., Zhang, J.G., and Yang, G.C. (1994). 2n prime-sequence code and its optical CDMA coding architecture. IEE Electronics Letters **30**(6), 509–510.

132. Labs, B. Bellcore traces. Available at `http://ita.ee.lbl.gov/html/contrib/BC.html`

133. Laevens, K. and Bruneel, H. (2003). Analysis of a single-wavelength optical buffer. In: IEEE Infocom 2003, vol. 3, pp. 2262–2267. IEEE.

134. Lavrova, O.A., Rau, L., and Blumenthal, D.J. (2002). 10-Gb/s Agile wavelength conversion with nanosecond tuning times using a multisection widely tunable laser. IEEE Journal of Lightwave Technology **20**(4), 712–717.

135. Lee, S.W. and Green, D.H. (1998). Coding for coherent optical CDMA networks. IEE Proceedings-Communication **145**(3), 117–125.

136. Leuthold, J., Besse, P.A., Eckner, J., et al. (1998). All-optical space switches with gain and principally ideal extinction ratios. IEEE Journal of Quantum Electronics **34**(4), 622–633.

137. Li, B. and Chu, X. (2003). Routing and wavelength assignment vs. wavelength converter placement in all-optical networks. IEEE Optical Communication Supplement, IEEE Communications Magazine **41**(8), S22–S28.

138. Li, J. and Qiao, C. (2004). Schedule burst proactively for optical burst switched networks. Computer Networks **44**(5), 617–629.

139. Li, J., Qiao, C., Xu, J., et al. (2004) Maximizing throughout for optical burst switching networks. In: Proceedings of IEEE INFOCOM 2004.

140. Li, L. and Somani, A. (1999). Dynamic wavelength routing using congestion and neighborhood information. IEEE/ACM Transactions on Networking **7**(5), 779–786.

141. Lin, Y.M., Way, W.I., and Chang, G.K. (2000) A novel optical label swapping technique using erasable optical single-sideband subcarrier label. IEEE Photonics Technology Letters **12**(8), 1088–1090.

142. Listanti, M., Eramo, V., and Sabella, R. (2000). Architectural and technological issues for future optical internet networks. IEEE Communications Magazine **38**(9), 82–92. DOI 10.1109/35.868147.

143. Ljolje, M., Inkret, R., and Mikac, B. (2005) A comparative analysis of data scheduling algorithms in optical burst switching networks. In: Proceedings of ONDM 2005, pp. 493–500.

144. Ma, X. and Kuo, G. (2003). Optical switching technology comparison: Optical MEMS vs. other technologies. IEEE Communications Magazine **41**(11), 16–24.

145. Maier, G. and Pattavina, A. (2001). Generalized space-equivalent analysis of optical cross-connect architectures. IEEE/OSA Journal Lightwave Technology **1**(4), 159–168.

146. Maimour, M. and Pham, C. (2002). Dynamic replier active reliable multicast (DyRAM). In: Proceedings of the 7th IEEE Symposium on Computers and Communications (ISCC).

147. Mak, M. and Tsang, H. (2000). Polarization-insensitive widely tunable wavelength converter using a single semiconductor optical amplifier. IEE Electronics Letters **36**, 152–153.

148. Makihara, M., Sato, M., Shimokawa, F., et al. (1999). Micromechanical optical switches based on thermo-capillarity integrated in waveguide substrate. IEEE Journal of Lightwave Technology **17**(1), 14–18.

149. Malis, A. and Simpson, W. (1999). PPP over SONET/SDH. RFC 2615, Internet Engineering Task Force.

150. Mannie, E. and Papadimitriou, D. (2004). Generalized multi-protocol label switching (GMPLS) extensions for synchronous optical network (SONET) and synchronous digital hierarchy (SDH) control. RFC 3946, Internet Engineering Task Force.

151. Martini, B., Baroncellia, F., and Castoldi, P. (2005). A novel service oriented framework for automatically switched transport network. International Symposium on Integrated Network management (IM 2005, 9th IFIP/IEEE, Nice).

152. Meagher, B., Chang, G.K., Ellinas, G., et al. (2000). Design and implementation of ultra-low latency optical label switching for packet-switched WDM networks. IEEE Journal of Lightwave Technology 18(12), 1978–1987.

153. Mecozzi, A. and Mork, J. (1997). Saturation induced by picosecond pulses in semiconductor optical amplifiers. Journal of Optical Society of America B 14(4), 761–770.

154. Menon, V.M., Tong, W., Li, C., et al. (2003). All-optical wavelength conversion using a regrowth-free monolithically integrated sagnac interferometer. IEEE Photonics Technology Letters 15(2), 254–256.

155. Mikkelsen, B., Vaa, M., Poulsen, H.N., et al. (1997). 40 Gbit/s all-optical wavelength converter and RZ-to-NRZ format adapter realized by monolithic integrated active michelson interferometer. Electronics Letters 33(2), 133–134.

156. Mikkelsen, B., Vaa, M., Storkfelt, N., et al. (1995). Monolithic integrated michelson interferometer with SOAs for high-speed all-optical signal processing. ofc TuH4, 13–14.

157. Mokhtar, A. and Azizoglu, M. (1998). Adaptive wavelength routing in all-optical networks. IEEE/ACM Transaction on Networking 6(2), 197–206.

158. Mukherjee, B.: Optical Communications Networks. McGraw-Hill, New York (1997).

159. Mukherjee, B., Banerjee, D., Ramamurthy, S., et al. (1996). Some principles for designing a wide-area WDM optical network. IEEE/ACM Transactions on Networking 4(5), 684–696. DOI 10.1109/90.541317.

160. Muretto, G. and Raffaelli, C. (2006). Performance evaluation of asynchronous multi-fibre optical packet switches. In: Proceedings of ONDM 2006. Copenhagen, DK.

161. Nakamura, S., Ueno, Y., and Tajima, K. (2001). 168-Gb/s all-optical wavelength conversion with a symmetric-Mach–Zehnder-type switch. IEEE Photonics Technology Letters 13(10), 1091–1093.

162. Nakamura, S., Ueno, Y., Tajima, K., et al. (2000). Demultiplexing of 168-Gb/s data pulses with a hybrid-integrated symmetric Mach–Zehnder all-optical switch. IEEE Photonics Technology Letters 12(4), 425–427.

163. Nejabati, R., Klonidis, D., Simeonidou, D., et al. (2005). Demonstration of user-controlled network interface for sub-wavelength bandwidth-on-demand service. In: Proceedings of Optical Fiber Communication Conference (OFC).

164. Nejabati, R., Klonidis, D., Zervas, G., et al. (2006). Demonstration of a complete and fully functional end-to-end asynchronous optical packet switched network. In: Proceedings of Optical Fiber Conference.

165. Networks, M.O. (2002). Myths and realities about 40G optical technology. White Paper.

166. Neukermans, A. and Ramaswami, R. (2001). MEMS technology for optical networking applications. IEEE Communications Magazine 10(1), 62–69.

167. Nord, M. (2004). Waveband based multi-plane optical packet switch with partially shared wavelength converters. Proceedings of 8th Working Conference on Optical Network Design and Modeling (ONDM), pp. 1–19.

168. Norros, I. (1995). On the use of fractional Brownian motion in the theory of connectionless networks. IEEE Journal on Selected Areas in Communications 13(6), 953–962.

169. N. Wada, Chujo, W., and Kitayama, K. (2001). 1.28 Tbit/s (160 Gbit/s × 8 wavelengths) throughout variable length packet switching using optical code based label switch. In: 27th European Conference on Optical Communication (ECOC 2001). Amsterdam, Netherlands, vol. 6, no. 2, pp. 62–63.

170. Odlyzko, A.M. (2003). Internet traffic growth: Sources and implications. In: Optical Transmission Systems and Equipment for WDM Networking II, B.B. Dingel, W. Weiershausen, A.K. Dutta, and K.-I. Sato, eds., Proceedings of SPIE, vol. 5247, pp. 1–15.

171. OIF-E-NNI-Sig-01.0: Intra-Carrier E-NNI Signaling Specification (2004).

172. OIF-ENNI-OSPF-01.0: External Network-Network Interface (E-NNI) OSPF-Based Routing—1.0 (intra-Carrier) Implementation Agreement (2007).

173. OIF-G-Sig-IW-01.0: Signaling Protocol Interworking of ASON/GMPLS Network Domains (2008).

174. OIF-UNI-01.0-R2-Common: User Network Interface (UNI) 1.0 Signaling Specification, Release 2: Common Part (2004).

175. OIF-UNI-01.0-R2-RSVP: RSVP Extensions for User Network Interface (UNI) 1.0 Signaling, Release 2 (2004).

176. OIF-UNI-02.0-Common: User Network Interface (UNI) 2.0 Signaling Specification: Common Part (2008).

177. OIF-UNI-02.0-RSVP: User Network Interface (UNI) 2.0 Signaling Specification: RSVP Extensions for User Network Interface (UNI) 2.0 (2008).

178. Okamoto, S., Otani, T., Sone, Y., et al. (2006). Field trial of signaling interworking of multi-carrier ASON/GMPLS network domains. In: Proceedings of OSA Optical Fiber Communications Conference OFC 2006, pp. 1–13.

179. Olsson, B.E., Ohlen, P., Rau, L., et al. (2000). Wavelength routing of 40 Gbit/s packets with 2.5 Gbit/s header erasure/rewriting using an all-fiber wavelength converter. IEE Electronics Letters 36(4), 345–347.

180. O'Mahony, M., Simeonidou, D., Hunter, D., et al. (2001). The application of optical packet switching in future communication networks. IEEE Communications Magazine 39(3), 128–135.

181. Ornan Gerstel, R.R. (2000). Optical layer survivability: A services perspective. IEEE Communications Magazine 38(3), 104–113.

182. Orphanoudakis, T.G., Drakos, A., Matrakidis, C., et al. (2007). A hybrid optical switch architecture with shared electronic buffers. In: Proceedings of International Conference on Transparent Optical Networks ICTON.

183. Overby, H. (2004). Performance modelling of synchronous bufferless OPS networks. In: Proceedings of International Conference on Transparent Optical Networks ICTON, vol. 1, pp. 22–28.

184. Overby, H. (2005). Quality of service differentiation: Teletraffic analysis and network layer packet redundancy in optical packet switched networks. Ph.D. thesis, Department of Telematics, Norwegian University of Science and Technology.

185. Overby, H., Nord, M., and Stol, N. (2006). Evaluation of QoS differentiation mechanisms in asynchronous bufferless optical packet switched networks. IEEE Communications Magazine 44(8), 52–57.

186. Overby, H. and Stol, N. (2004). Quality of service in asynchronous bufferless optical packet switched networks. Kluwer Telecommunication Systems 27(2–4), 151–179.

187. Papadimitriou, D., Ong, L., Sadler, J., et al. (2005). Requirements for generalized MPLS (GMPLS) signaling usage and extensions for automatically switched optical network (ASON). RFC 4139, Internet Engineering Task Force.

188. Papadimitriou, D., Ong, L., Sadler, J., et al. (2006). Evaluation of existing routing protocols against automatic switched optical network (ASON) routing requirements. RFC 4652, Internet Engineering Task Force.

189. Papadimitriou, G., Papazoglou, C., and Pomportsis, A. (2003). Optical switching: Switch fabrics, techniques and architectures. IEEE Journal of Lightwave Technology 21(2), 384–390.

190. Parker, C. and Walker, S. (1999). Design of arrayed-waveguide gratings using hybrid Fourier–Fresnel transform techniques. IEEE Journal on Selected Topics in Quantum Electronics 5(5), 1379–1384.

191. Patel, N., Rauschenbach, K., and Hall, K. (1996). 40-Gb/s cascadable all-optical logic with an ultrafast nonlinear interferometer. Optics Letters 21(18), 1466–1468.

192. Patel, N., Rauschenbach, K., and Hall, K. (1996). 40-Gb/s demultiplexing using an ultrafast nonlinear interferometer (UNI). IEEE Photonics Technology Letters 12(8), 1695–1697.

193. Patel, N.S., Hall, K.L., and Rauschenbach, K.A. (1998). Interferometric all optical switches for ultrafast signal processing. Applied Optics 37(14), 2831–2842.

194. Pattavina, A. (2005). Architecture and performance of optical packet switching nodes for Ip networks. Journal of Lightwave Technology 23(3), 1023–1032.

195. Pattavina, A. (2005). Multiwavelength switching in Ip optical nodes adopting different buffering strategies. Optical Switching and Networking **1**(1), 66–75.
196. Perrier, P. (2000). Optical cross connects—Part 2: Enabling technologies. Fiber optics online **1** (http://www.fiberopticsonline.com).
197. Phung, M., Chua, K., Mohan, G., et al. (2005). On ordered scheduling for optical burst switching. Computer Networks **48**(6), 891–909.
198. Prucnal, P. and Santoro, M. (1986). Spread spectrum fiber optic local area network using CDMA and optical correlation. IEEE Journal of Lightwave Technology **4**(5), 30–314.
199. Qiao, C. and Yoo, M. (2000). Choices, features and issues in optical burst switching (OBS). Optical Networking Magazine **1**(4), 36–44.
200. Qiao, C., Wei, W., and Liu, X. (2006). Extending generalized multiprotocol label switching (GMPLS) for polymorphous, agile, and transparent optical networks (PATON). IEEE Communications Magazine **44**(12), 104–114.
201. Qiao, C. and Yoo, M. (1999). Optical burst switching (OBS): A new paradigm for an optical Internet. Journal of High Speed Networks **8**(1), 69–84.
202. Raffaelli, C. (2000). Design of a multistage optical packet switch. European Transactions on Telecommunications **11**(5), 443–451.
203. Raffaelli, C. and Savi, M. (2006). Performance modelling of synchronous buffer-less optical packet switch with partial wavelength conversion. In: Proceedings of IEEE ICC 2006. Istanbul, Turkey.
204. Raffaelli, C., Savi, M., and Stavdas, A. (2006). Sharing wavelength converters in multistage optical packet switches. In: Proceedings of IEEE HPSR. Poznan, PL.
205. Raffaelli, C. and Zaffoni, P. (2003). Packet assembly at optical packet network access and its effect on TCP performance. In: Proceedings of HPSR High Performance Switching and Routing 2003. Torino, Italy.
206. Raffelli, C. and Muretto, G. (2006). Combining contention resolution schemes in WDM optical packet switches with multifiber interfaces. Journal of Optical Networking **6**(1), 74–89.
207. Ramamurthy, B. and Mukherjee, B. (1996). Wavelength conversion in WDM networking. IEEE Journal on Selected Areas in Communications **16**(7), 868–880.
208. Ramantas, K., Vlachos, K., González de Dios, O., et al. (2008). Window-based burst assembly scheme for TCP traffic over OBS. OSA Journal of Optical Networks **7**(5), 487–495.
209. Ramaswami, R. and Sirvajan, K. (1995). Routing and wavelength assignment in all-optical networks. IEEE/ACM Transactions on Networking **3**(5), 489–500.
210. Ramaswami, R. and Sirvajan, K. (1996). Design of logical topologies for wavelength-routed optical networks. IEEE Journal on Selected Areas in Communications **14**(5), 840–851.
211. Ramaswami, R. and Sivarajan, K. (2001). Optical Networks: "A Practical Perspective". 2nd ed. Morgan Kaufman, San Francisco, CA.
212. Renaud, M., Bachmann, M., and Erman, M. (1996). Semiconductor optical space switches. IEEE Journal of Selected Topics in Quantum Electronics **2**(2), 277–288. DOI 10.1109/2944.577378.
213. Reviriego, P., Hernández, J.A., and Aracil, J. (2007). Analysis of average burst-assembly delay and applications in proportional service differentiation. Photonic Network Communications **14**(2), 183–197.
214. Reviriego, P., Hernández, J.A., and Aracil, J.: Assembly admission control based on random packet selection at border nodes in optical burst-switched networks. Photonic Network Communications http://dx.doi.org/10.1007/s11107-008-0168-4
215. Rosberg, Z., et al. (2003). Performance analyses of optical burst switching networks. IEEE JSAC **21**(7), 1187–1197.
216. Rosberg, Z., Vu, H.L., Zukerman, M., et al. (2003). Blocking probabilities of optical burst switching networks based on reduced load fixed point approximations. In: Proceedings of INFOCOM 2003, pp. 2008–2018.
217. Rosen, E.C., Viswanathan, A., and Callon, R. (2001). Multiprotocol label switching architecture. RFC 3031, Internet Engineering Task Force.

218. Rostami, A. and Wolisz, A. (2007). Impact of edge traffic aggregation on the performance of FDL-assisted optical core switching nodes. In: Proceedings of IEEE International Conference on Communication (ICC).

219. Rostami, A. and Wolisz, A. (2007). Modeling and synthesis of traffic in optical burst-switched networks. Journal of Lightwave Technology 25(10), 2942–2952.

220. Runser, R., Zhou, D., Coldwell, C., et al. (2001). Interferometric ultrafast SOA-based optical switches: From devices to applications. Optical Quantum Electronics 33(7–10), 841–874.

221. Bregni, S., Pattavina, A. and Vegetti, G. (2003). Architecture and performance of AWG-based optical switching nodes for IP networks. IEEE Journal on Selected Areas in Communications 21(7), 1113–1121.

222. Okamoto, S., Watanabe, A. and Sato, K.I. (1996). Optical path cross-connect node architectures for photonic transport network. IEEE/OSA Journal of Lightwave Technology 14(6), 1410–1422.

223. Sander, V., et al. (2004). Networking issues of grid infrastructures. Grid Forum Draft, GHPN-RG GFD-I.037.

224. Santop, M.A. and Prucnal, P. (1987). Asynchronous fiber optic local area network using CDMA and optical correlation. IEEE Proceedings 75(10), 1336–1338.

225. Segatto, M.E.V., Kashyap, R., Maxwell, G.D., et al. (2000). Multi Gbit/s bit parallel WDM transmission using dispersion managed fibers. IEEE Photonics Technology Letters 17(8), 995–997.

226. Shen, S. and Weiner, A.M. (1999). Demonstration of timing skew compensation for bit-parallel WDM data transmission with picosecond precision. IEEE Photonics Technology Letters 11(5), 566–568.

227. Shimokawa, F., Sakata, T., Makihara, M., et al. (2003). High-speed switching operation in a thermocapillarity optical switch for application to photonic networks. NTT Technical Review Selected Papers 1(7), 14–18.

228. Shinohara, H. (2007). FTTH experiences in Japan. OSA Journal of Optical Networking 6(6), 616–623.

229. Shun, Y., Mukherjee, B., Yoo, S., et al. (2003). A unified study of contention-resolution schemes in optical packet-switched networks. Journal of Lightwave Technology 21(3), 672–683.

230. Simeonidou, D., et al. (2004). Optical network infrastructure for Grid. Grid Forum Draft, GFD-I.036.

231. Simeonidou, D., et al. (2007). GridFTP v2 protocol description. Grid Forum Draft, GFD.47.

232. Simpson, W. (1994). PPP in HDLC-like framing. RFC 1662, Internet Engineering Task Force.

233. Simpson, W. (1994). The point-to-point protocol (PPP). RFC 1661, Internet Engineering Task Force.

234. Sokoloff, J.P., Prucnal, P.R., Glesk, I., et al. (1993). A terahertz optical asymmetric demultiplexer (TOAD). IEEE Photonic Technology Letters 5(7), 787–790.

235. Soulage, G., Doussiere, P., Jourdan, A., et al. (2004). Clamped gain travelling wave semiconductor optical amplifier as a large dynamic range optical gate. In: Proccedings of ECOC.

236. Stavdas, A., Manousakis, M., Scahill, C., et al. (2001). Design and performance of free-space concave grating demultiplexers for ultrawideband WDM networks. Journal of Lightwave Technology 19(11), 1777–1784.

237. Stavdas, A., Sygletos, S., O'Mahony, M., et al. (2003). IST-DAVID: Concept presentation and physical layer modelling of the metropolitan area network. Journal of Lightwave Technology 21(2).

238. Stavdas, S. (2003). Architectures, technology, and strategy for gracefully evolving optical packet switching networks. Optical Networks Magazine 4(3), 92–107.

239. Stevens, T., Leenheer, M., Turck, F., et al. (2006). Distributed job scheduling based on multiple constraints anycast routing. In: Proceedings of IEEE Broadnets 2006.

240. Stevens, W. (1994). TCP/IP Illustrated, Volume 1: The Protocols. Adison-Wesley, New York.

241. Stubkjaer, K.E. (2000). Semiconductor optical amplifier-based all-optical gates for high-speed optical processing. IEEE Journal of Selected Topics in Quantum Electronics 6(6), 1428–1435.

242. Subramaniam, S. and Barry, R.A. (1997). Wavelength assignment in fixed-routing WDM networks. In: Proceedings of the IEEE Internatinal Conference on Communications (ICC 1997), vol. 1, pp. 406–410.
243. Suzuki, K., Iwatsuki, K., Nishi, S., et al. (1994). Error-free demultiplexing of 160 Gbit/s pulse signal using optical loop mirror including semiconductor laser amplifier. Electronics Letters 30(18), 1501–1503.
244. Sze, S. (1981). Physics of Semiconductor Devices, 2nd ed. Wiley-Interscience/McGraw Hill, New York.
245. Tajima, K. (1993). All-optical switch with switch-off time unrestricted by carrier lifetime. Japanese Journal of Applied Physics 32(12A), L1746–L1749.
246. Tajima, K., Nakamura, S., and Ueno, Y. (2001). Ultrafast all-optical signal processing with symmetric Mach–Zehnder type all-optical switches. Optical Quantum Electronics 33(7–10), 875–897.
247. Tan, S., Mohan, G., and Chua, K. (2003). Algorithms for burst rescheduling in WDM optical burst switching networks. Computer Networks 41(1), 41–55.
248. Tancevski, L., Yegnanarayanan, S., Non, G.C., et al. (2000). Optical routing of asynchronous, variable length packets. IEEE Journal on Selected Areas in Communications 18(10), 2084–2093.
249. Tang, J. and Shore, K. (1998). Strong picosecond optical pulse propagation in semiconductor optical amplifiers at transparency. IEEE Journal of Quantum Electronics 34(7), 1263–1269.
250. Tančevski, L., Bazgaloski, L., Andonovic, I., et al. (1994). Incoherent asynchronous optical CDMA using gold codes. IEE Electronics Letters 30(9), 712–723.
251. Tančevski, L., Tamil, L., and Callegati, F. (1999). Nondegenerate buffers: An approach for building large optical memories. IEEE Photonics Technology Letters 11(8), 1072–1074.
252. Tian, Y. and Xu, K. (2005). TCP in wireless environments: Problems and solutions. IEEE Communications Magazine 43(3), 27–32.
253. Todimala, A. and Ramamurthy, B. (2003). Congestion-based algorithms for online routing in optical WDM mesh networks. In: Communication, Internet and Information Technology, pp. 43–48.
254. Turner, J.S. (1999). Terabit burst switching. Journal of High Speed Networks 8(1), 3–16.
255. Tzanakaki, A. and O'Mahony, M. (2000). Analysis of tunable wavelength converters based on cross-gain modulation in semiconductor optical amplifiers operating in the counter propagating mode. IEE Proceedings Optoelectronics 147, 49–55.
256. Valcarenghi, L., Foschini, L., Paolucci, F., et al. (2006). Topology discovery services for monitoring the global grid. IEEE Communications Magazine 44(3), 110–117.
257. Van Mieghem, P. and Kuipers, F.A. (2004). Concepts of exact quality of service algorithms. IEEE/ACM Transactions on Networking 12(5), 851–864.
258. VanBreda, M. (2005). Architectures for end-to-end video delivery. Broadband World Forum. URL http://www.iec.org/events/2005/bbwf/presentations/index.html.
259. Varvarigos, E.A. and Sharma, V. (2000). The ready-to-go virtual circuit protocol: A loss-free protocol for multigigabit networks using FIFO buffers. IEEE/ACM Transactions on Networking 5(5), 705–718.
260. de Vega Rodrigo, M. and Remiche, M.A. (2007). Planning OBS networks with QoS constraints. Photonics Network Communications 14(2), 229–239.
261. Vokkarane, V., Haridoss, K., and Jue, J. (2002). Threshold-based burst assembly policies for QoS support in optical burst-switched networks. In: Proceedings of SPIE/IEEE OPTICOMM, pp. 125–136.
262. Wada, N., Cincotti, G., Yoshima, S., et al. (2006). Characterization of a full encoder/decoder in the AWG configuration for code-based photonic routers—Part II: Experiments and applications. IEEE/OSA Journal of Lightwave Technology 24(1), 113–121.
263. Wada, N., Harai, H., and Kubota, F. (2003). 40 Gbit/s interface optical code based photonic packet switch prototype. In: Proceedings of Optical Fiber Communications Conference OFC 2003.
264. Wada, N. and Kitayama, K. (1999). A 10 Gbit/s optical code division multiplexing using 8-Chirp optical bipolar code and coherent detection. IEEE Journal of Lightwave Technology 17(10), 1758–1765.

265. Wang, D., Shao, Y.B., and Shao, Q. (2002). Reconfigurable optical add/drop multiplexers (R-OADMs): A key network element for the all-optical network. Optical Switching and Optical Interconnection II, Proceedings of SPIE **4907**, 16–22.

266. Wei, J.Y. and MacFarland, R.I. (2000). Just-in-time signaling for WDM optical burst switching networks. IEEE/OSA Journal of Lightwave Technology **18**(12), 2019–2037.

267. White, I.a., Penty, R., Webster, M., et al. (2002). Wavelength switching components for future photonic networks. IEEE Communications Magazine **40**, 74–81.

268. White, I.M., Wonglumsom, D., Shrikhande, K., et al. (2000). The architecture of HOR-NET: A packet-over-WDM multiple-access optical metropolitan area ring network. Computer Networks **32**(5), 587–598.

269. Wolfson, D., Fjelde, T., Kloch, A., et al. (2000). All-optical wavelength conversion scheme in SOA-based interferometric devices. Electronics Letters **36**(21), 1794–1795. DOI 10.1049/el:20001245

270. Wong, E. and Zukerman, M. (2006). Analysis of an optical hybrid switch. IEEE Communications Letters **10**(2), 108–110.

271. Xiong, Y., Vandenhoute, M., and Cankaya, H. (2000). Control architecture in optical burst-switched WDM networks. IEEE Journal on Selected Areas in Communications **18**(10), 1838–1851.

272. Xu, J., Qiao, C., Li, J., et al. (2004). Efficient burst scheduling algorithms in optical burst-switched networks using geometric techniques. IEEE Journal on Selected Areas in Communications **22**(9), 1796–1811.

273. Yao, S., Mukherjee, B., and Dixit, S. (2000). Advances in photonic packet switching: An overview. IEEE Communications Magazine **38**(2), 84–94.

274. Yariv, A. (1997). Optical Electronics in Modern Communications. 5th ed. Oxford University Press, New York.

275. Yoo, M. and Qiao, C. (1997). Just-enough-time (JET): A high speed protocol for bursty traffic in optical networks. IEEE/LEOS Technol. Global Information Infrastructure **1**(1), 26–27.

276. Yoo, M., Qiao, C., and Dixit, S. (2000). QoS performance of optical burst switching in IP over WDM networks. IEEE Journal of Selected Areas in Communications **18**(10), 2062–2071.

277. Yoo, S. (1996). Wavelength conversion technologies for WDM network applications. IEEE Journal of Lightwave Technology **14**(6), 955–966.

278. Yu, X., Chen, Y., and Qiao, C. (2002). Study of traffic statistics of assembled burst traffic in optical burst switched networks. In: Proceedings of SPIE/IEEE OPTICOM pp. 149–159.

279. Zalesky, A., Vu, H.L., Rosberg, Z., et al. (2006). OBS contention resolution performance. Performance Evaluation **64**(4), 357–373.

280. Zerva, G., Nejabati, R., Simeonidou, D., et al. (2006). QoS-aware ingress optical grid user network interface: High-speed ingress OBS node design and implementation. In: Proceedings of Optical Fiber Communication Conference (OFC).

281. Zhang, M., Wang, L., and Ye, P. (2005). All-optical XOR logic gates: Technologies and experimental demonstrations. IEEE Communications Magazine **43**(45), S19–S24.

282. Zhang, T., Lu, K., and Jue, J.P. (2006). Shared fiber delay line buffers in asynchronous optical packet switches. IEEE Journal on Selected Areas in Communications **24**(4), 118–127.

283. Zhang, X. and Qiao, C. (1998). Wavelength assignment for dynamic traffic in multi-fiber WDM networks. In: Proceedings of the Seventh IEEE International Conference on Computer Communications and Networks (ICCCN 1998), pp. 479–485.

284. Zhang, Z. and Campora, A. (1995). A heuristic wavelength assignment algorithm for multi-hop WDM networks. IEEE/ACM transactions on Networking **3**(3), 281–288.

285. Zhou, D., Wang, B.C., Runser, R.J., et al. (2001). Perfectly synchronized bit-parallel WDM data transmission over a single optical fiber. IEEE Photonics Technology Letters **13**(4), 382–384.

286. Zhu, X. and Khan, J. (2003). Queuing models of optical delay lines in synchronous and asynchronous optical packet-switched networks. Optical Engineering **42**(6), 1741–1748.

Index